FUTURE OF
THE FOREST

A volume in the

Cornell Series on Land: New Perspectives on Territory, Development, and Environment

Edited by Wendy Wolford, Nancy Lee Peluso, and Michael Goldman

A list of titles in this series is available at cornellpress.cornell.edu.

FUTURE OF THE FOREST

Struggles over Land and Law in India

Anand P. Vaidya

CORNELL UNIVERSITY PRESS   ITHACA AND LONDON

First published 2025 by Cornell University Press

Librarians: A CIP catalog record for this book is available from the Library of Congress.

ISBN 9781501780493 (hardcover)
ISBN 9781501780509 (paperback)
ISBN 9781501780523 (epub)
ISBN 9781501780516 (pdf)

Contents

Preface: The Problem of the Forest

I was still waking up one morning in September 2011 in my apartment in Delhi when I got the phone call. I hadn't yet made coffee, checked my email, or made the various last-minute arrangements that were necessary before I traveled the next day. I was planning to go to Ramnagar, the village in which I had been carrying out fieldwork for eleven months at that point. My phone rang. It was Geeta, the activist who had first brought me to Ramnagar. "Anand, you have to come immediately," she said. "They have destroyed Ramnagar."

I caught an overnight train to Mughal Sarai, a train junction on Uttar Pradesh's eastern border. From there it was a bumpy six-hour bus ride south: out of the agricultural Gangetic valley and over the Kaimur hills into air that was increasingly thick and milky, the result of the cement manufacturing and coal mining that defined the Duddhi region's political economy. Most land here was owned by the Forest Department, but there was little vegetation. A few *sal* and *khair* trees and the occasional scrub were scattered around the hills, but most of their tree cover had been lost, cut and sold off over many decades.

I got down in Govindnagar, a village of four thousand people arranged around the small Son River. The Ramnagaris had come here when their village was destroyed: they had grown up here, and most still had families here that they could return to. Ramnagar was two kilometers up the dry, reddish hills that rose to the north of Govindnagar. The scene in Govindnagar looked as it usually did: dominant-caste men were sitting in plastic chairs arranged on the dirt road in front of their *pakka* houses, built of brick and cement blocks and painted in bright colors. These men looked me up and down as I walked past them on my way to Ram Lakhan's brother's earthen home in Govindnagar's Dalit hamlet.[1] Inside the home, the mood was somber. Ram Lakhan was sitting on a cot inside, with his wife Baldev, his friend Balraj, and Geeta, the activist from Delhi who had first brought me here. Ram Lakhan was in his forties, although he did not know his exact age. He was dressed in a faded white kurta and, like Balraj, had a colored cotton scarf draped over his neck. He had emerged as one of the leaders of the Sangathan movement for forest rights in Ramnagar. Geeta was in her forties as well. She had been raised in a city in the western part of the state and had become involved in leftist forest politics while she was at university.

I took a place on a second cot in the hut, and Baldev offered me a cup of sweet tea brought from the chai stall down the road. Geeta already had a cup in her hand, but the others were not partaking. Ram Lakhan had told me once that he believed tea makes one too weak for labor. Once we were settled, Ram Lakhan and Geeta began to tell me what had happened to Ramnagar.

Five days earlier on the afternoon of September 10, I learned, the two hundred-odd residents of Ramnagar saw a group of men coming up the hills from Govindnagar. The Ramnagaris recognized these men as members of the land-owning dominant Yadav caste from Govindnagar. The men had sticks in their hands, and they were yelling and cursing, "This land is forest land, not your land!" They set fire to the thatched roofs of the Ramnagaris' earthen homes and smashed the walls with metal implements. Later that day, they brought buffaloes to eat the wheat and potato plants that were coming up in the Ramnagaris' fields. The rains had been good that year, and the Ramnagaris had expected a good harvest.

The attacks went on for two more days. The Ramnagaris knew better than to call the police or the Forest Department, whom they expected would side with the dominant-caste attackers. On the third day, a representative from the Bahujan Samaj Party, the pro-Dalit party that was in government in the state of Uttar Pradesh, arrived and helped put a stop to the attacks. But the damage had already been done: some 70 of the village's 120 homes had been destroyed, and the crops ruined. It didn't seem safe to return and rebuild; the attackers could come back at any moment, and they seemed to have the tacit backing of someone powerful in the state—bureaucrats, Forest Department officials, some politicians, perhaps. Instead, the devastated Ramnagaris moved in with their families in Govindnagar.

Ramnagar had been built over the previous five years by landless Dalits and Adivasis from Govindnagar.[2] In 2007, Geeta and a group of local left activists had arrived in Govindnagar and told the landless Dalits and Adivasis of the village about a new national law that had been passed in Delhi, the Forest Rights Act. The new law, the activists said, would allow the Dalits and Adivasis to claim the forests surrounding Govindnagar, which, the activists argued, rightfully belonged to them. Over the following two years, Ramnagar was built: the villagers lacked formal titles, water, electricity, and a school, but with their own village and land they no longer had to work on the fields of their dominant-caste neighbors.

The men who destroyed Ramnagar, however, cited the same Forest Rights Act as they attacked. Among the attackers were members of a village-level committee that was created through the Forest Rights Act to protect the forests surrounding villages. The Ramnagaris, they claimed, were nothing more than encroachers on forest land, and so, to protect the forest, the village had to be razed to the ground.

How could one law be used both to build a village and to destroy it? This book is about that law—the Forest Rights Act, or, as it is officially known, the Scheduled Tribes and Other Traditional Forest Dwellers (Recognition of Forest Rights) Act—and how it came to be available to both the Ramnagaris and their attackers.* Passed by India's Parliament in December 2006, the Forest Rights Act had been in existence for four years when Ramnagar was attacked. Over nine pages, the law sets out to bring about the largest redistribution of property that independent India has seen, allowing the uncounted hundreds of millions of people who live in the country's forests or who depend on the forests for their livelihoods to claim property and use rights to the forest. And yet those rights, as the Ramnagaris learned, were not settled by the passage of the law. Instead, the question of who exactly could claim those rights and how they could do it was being answered through the destruction of their village.

I argue that the Forest Rights Act was the latest in a long series of attempts to solve what I call the problem of the forest, the problem of the extension of property to a group of people, forest dwellers, whose presence had been defined by the denial of property rights. Since the nineteenth century, people like the Ramnagaris who live in forests have found that they have been unable to enforce their claims to the land on which they live. The new law was a product of collective action on a national scale to solve the problem of the forest—and in Ramnagar, these efforts were being undone through further collective action, carried out by a group that was citing a second interpretation of the same law. This book tells the story of Ramnagar's making and unmaking. To do so, it also tells the story of a national movement and an ambiguous law, which was passed in New Delhi and would make and unmake forests across the country.

---

* The full text of the Scheduled Tribes and Other Traditional Forest Dwellers (Recognition of Forest Rights) Act, 2006, along with the rules and guidelines for its implementation, is available at https:// tribal.nic.in/downloads/FRA/FRAActnRulesBook.pdf.

Acknowledgments

The generosity of many people over many years has brought this book into being. My first thanks are to the villagers of Ramnagar, whose hospitality under profoundly trying circumstances I can only hope to be able to reciprocate. I hope that this book will be able to contribute in some way to their struggle. The activists of the Sangathan brought me to Ramnagar and, along with the Ramnagaris, shared their homes, meals, and visions for a more just forest and world. They provided living examples of how to see the world as it is and as it could be, how to find and open the cracks of possibility in the social order.

Ragini Behen and the staff of the Banwasi Seva Ashram provided me with food, a room of my own, and answers to many questions. I could not have conducted this research without them.

The research that forms the foundation of this work was carried out during my time at Harvard University. Ajantha Subramanian has been an extraordinary mentor and a model for a politically engaged and principled life as a scholar. Steve Caton introduced me to a more expansive understanding of language and communication in the world. Asad Ahmed encouraged me to think more carefully about law and language, and to read everything twice. Mahesh Rangarajan has been an ongoing mentor and guide through the world of Indian forest history and politics. K. Sivaramakrishnan provided crucial advice at an early stage of my research and has continued to be generous with his time and guidance.

The essential form of this book and its argument emerged over late-night conversations in Cambridge in an apartment on Inman street with Naor Ben-Yehoyada, Alireza Doostdar, Alex Fattal, Tilsa Ponce, and Emrah Yıldız. Claudio Sopranzetti's friendship, his food, and his relentless, critical engagement have sustained my intellectual life. Dilan Yıldırım has been such an important interlocutor over such a range of topics over the years that it would be impossible to trace exactly the shape of her influence. Many other mentors and comrades at Harvard and in Cambridge have left their mark on this book, including Sam Asher, Felicity Aulino, Sai Balakrishnan, Philip Cartelli, Kerry Chance, Rebecca Chang, Juana Dávila, Namita Dharia, Sally Falk Moore, Susan Farley, Marianne Fritz, Bridget Hanna, Nicholas Harkness, Michael Herzfeld, Jason Jackson, Hayden Kantor, Anush Kapadia, Julie Kleinman, Ekin Kurtiç, Darryl Li, Jared McCormick, Dinyar Patel, Federico Pérez Fernández, Sanjay Pinto,

Mircea Raianu, Ivette Salom, Caterina Scaramelli, Benjamin Siegel, Joshua Specht, and Namita Wahi.

In Delhi I was fortunate to have the friendship and support of Raghu Karnad, Shruti Ravindran, Sonal Shah, and Anmol Tikoo. Lilly Irani has been a co-conspirator since the earliest months of fieldwork, as a flatmate, an intellectual sounding board, and a friend. G. D. Agrawal, K. C. Deo, Debi Goenka, Shankar Gopalakrishnan, Shomona Khanna, Ashish Kothari, Mark Poffenberger, Pradip Prabhu, Archana Prasad, Vasant Saberwal, Madhu Sarin, N. C. Saxena, Nitin Sethi, and B. D. Sharma were all generous with their time and their ideas. Arshiya Bose was the first to point me to the Forest Rights Act as an interesting question for an ecologically minded anthropologist, and it has been my good fortune to have been able to continue our conversation over the years. M. Rajshekhar indulged my inner investigative journalist and provided me with countless leads, documents, and theories.

Among the other friends who I have been fortunate to have learned from and whose ideas have shaped this book are Dwai Banerjee, David Bateman, Kishor Bhat, Lisa Björkman, Rishidev Chaudhuri, Sandipto Dasgupta, Navyug Gill, Radhika Govindrajan, Brandon Hamilton, Mik Kinkead, Michael Levien, Andrew Liu, Debashree Mukherjee, Karuna Nundy, Poulami Roychowdhury, Mihir Sharma, Nishita Trisal, and Bharat Venkat. My conversations with Begüm Adalet began many years ago, and she has helped shape every chapter of this book. Bruce Grant introduced me to anthropology when I was an undergraduate, and it has been my good fortune that he hasn't stopped sharing his wisdom with me since.

Funding from the Norwegian Research Council provided me with time and resources to work on this book. More important, it brought me into conversation with Alf Gunvald Nilsen and Kenneth Bo Nielsen to think through Gramsci, social movements, and the politics of the conjuncture in India.

My colleagues and students at Reed College have provided a lively and collegial home to finish the writing of this book. Over long walks and drinks with Paul Silverstein, he helped me find my feet as a teacher and as a scholar. Charlene Makley has been a wonderful mentor, welcoming me into the department and to several of her many projects at Reed and beyond. LaShandra Sullivan and Betsey Brada provided me with opportunities to talk through arguments and syllabi alike. One long conversation over a long evening at Radhika Natarajan and Paddy Riley's home helped me pin down the central argument of the book. I also owe thanks to Miishen Carpentier, Nejat Dinç, Emily Hebbron, Yaejoon Kwon, Alejandra Roche Recinos, and Darcy Tanner. Dan Plekhov expertly produced the map, with careful attention to the political nuances of mapmaking. Lilia Noger-Onstott provided a very helpful early reading of the manuscript. In Portland, I am grateful for the friendships of Victor Cazares, Pinky Hota, Barbie Malaran, Asa Natarajan, Yalçın Özkan, Grace Peck, Aurora Pérez-Salom, Guillermo Pérez-Salom, Vincent Pham, Bertha Rangel, Ivette Salom, Alpen Sheth, Mrinalini Tankha, and Sameer ud Dowla Khan. Over many years of friendship, Federico Pérez Fernández has provided me with his thoughtful advice and support. By this point, I suspect that he has read every chapter of this book twice, and I only hope I can repay him for his care and generosity.

The research for this book was carried out with support from the Cora Du Bois Charitable Trust, a Fulbright-Nehru fellowship, the Lakshmi Mittal and Family South Asia Institute, the Norwegian Research Council, the Radcliffe Institute for Advanced Studies, a Reed College Sabbatical Fellowship, the Wenner-Gren Foundation, and the Wenner-Gren Osmundsen Initiative. Portions of this book have been published as articles in *Seminar* (2017) and *Focaal* (2023). Portions of chapter 2 were previously published as "'Word Traps' and the Drafting of India's Forest Rights Act," in *Staking Claims: The Politics of Social Movements in Contemporary Rural India*, edited by Uday Chandra and Daniel Taghioff (Oxford University Press, 2016), used by permission of Reed College. Portions of the preface and introduction were previously published as "New Villages for Old: Collective Action and Conditional Futures after India's Forest Rights Act," *Political and Legal Anthropology Review* 45, no. 1 (2022).

I want to thank my editors at Cornell University Press and the Series on Land: Michael Goldman, Mahinder Singh Kingra, Nancy Lee Peluso, and Wendy Wolford. Michael in particular has provided help through the entire writing process with everything from the book's argument and framing to its structure. My developmental editor, Holliana Bryan, provided invaluable feedback and suggestions from the sentence level to the book's larger argument. Blair Peruniak shared critical feedback and edits with me and made the index for the book.

My partner Jyothi Natarajan is in every page of this book. She has brought her adventurous intellect and editor's eye as she's helped with every sentence and every thought, and the life that we have together has sustained me through this too long process. My brother Vivek and my sister Anjali have been close friends, intellectual sparring partners, and generous supports. I thank Miriam Jacobs, Gaurav Mendiratta, Kavya Mendiratta, Sudha Natarajan, Murali Natarajan, Vani Natarajan, Nick Parkinson, Akanksha Vaidya, Anita Vaidya, and Manushka Vaidya. I thank my parents, Beverly and Prabhakar. Their love has carried me through life. No one was more excited for this book than my father, who passed away before it was complete. I dedicate it to him.

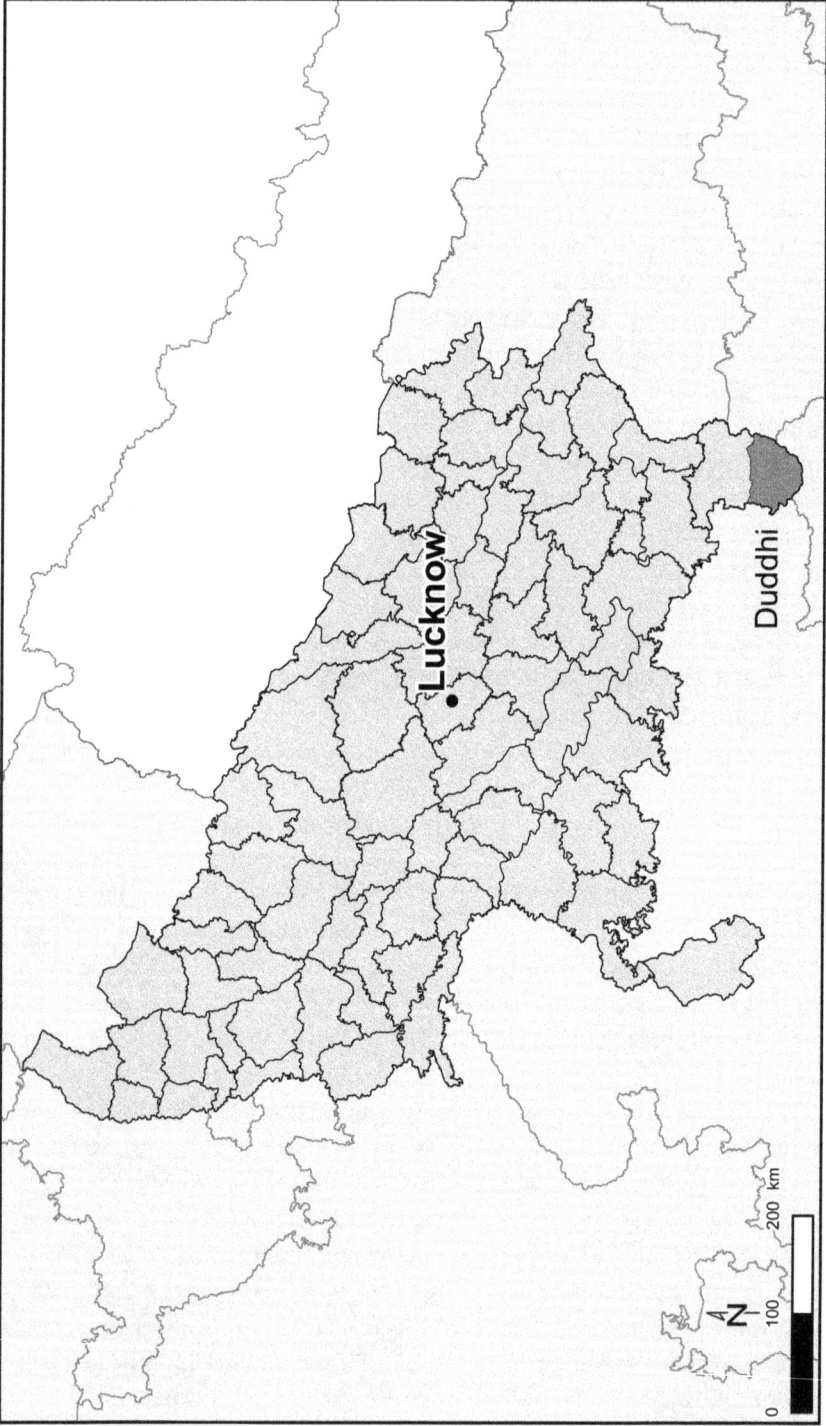

MAP 1. Map of Uttar Pradesh.

FUTURE OF
THE FOREST

INTRODUCTION

In October 2002, India's Forest Department began a drive to evict people who were living in the country's forests. In forest villages from Maharashtra to Tamil Nadu, guards arrived at people's homes and started to force people out. A man named Kalla, from Banswada district in Rajasthan, would describe his family's eviction this way:

> I had gone out on mazdoori [labor] work. My wife was at home alone. A group of 20–25 persons from the forest department including the beatguard and ranger came there. We had houses in the forest, our ancestors used to stay there and the forest department people came to evict all the eight houses. People chased them away but they cornered our daughter and forcibly took her signature. They came back after eight days and destroyed all the produce of cotton, maize and grain and they took away things from our house. They have even taken away my water pump. They threatened us saying that this is not your ancestors' property. I said to them that my forefathers have lived and died in this place.
>
> We pleaded with them saying, "Please leave us at least a little grain to eat, sahib." They ignored this, took away some of the grain and destroyed the rest. I rushed to the police station to lodge a complaint. They told me that this concerns the forest department, not the police. Then we went to the Collector. He also told us to leave. Then when the area manager came we showed him our "pattas" and he said they were

false pattas. But we said to him that these pattas had been issued by him himself. They are not ready to accept the pattas and they are not ready to show us the area maps. They even arrested ten of us and took us to jail. (Campaign for Survival and Dignity 2003, 97)

Kalla's signed pattas, or land deeds, were supposed to have exempted his family from the eviction order: they were proof that his family's home had been regularized. This deed was a written document, signed by an authorized official, that ostensibly provided proof that the owner did, indeed, have rights to the land. In Indian forests like the one in which Kalla and his family lived officials would periodically "regularize" the holdings and rights of residents: in response to political mobilizations, new state laws, or directives from higher officials, they would grant deeds, or pattas, that provided written proof of residents' land rights. Yet Kalla's pattas, which were meant to prevent eviction, failed that day. This record of what Derrida (1988) has called a "signature-event," marking an agreement by the official that the land belonged to Kalla's family, was ignored, the official denied that the signature was his or that the event had taken place, and the eviction was carried out. Those who would not leave their homes were arrested.

Kalla's was one of roughly three hundred thousand families that would be evicted across the country between 2002 and 2003 (Drèze 2005), as forest guards carried out orders that had been sent down from the national Ministry of Environment and Forests in New Delhi. As a result of those orders, people who lived in forest settlements that had not been regularized—or, in the case of Kalla's family, people whose regularized holdings would not be recognized—were to be evicted.

Over the following years, however, conditions would change radically for the millions of people who live in forests in India. A new national movement would halt the evictions within the year and, three years later in 2006, it would pass a law that would allow Kalla and millions of others to claim rights to forest land—a law that would set off one of the largest redistributions of land that India or any other country had seen. That law was the Scheduled Tribes and Other Traditional Forest Dwellers (Recognition of Forest Rights) Act, which is popularly known as the Forest Rights Act (FRA). This book is an account of the Forest Rights Act and the transformations it brought to many millions of India's forest dwellers and the land they live on.

Hundreds of millions of people live on the quarter of India's land area that is state forest land. For most of these forest dwellers, the land is also a source of livelihood: the forests are full of agriculture, small fields growing lentils, wheat, potatoes, and many other crops. Millions of people who live inside or near the forest depend on this land, using it to graze their animals and to gather sticks for firewood, *tendu patta* leaves to make the wrappers for beedi cigarettes, or *mahua* flowers to make wine. This land has also been a valuable site of extraction: the colonial Forest Department sought revenue through the sale of its timber, and in the twentieth century, coal companies have found India's largest bauxite seams underneath forest land.

No reliable survey has been conducted of the people who lived without rights in India's forests before the passage of the FRA in 2006. Estimates put 60 percent of landless forest dwellers—somewhere between seventy to one hundred million people—in the legal category of Scheduled Tribes, and of the remaining 40 percent, many if not the majority in the legal category of Scheduled Castes (Guha 2007; Sahoo and Sahu 2019; Jahan 2023). These legal categories emerge out of colonial ethnographic attempts to account for two groups: according to this view, members of Scheduled Castes (i.e., members of the formerly "untouchable" castes) fell within but at the bottom of the Hindu caste hierarchy, while members of Scheduled Tribes, who often lived in designated forest areas away from India's urban and agrarian settlements, fell outside of the caste hierarchy altogether.[1] The legal category of Scheduled Castes corresponds roughly to the political category Dalit, or the oppressed, a term coined by the nineteenth-century anticaste reformer Jotiba Phule which has gained deep affective and political salience. The category of Scheduled Tribes in turn corresponds roughly to the political category Adivasi, or indigenous, a term that gained currency over the twentieth century as Adivasi leaders began to locate themselves in relation to a transnational movement of indigenous people (see Xaxa 1999; Niezen 2003).

The Forest Rights Act would enable enormous changes to the order of caste and property in India's forests, but it was a short nine-page text written without consensus about exactly what those changes would be. The draft bill would be amended many times to accommodate conflicting visions of the forest and the people who live in it: the narratives of conservationists, of political parties, of organizations representing forest dwellers. The law would need to be able to travel across contexts, with its procedures and categories being fit to new specifics. It would have to be legible through multiple conflicting narratives. The law would have to be able to undo Kalla's dispossession. Conservationists would need to be satisfied that the law would protect the forest. Politicians in the ruling United Progressive Alliance government saw the law as an effort to counter a Maoist insurgency that was taking hold in India's forests, but they invited activists who had been associated with the revolutionary Left to write the bill's first draft. The law would have to fulfill goals associated both with the insurgency, by redistributing forest property as a step toward revolution, and with counterinsurgency, by persuading the armed insurgents to put down their weapons.

In this book, I track these movements and changes, following the law as it was created and as it made its way to two neighboring villages in the Central Indian forest belt, which I call Govindnagar and Ramnagar. The FRA was passed in an attempt to solve what I call the problem of the forest—that is, the problem of the extension of property to a group of people, forest dwellers, whose presence had been defined by an absence of property rights. From the nineteenth century on, the people who live in forests have found that they have been unable to enforce their claims to the land that they live on and the products of it that they use. The problem of the forest is thus also a problem of the state: the forests have seen a long history of political authority that is absent or fractured, but when it has acted, it has overwhelmingly acted on behalf of the powerful. As they were for Kalla, property laws in the forest have tended to be interpreted to the detriment of marginal forest dwellers. The ability to claim and hold land was inseparable from a claim to substantive citizenship, from a status as a subject with rights enforceable by the state.

If the many years of residence that Kalla and his family had in the forest could be made irrelevant, and their deed to the land could be ignored, then the question that faced forest dwellers and forest rights activists was how to gain the political authority to enforce claims for those who did live on the land. This political authority would be sought in the name of the law, but it would be gained through collective action. The slow, halting, and contradictory process through which this authority would be claimed is the story of this book.

Property and Dispossession

The dispossession of India's forest dwellers began in the second half of the nineteenth century with the establishment of the colonial Forest Department and the passage of a series of laws that would allow the department to claim possession of land through eminent domain. Many areas were dense with valuable trees such as teak, but the land that would be claimed was defined less by its specific ecology than by the absence of enforceable property claims, turning it into a *terra nullius* without settlers (Kapila 2022).[2] Much of this land had been classified as uncultivated waste before its reclassification by the Forest Department, and the arrival of fences in the forest (Rangarajan 1996) marked the introduction of a new regime of property. Over the following decades, the Forest Department went on to claim nearly a quarter of the country's land area, but only in rare cases did it grant legal recognition to the rights of the people who lived on that land. As a result, forest dwellers became vulnerable to dispossession for the sake of forestry, dams, and industry.

The Indian Forest Service was established through the Indian Forests Act of 1865 with the right to claim land "for the better management and preservation of Forests" (36). The questions of what management and preservation entailed, however, and what rights if any the people who lived in forests should have were debated in the early years of the Forest Service. These debates circled around contradictions between the goals of forest conservation, extraction of timber for government revenue, and the recognition of what were described as the customary rights of forest dwellers—and they would be framed in the legal language of property (see Guha 1990; Rangarajan 1994; Grove 1996; Philip 2003; Weil 2006).

The first Inspector General of Forests, the head of the newly established Indian Forest Service, was the German botanist Dietrich Brandis, who argued for the recognition of what he saw as the traditional and customary forms of conservation among forest dwellers. In the drafting of the 1878 Indian Forest Act, however, he would be sidelined by the Conservator of Forests for Punjab B. H. Baden-Powell, who sought to strengthen the state's claim on forest land.[3] As Baden-Powell would later put it, if the forest "is to be either managed or protected," it must be understood in terms of clearly defined and bounded rights of property:

> For if you realise the idea of a forest estate to be cared for as a piece of property and protected by law, you will also acknowledge that a "piece of property," if it is to be either managed or protected, must be defined as to its limits, and all questions of right and obligation arising in those limits must be settled. If that is not done, the forest is still in a fluid, uncrystallised state; it hardly deserves to be called "property," and in consequence any real conservancy will be unattainable. (1893, 4)

Chaudhry (2016) has argued that these debates had consequences beyond the forests; that legislators and administrators were forced to redefine the "bundle of rights" that property consisted of in India when they began to grapple with forest land, precisely because forests had yet to be made property. Baden-Powell thus proposed that property rights be disaggregated, with possession distinguished from rights to use, cultivate, and transfer. The task of legislation was to manage forests—whether for conservation or revenue—while taking account of the varied and more limited rights that forest dwellers might hold.

Such disaggregated and limited rights would be recognized in the 1878 Indian Forest Act, which created three classes of forests: (1) reserved forests, in which customary rights were to be either extinguished or transferred to other areas and recast as "privileges" rather than rights; (2) protected forests in which both rights and privileges were to be recorded but not recognized; and (3) village forests, within which customary rights could be recognized but only following the area's prior designation as a reserved forest. To the extent that forest dwellers' rights were recorded, therefore, they were now for the most part reframed as "privileges." The state's right to forests was consolidated by the Indian Forest Act of 1927, which maintained these three categories of forests and attempted to increase government revenues through licenses and duties on the sale of timber. Under the 1927 law, the Forest Department was required to "survey and settle" existing customary rights as it claimed land, but in most cases it did not do so, leaving the millions of people who lived on or depended on the forests without property rights to those forests or the legal right to use the land on which they lived.

With the expansion of Forest Department control, negotiation between different uses of the forest has proceeded over the years through a series of claims to the land in the legal language of property. Historically, some of these claims to property have been more successful than others, most notably those of the Forest Department. In many places, the claims of those seeking to build large dams and coal mines have triumphed over those made by Adivasi and low-caste forest dwellers. In others, claims by dominant-caste groups have led to their gaining rights over larger and more fertile holdings, while those of Adivasi and low-caste forest dwellers were either ignored or yielded smaller, less fertile holdings. Such distributions and redistributions of land have shaped work relations in the forests, compelling low-caste forest dwellers to find work with the Forest Department, the largest landowner, in cement factories and in coal mines, and on the fields of dominant-caste families with larger holdings.

Efforts by lower-caste and Adivasi forest dwellers to claim property rights over the years met limited success. A series of laws was passed over the twentieth century, each ostensibly allowing forest dwellers to claim greater rights to the forest, but as the late forest rights activist B. D. Sharma (2010, 2) puts it, these laws made up "an unbroken history of broken promises." Across geographies and historical regimes of accumulation, from the colonial to the neoliberal "land grab" (see Li 2011; Sampat 2015; Levien 2018; Goldman 2020; Kodiveri 2024), land rights were assigned inconsistently, often to members of dominant-caste rather than low-caste or Adivasi forest dwellers, and dispossession continued.

The problem of the forest is the problem that property claims made by low-caste and Adivasi forest dwellers failed, again and again, despite the passage of laws and the issuing of deeds. The problem of the forest is then a problem of how property is claimed and of what these claims do. The "bundle of rights" that a property relation consists of is a famously fluid assemblage, one that includes historically and situationally shifting rights to exclude, use, and possess (see Verdery 2003; Riles 2004); that defines relations between people and things and thereby defines both people and things (Strathern 1999).

When property claims are made through the law, however, they invoke the state, both to recognize and enforce those claims. One need not follow Locke ([1690] 2003) in seeing the state as existing in order to enforce property claims to recognize that, as Cronon (1983) has pointed out, every property claim implies the presence of the state to enforce it. Attempts to claim land for those who have faced decades or centuries of dispossession have gone hand in hand, then, with attempts to reorganize their relationship to the state, whether for low-caste and indigenous residents of India's forests, for black smallholders in independent Zimbabwe (Moore 2005), for working-class residents of informal settlements in São Paulo (Holston 2009), or for peasants in Paraguay's border regions (Hetherington 2009). Such attempts to claim land have also been attempts to claim substantive citizenship.

Yet, to return to Kalla and his family, for Indian forest dwellers, claims to land that had been recognized by the state were not enough to prevent dispossession. If "the idea of property acts powerfully in the contemporary world" (Verdery 2003, 15) then what sort of a problem is it when a claim to property *fails* to act, as it failed for hundreds of thousands of forest dwellers? What caused this failure, and under what circumstances might such a claim succeed? What would allow a reconfiguration of forest dwellers' relationship to the state? Would success require armed struggle? Civil disobedience? The intervention of the courts?

The movement for forest rights has been a series of attempts made by forest dwellers to answer this question, to produce a diagnosis of the problem of the forest and a cure. The movement led to a new law, but the law alone would not secure property rights for India's forest dwellers. The law was a product of collective action, and the answers that have been provided to the problem of the forest have been delivered through collective action. Collective action, which I understand to be actions whose effects can be understood only in relation to the collection of people involved in them, acted on multiple scales to produce the Forest Rights Act and would reorganize the relationship between forest dwellers, their land, and political authority in India. Collective demands for property through the law that drew on older narratives associated with the forest rights struggle would make their way into the law's text. As that text traveled and was brought into political practice, these collective demands would reshape what property meant in forests: by claiming land—and the rights to live on it, to cultivate it, to gather leaves and branches from it, and to conserve it—India's forest dwellers would reshape their own livelihoods, the contours of their political coalitions, and the terms of social life in forests.

But it was not only forest dwellers who were engaged in collective action around the FRA. The conflicts that accompanied the law's drafting produced a conflicted and ambiguous text that could be cited not only in the collective action that built Ramnagar but also in the collective attack that destroyed the village in 2011, described in the preface. The law could thus provide grounds for a reassertion of dominant-caste property rights, and these grounds in Ramnagar would be accepted by local bureaucrats and police. For elite environmentalists, the law could be a vehicle for a strengthened participatory conservation regime in the country's forests. The law would provide, in years to come, the means for a resurgent Hindu-nationalist politics to expand its Adivasi electorate. The contests over the law's drafting and passage—over word choices, over provisions, over whether the law should be passed at all—were articulated by (often elite) individuals, but they spoke as representatives of larger acting collectives, whether political movements, caste groups, or the Indian nation.

The problem of the forest was not solved by the law then: the FRA was not a technical or antipolitical fix to a problem. Nor did it shift forest politics to an individuated and elite domain of liberal rights and away from the political practices of the many (Chatterjee 2004). To the contrary, the FRA shifted collective politics to the terrain of a new, ambiguously worded law. This book traces the struggles over this terrain as a series of studies and experiments, collectives coming into being and fading away in efforts to rearrange relationships between people, things, and the state in the forest. The rest of this introduction presents these elements in their overlapping configurations, working through property, law, and collective action as each relates to questions of political authority and struggle in the FRA.

Property and Authority

The 2002 eviction drive left Kalla's family and many thousands of other forest dwellers homeless, but it also catalyzed the movement for the FRA that promised to resolve the problem of the forest: it promised to bring enforceable property rights to people whose presence on forest land had been marked by the absence of enforceable property rights.

The FRA was meant to bring such rights to the forest—or, as it was put in the law, to recognize forest dwellers' already existing but unrecognized rights—by allowing residents to claim up to four hectares of land per family. Under the law, they are also allowed use rights to the forest—for example, forest dwellers can graze animals and harvest plants that fall under the category of "minor forest produce," although the law prohibits them from felling trees. The rights that the FRA recognizes are distinct from the property rights that exist in much of India: they cannot be transferred or sold, but they can be passed on to descendants. To prevent people from moving onto forest land to claim rights after the FRA's passage, the law establishes cutoff dates for eligibility. Members of Scheduled Tribes must demonstrate that they have occupied forest land before December 13, 2005. The law establishes a higher bar for the millions of forest dwellers who are not members of Scheduled Tribes, who must prove seventy-five years of residence. The law also grants conservation authority to communities who live in forests, who for the first time must be consulted before forest land is to be sold to other parties or diverted to other uses. Communities are also able to claim forest rights together, without dividing their land into individual plots.

To date, more than two million families have successfully claimed rights through the FRA and gained pattas of their own. The meanings of these rights, the bundle of sticks that the pattas confer, are themselves subject to ongoing negotiations and contestations, both in individual villages and in national politics. In 2019, the Supreme Court ordered the eviction of all forest dwellers whose claims had not been settled, although the order was ultimately stayed. In 2022, the Union government announced new rules that would allow private companies to harvest timber without consulting communities who had gained rights through the FRA, which was in apparent violation of the law. The meaning of the legal text, what rights it confers to whom and how they are to be enforced, continues to be shaped through the collective action of low-caste and Adivasi forest dwellers, but also by political parties, landowning dominant-caste organizations, conservationists, and others.

Not everyone who has made claims through the FRA has been successful. Some 45 percent of all the rights claims that have been made through the law, the claims of some 1.75 million families, have been rejected (Sharma 2020). Among those 1.75 million families were the residents of the village Ramnagar. Ramnagar was settled on the promises made by the FRA, that forest dwellers would at last have their rights recognized and that a new relationship to the state would follow, but the law did not resolve the problem of the forest on its own. The Ramnagaris would see their claims rejected and their village destroyed by the dominant-caste landowners for whom they had previously worked—dominant-caste landowners who, in destroying Ramnagar, were themselves claiming to be implementing the FRA. The story of the Ramnagaris' struggle for the recognition of their rights to the forest is one of politics, of collective action at multiple scales, from New Delhi to a pair of villages in the forest, as it has interacted with a law.

Property and Insurgency

The problem of property in India's forests has ecological consequences. India's forests, at nearly a quarter of the country's land area, are a critical carbon sink: they hold an estimated 7,124 million metric tons of carbon (TERI 2020). India, with 2.4 percent of the world's land area, is home to 7–8 percent of all the world's recorded species—and forests are home to many of them. In the 1980s and 1990s, an average of 15,500 hectares of forest were formally diverted each year, removing them from Forest Department control and allowing them to be put to other uses. A third of the diverted area went to mining, with the rest going to irrigation, power plants, dams, roads, and other purposes (Joshi and Singh 2003).

Yet to limit the forests to their ecologies would be to miss the many conflicting meanings and investments that humans have given them, and the place of law in both mediating these conflicts and transforming them. As Gopalakrishnan (2010a) points out, the diversion of forest land—which allows it to be purchased at prices substantially below market rates—has functioned as an enormous subsidy for Indian capital, and the tens of millions of migrants from forests have provided a pool of cheap labor. In parallel to an intensifying accumulation by dispossession (Harvey 2003), the multiple strains of India's militant Maoist movement found their way to the forest belt from the late 1970s on. The movement aims to wage a guerrilla "people's war" against the Indian state as a path toward socialism. Maoists found in forests both geographic refuge from state surveillance with their hills and trees and a receptive audience: the millions of people who lived without legal rights to the land they lived on, and who were therefore easily evicted to make way for dams, factories, and mines. Forest Department officials and local landowning and mercantile elites were the local targets in such areas, which became strongholds as the strands of the Maoist movement grew to a reported fourteen thousand full-time guerrillas by 2010, active across 180 of India's 718 districts (*The Economist* 2010). In 2010, Prime Minister Manmohan Singh would famously call the movement "the biggest internal security challenge facing our country" (*The Hindu* 2010).

India is not the only country that has seen forest-based insurgencies in recent decades: Colombia's FARC (the Revolutionary Armed Forces of Colombia), Peru's Shining Path, the Allied Democratic Forces in the Democratic

Republic of Congo and Uganda, and Communist movements in Thailand and Malaysia have all found territory and constituencies in forests (see Peluso and Vandergeest 2011). As in Colombia, Thailand, and the Democratic Republic of Congo, state counterinsurgency tactics in India have included both the use of force and the use of law: laws that redistributed land, specifically, and that it was hoped would bring consent and hegemony to forests. As the politician Kishore Chandra Deo, who had served as the chair of the Joint Parliamentary Committee that shepherded the FRA through Parliament, told me in a 2012 interview, the government had seen the FRA as a response to the forest-based Maoist movement.

By recognizing forest dwellers' property and use rights, they hoped the law would preempt the insurgency. The law, in other words, would not only bring rights to forest dwellers: it also would secure their consent for the Indian state. The FRA was a response to a failure of state hegemony in forest areas, and the text that emerged opened up a new arena of hegemonic contestation, this time on legal and linguistic grounds. Conflicting political visions made their way into the text of the law, and political projects that had been associated with left-wing insurgency found their way into a law that aimed to curb that insurgency.

The FRA was a response, then, to a challenge to the Indian state's monopoly on legitimate violence. In establishing a new set of rules that would govern the relationship between forest-dwelling people and the forest they dwelled in, it was hoped that those people who might have joined the Maoist insurgency would not. And yet, violent contentious politics seem to follow the FRA wherever it goes. Far from replacing nonstate violence with the rule of law, the FRA brought many possible rules into play, backed by every form of politics, including violence.

Laws, Threats, and Traps

The FRA emerged over months of conflict between distinct organizations, politicians, bureaucrats, and lobbyists, all seeking to create a legal text that would produce distinct arrangements of people, property, and forests. These visions coexist in the text as contradictory possible readings, possible configurations of forests and people that can be grounded in the act.

The problem of how laws will be interpreted and used is not limited to the FRA. Legal scholars (e.g., Cover 1983; West 1993; Brooks and Gewirtz 1998) have long been aware that laws are often interpreted through the use of nonlegal narratives that function less as sets of rules than as intermediary cotexts (Silverstein and Urban 1996): theories or histories that frame the problems the law addresses and solutions to those problems that the law provides. Sivara-makrishnan (1995) has shown, for example, that a selective and strategic production of narratives of India's forests has long played a powerful role in justifying forest administration.

The FRA was written, however, to be read through narratives that were not present in its text, narratives about the relationship between people, forests, and property that circulated through political movements. Its many authors allowed for these extralegal readings through what the bureaucrat R. Gopal-akrishnan who helped to usher the drafting of the bill called "word traps," that is, words and phrases that appeared innocuous in their referential meaning but that allowed readers to fit the text into politicized narratives of the forest. Such word traps allowed the laws' authors to act on behalf of their constituencies by placing the rules according to which the law was to be interpreted within the text as a *potential*. The authors of laws can enable extralegal narrative framings in the law's text itself, either by providing such a framing themselves (in a law's preamble, for instance) or by embedding words or phrases that do not change the strictly referential meaning of the law, but that invoke already circulating extralegal cotexts. The authors of the FRA thus took advantage of a prolifera-tion of moralized narratives of property, people, and forests in India by insert-ing words and phrases that would allow it to be interpreted not according to its strict legal provisions, but instead as the redemption or culmination of moral-ized histories. The FRA, in other words, was written in order to be interpreted not only in bureaucracies and courts, but also by organized groups of landless forest dwellers and to aid in organizing such groups.

Laws may be written by a small number of people in a small number of rooms and places, but those people both invoke and make claims to represent larger constituencies and they anticipate possible uses and effects of the law as they negotiate and fight for particular wordings. The voices that make their way into the law are not equivalent: they may be better suited for one particular purpose than another, and they may index and invoke different times, places, and ideol-ogies. Mikhail Bakhtin (1982) called these amalgams "chronotopes." Chrono-topes, Agha (2007) argues, should be understood as participation frameworks: they outline the time and space in which action will take place and the roles that will take part in this action, while leaving open the subjects of those roles. Laws' voices simultaneously invoke two chronotopes, two configurations of time and space: the time and space of the problems of the past that the law claims to redress and the time and space of the future that the law brings into being.

A law like the FRA purports to be universal, to apply evenhandedly and nonarbitrarily to events that have not yet taken place. The act emerged, how-ever, out of specific events, such as Kalla's family's dispossession in Rajasthan in 2002. These events had to be fit within nonspecific categories to build the larger coalition that could exert collective action on a scale that would force Parliament to pass a law. The FRA's word traps are a means of narratively connecting pasts and futures, fitting events to generalizable concepts that can travel across time and space and enable collective action at a scale that can pass a law to rearrange forest property across India.

The narratives that tied together disparate violent events in the FRA held a second set of more specific social valences as they were debated and written, although these specific valences could not make their way into the law's evenhanded text. The question of who exactly had done what to whom was raised again and again: Was it the colonial state, the courts, the government, the Forest Department, or dominant castes who had denied forest dwellers their rights? Was it Adivasis or all forest dwellers of all castes who had suffered? Roles for guilty and aggrieved parties were produced and contested. Histories of the forests that were fought over were themselves contested. These were contests over chronotopes, over the time and space of discourse, and the participation frameworks through which one might pick up that discourse and bring it to bear on a specific social situation.

Legal narratives, however, also carry with them compulsion, the ability to act on those social situations. Law's narratives are contingent on future events and carry the threat of force if certain other future events do not follow: as they are brought into social life, laws become attached to conditions and are made to carry specific threats—often threats to be carried out by state actors, such as courts, police, or Forest Department officers. In the case of the FRA, as it cued up chronotopes of forests and people and entered the many relations of force that cross the forests, the threats that it would produce would intervene in long histories of conflict over forest land and resources, as in Ramnagar and Govindnagar.

Legal meaning, as critical legal scholars (e.g., Trubek 1984; Solum 2010) have shown, is indeterminate: laws are made and remade both by formal authorities and ordinary people as they are interpreted, applied selectively, and ignored. And yet, an approach that emphasizes the agency of individuals in legal interpretation can lose sight of this rule-like capacity to constrain and coerce, as well as the common belief in the consistency and legitimacy of at least some legal rules. In 1978, Sally Falk Moore proposed that the indeterminacy of laws actually reflected a feature of social life more broadly; that "inconsistency, ambiguity, discontinuity, contradiction, paradox, and conflict" (49) in fact characterized all social and cultural orders. Regularities of symbolic form—whether of the FRA, a ritual, or even form in the built environment—can present the appearance of consistency in situations of political and social conflict and change. Moore called for an attention, therefore, to the practices through which situations are either regularized or adjusted, seeing the relative determinacy of certain social situations as a tentative achievement that is always vulnerable to challenges that may even appear as formal continuity. Processes of renewal claiming to preserve a given form can become processes of change, as the content attached to the form is shifted.

Moore's shift of focus, guiding analytic attention away from the search for an inherent character to laws and toward the practices that fix and unsettle legal meaning, raises new questions as the FRA makes its way to India's forests. The FRA was both a product of struggle and conflict and an effort to fix the relationship between people and the forests around them. The FRA is a text, ratified by Parliament, that, its drafters hoped, could be reproduced and circulated across India without changes to its meaning. Its drafters disagreed over what that meaning was, but each hoped that its meaning would be fixed, that it would rearrange the relationship between people and the forests in specific ways. The law's word traps allowed for several such conflicting attempts to fix the law's meaning: they would delegate the regularization of legal meaning to other groups who were equipped with the narratives and political capacity to carry out the collective action needed to bring about specific relations of people and property in the forest.

To follow the production and circulation of the new law requires, then, an attention to the lives of the text both as an artifact that constrains the possibilities of its interpretation and as it contains within itself new political possibilities (see Messick 1996; Riles 2006; Hetherington 2011; Hull 2012). *Future of the Forest* thus tracks both what Silverstein and Urban (1996) call "entextualization" and "contextualization," the processes through which the text is written and through which it is read and cited to be brought into social and political life. These processes are linked by a text, but the sites of the text's contextualization are not limited to trained judges in courtrooms or to bureaucrats in their offices, to name two sites in which legal interpretation is relatively restricted and regimented.[4] Alongside such authorized channels, the text circulates through social movements, including the Sangathan, which foster their own interpretive practices and narrative frames. As we will see, the text itself, through the struggles that produced it, enables both its interpretive fixing and its unfixing, its opening up to new possible readings and uses.[5]

Tracking the FRA as it makes its way to India's forests produces a second problem for a study of the production of legal meaning. If, following decades of insurgency, Ramnagar and the forests were a domain in which state hegemony had little grip, in which disputes were settled through coercion rather than consent and no shared world of legal forms exists, then how could legal meaning ever take shape? The new law could be seen as a bid for hegemony, an attempt to produce a shared world of legal forms by providing a set of terms via a legal text through which certain disputes could be resolved or, as William Roseberry puts it, "a common language or way of talking about social relationships that sets out the central terms around which and in terms of which contestation and struggle can occur" (1994, 361). And yet, beyond a recognition of the legitimacy of the law, very little was in fact shared: how the law was to be interpreted, who was to be in charge of producing authoritative interpretations, and in what forum disputes over its interpretation should be settled. How, then, can we understand the story that leads from the FRA to Ramnagar's destruction? One answer, I suggest, lies in the central place of collective action in this story.

Collective Action and the Law

Collective action, often contentious and at times violent, has marked the entire life of the Forest Rights Act, from the movements that pushed for its passage to fights over villages like Ramnagar. It is through this collective action that the law's meaning has taken shape. In this book, I use collective action to mean actions whose effects can be understood only in relation to the collection of people involved. A strike, for example, depends for its efficacy on the participation of a large portion of a workforce. Elections, rallies, and sit-ins similarly operate through the large number of people participating in them. The FRA was a response to the problem of the forest that took shape through collective action, the act would be passed and brought into social life through collective action, and after its destruction Ramnagar would ultimately be rebuilt and would remain through the effects of collective action.

Collective action is not new to anthropology or to the social sciences. Political anthropologists have long recognized the importance of collective or group action in political practice (e.g., Evans-Pritchard 1940; Gluckman 1940). Threats and checks between groups maintained and destabilized balances of forces for early political anthropologists, who implicitly treated the present as defined against future collective action. Within anthropological literature on social movements, a rich body of work has studied collective action (e.g., Edelman 1999; Nash 2001; Tsing 2004). In Li (2007), for example, collective action is treated as a capacity of some but not all subaltern groups, produced through the historical contingencies of kinship networks, rituals, and charismatic leaders. A rich body of work on politics in South Asia has studied collectives in relation to language and media, as they are produced through address as publics (e.g., Bate 2009; Cody 2013) and as crowds (Chowdhury 2019).

By focusing on the effects of collective action, I hope to avoid a methodological individualism that has preoccupied much work on collective action.

Scholars in sociology, economics, and political science who have been concerned with understanding the motivations behind individuals' participation in collective action have attempted to explain it through shared grievances, ideologies, norms, or identifications (e.g., Smelser 1963; Ostrom 1998; Tarrow 1998). As I discuss in later chapters, however, the shapes and motivations of the collectives that produced Ramnagar were themselves varied and unfixed, shifting as futures became more and less possible. An identification as "Dalit Adivasis," drawing together lower castes and indigenous people, took form and then faded as a future of land rights in Ramnagar became more and then less possible, following the destruction of the village. As in Richland's (2008) ethnography of the emergence of tribal traditions and jurisprudence in the Hopi Tribal Court, the contours of community were themselves negotiated in the citation of community-specific law.

Through an attention to these ongoing enactments of collective action, therefore—to the capacity of collective action to produce both new futures and new collectives—I hope to avoid an emphasis on longue-durée social structures. I treat collectives instead as tentative achievements that are oriented toward futures, toward the achievement of a rule-like regularity of legal interpretations. The groups that took shape to create the FRA—the groups that settled and that destroyed Ramnagar—were not predetermined by the region's social structures, but instead came into being through collective action and the futures it made. This book, then, examines the capacity of the collective action that produced the FRA at each moment of its life to make and remake not only the law, but also the social and ecological worlds in which the law came into being.

The future has come into anthropologists' sight over the last decade, as efforts to place our research in time have built on an older historical turn to examine how our interlocutors relate to what is to come. Such prefiguration of futures as utopias and as threats is central to the work of collective action. Collective action can be seen as acting twice: once in its moment of occurrence and again in the threats and visions that it produces—of future attacks on Ramnagar if it were to be rebuilt, for example, or of electoral losses if the FRA were not to be passed by Parliament. Such futures, for the Ramnagaris and their attackers, and for the activists, bureaucrats, and politicians I discuss in this book, contain a wide range of visions, of land rights and threats of violence, that are all produced in and shape the present. These futures were not simply a set of paths that lay ahead but were a range of threats, counterthreats, and visions of justice that were already shaping the contours of daily life. Making other futures more or less possible, then, can make other presents more or less possible.

Some of these futures were only indicated; the implicit threat of a second attack on the village if it were rebuilt did not need to be spoken aloud by the attackers. Many of the law's futures would be explicitly articulated, however, demanded and discussed throughout the law's life. To track the life of the law, then, is to track the range of linguistic practices about those futures—a host of analyses, narratives, and political visions—as they make their way into a legal text, and then as that text travels through Parliament, moves across the country, and is brought into political practices.

If, as politician Kishore Chandra Deo told me, his government saw the FRA as a counterinsurgency measure, as an effort to provide forest dwellers with the ability to claim property so that they would not join the Maoist revolt, then we can see the law as an effort to recast insurgent political projects in the language of hegemony. In this effort, however, the government's project to gain state hegemony took on the language of an insurgency. Left forest activists who were familiar with being labeled Maoists themselves would write the first drafts of the law. Other leftist forest activists would lobby for the law's passage and, even as they considered its provisions insufficient to the task of finally providing justice to India's forest dwellers, they would see in it the potential for the beginning of a much larger, even revolutionary, redistribution of property in the country. These were not the only projects and movements that would find their way into the drafting process: environmentalist activists brought about dramatic revisions to the bill's text at a crucial stage, and political parties representing diverse caste coalitions would have their say over its provisions, as I discuss in chapter 2. The text's contextualization has brought it into new channels and institutions, including new political projects outside of the visions of the law's drafters: the law has not only traveled through the printed and bound texts, but through many parallel channels, from cellphone calls to rallies to word of mouth. These many channels have shaped the ways the law is deployed and used.

These practices of drafting, reading, and interpreting the law's text, however, all take place against a backdrop of forest-based insurgency and counterinsurgency, with struggles over the forest refracted into clauses and phrases in the law and fragments of text making their way back to forests to be contextualized in fights over land and use rights. This process can be usefully understood semiotically, as an ongoing process through which rules that shape social life in forests are made, picked up, reinterpreted, and remade: who can live where in the forest, who they would work for, what trees they can cut down, what flowers they can harvest. This is an ongoing, iterative process of rulemaking, in which meaning is produced neither through the individual choices of those interpreting the law nor through a stable authority tasked with its interpretation, but through collective action. The Forest Rights Act is made and remade through the collective action of those involved in struggles over the forest and the legal text, everyone from the dominant-caste men who attacked Ramnagar to the collection of bureaucrats, politicians, and activists who wrote the FRA. This collective action operates twice, both in its immediate effects and by pointing to a potential future of what the collective might do: they might attack the village again, or they might deny support in a crucial vote. Such threats, as they come to be understood as conditional—conditional on the villagers returning to Ramnagar to rebuild, for example—solidify into rules that shape life in the present.

The law emerged out of a vast mobilization of collective action, through a newly organized national campaign of forest dwellers, a national calculus on the part of politicians about voting patterns in the forests, and out of years of Maoist insurgency. One result of this mobilization was the creation of the law as a text, as a mobile, replicable artifact that could be read and reread to bring rules to bear on different forests and in different contexts. But the law contained within itself a range of voices and visions—word traps that in chapter 2 I describe as potential chronotopes, seeds that enable the law to be read through political narratives about forests and people that are not present within the text. Via the law's word traps, these potential chronotopes could be picked up, fit within extralegal narratives, and brought into political practice in places like Ramnagar as a result of a second effect of the mobilization: the nationalized movement itself. The movement for the Forest Rights Act produced more than a law. In its mobilization, an infrastructure of collective action took shape. This infrastructure could be mobilized to act again: it could make further demands regarding the law, but it could also carry the text with it to new forests across the country, and with the text it could bring para-texts, interpretations of the law and narratives about the longer forest struggle.

The collective action that would produce Ramnagar and destroy it had effects well beyond the interpretation of the law. Ramnagar and Govindnagar's ecologies would be transformed repeatedly through such collective action, as trees were planted and felled, as crops planted and destroyed, animals reared and then taken away. The shape of the ecology that the Ramnagaris would live in was being made and remade, through action oriented around reshaping property rights. A turn in environmental anthropology over the last two decades has usefully addressed the question of how people relate to the nonhuman, as scholars have urged anthropologists to expand the boundaries of the world that humans exist in to include nonhumans. A key insight of this work has been that humans' understandings of themselves are forged through relations with nonhumans: people relate to the nonhuman and understand themselves, in part, through these relations (see Haraway 2003; Paxson 2012; Kohn 2013). Such work on the coconstitution of humans and nonhumans echoes older scholarly discussions of the transformations of people and things when they exist in property relations. Scholars from Karl Marx ([1887] 1990) to

Marcel Mauss ([1925] 1990), and more recently Marilyn Strathern (1999) and Alain Pottage and Martha Mundy (2004) have argued that property relations, in establishing relations—often exclusionary—between things and people who possess them, redefine both the things and the people. In following the fate of the Forest Rights Act and Ramnagar, this book attempts to bring these insights together, to examine the mutually implicated transformations of relations between the Ramnagaris with one another and their larger social world, along-side and through the transformations of property relations with the nonhuman world around them.

Fieldwork in Motion

I was brought to Ramnagar through an interest in India's environmental poli-tics, which I had been convinced placed the urgent demands of ecological crisis and the equally urgent demands of addressing deep socioeconomic inequality at odds. What sense could it make to set aside land and resources for protected forests when so many people in India lacked shelter? And yet it was those same people, the poor and those marginalized on axes of caste and religion, who would likely bear the brunt of drought, deforestation, and climate crisis. The Forest Rights Act was a tremendously exciting effort to address both sides of this contradiction: the law set out to undo more than a century of dispossession in India's forests and to avert ecological disaster, by granting both rights as well as conservation authority to the people who live in the forests.

As I began my preliminary fieldwork in the summer of 2008, the law was unfolding in front of me, making its way across the country through new and old channels of kin networks, bureaucracies, movements, and nongovernmen-tal organizations (NGOs).[6] I could follow the new law as it came into effect, seeing how it transformed the lives of forest dwellers and the forests that they dwelled in. In June 2009, I met Geeta and Amit, the two conveners of what I call the Sangathan, or "movement," an organization spanning several states that had been present in the push for the FRA seven years earlier and was now working to help forest dwellers claim rights through the act across North and Central India.

We first met in Delhi, in Geeta's family's flat. Over tea, the two explained their organization to me, and invited me to an event that they were holding a few weeks later, in Lucknow, the state capital of Uttar Pradesh. Uttar Pradesh is India's largest state, and it had nearly two hundred million inhabitants in 2009. Geeta and Amit had set up a public meeting with representatives from the state government and with forest rights activists, including Ram Lakhan and other

Ramnagaris. They told me that I would be able to meet forest dwellers from across the state there and get a sense of the strides that their movement was making in helping people gain forest rights.

It was a hot summer afternoon when I made it to the Lucknow auditorium that hosted the public meeting. Under ceiling fans weakly trying to blow away the heat, three hundred or so people sat in foldout, cinema-style chairs. At any given moment, it seemed to me, roughly 10 percent of the audience was asleep. On stage, ten people sat in a row behind a lectern, to which each of them walked in turn to speak. The chief conservation officer of the state Forest Department was one of them, as was a minister in the state cabinet who belonged to the Bahujan Samaj Party (BSP), a party with a political platform that was explicitly in support of lower-caste communities. Village representatives stood and gave testimonials about harassment from their local forest departments, which frequently evicted them from their land and did not allow them to gather leaves, sticks, and fruit from the forest.

The minister, a tall man in a white kurta pajama with a loud voice and a thick mustache, stood up in the midafternoon and gave a fiery speech. He said that Mayawati, the BSP chief minister of Uttar Pradesh, supported the law and forest dwellers. The law, he said, was protection against the multinational corporations that were stealing forest land from Dalits and Adivasis, members of the lowest castes and indigenous people. The law was the fulfillment of the promise of India's independence: it gave the country's forest dwellers independence for the first time from the colonial laws that had taken away their land. Mayawati's support for the law was so strong, the minister said to loud applause, that she would ignore the requirement that forest dwellers who do not belong to the state category of Scheduled Tribes prove seventy-five years of residence in the forest.

It was at the Lucknow hearing that day that it first became clear to me that the meaning of the FRA was not fixed, and that I would not simply be observing a law as it came into effect. A representative of the chief minister of India's largest state was claiming that, as a result of its strong support for the law, his government would be ignoring one of its provisions, making the rights recognized by the law more easily available to all forest dwellers. This announcement could be reduced to electoral realpolitik: the primary constituency of the BSP are members of Scheduled Castes, some of whom live in forests. The party, in identifying itself with the new Forest Rights Act, needed to ignore a provision in the law that made it difficult to redistribute land to its primary constituency. Whatever the minister's motivations were, something new was emerging in the afternoon heat that day, reconfiguring the meaning of a law that I had assumed was fixed in ink on paper. The law, I began to see, was not restricted to the denotational meaning of its text. To remake the FRA in this case, a new coalition of people had to be brought together as a political force: state actors, activists, lawyers, journalists, and forest dwellers would reshape the law's meaning. I would come to realize that the law was being produced through collective action—that it was groups like this one coming together to make their own demands of the forest and tying those demands to the FRA that were shaping what the law meant. As they came together, these groups of people indicated what they *could* do—they could vote for certain political parties, they could destroy a village, they could claim land for Dalits who lived in the forests—and they would thereby remake both the law and the forest.

Movements require motion, Anna Tsing (2004) notes: to mobilize politically puts people in motion as they travel to new places with new comrades. This book, then, moves along with the movements that it studies. *Future of the Forest* tracks a law, the Forest Rights Act, as it came into being and as it made its way from Delhi to Ramnagar and Govindnagar. The activists who lobbied for the law moved: they met in Delhi in a crucial public hearing in 2002 and would travel back and forth from the capital to forests to meet with their organizations and allies as the movement for the new law gained force. In traveling between the forests and the country's capital, the activists followed tracks that had been built in the previous decades, as left activists and new circulations of capital made forests central to India's politics and political economy. To bring the law to the forests required further movement: trips by train and by jeep, text messages, phone calls, and emails all carried word of the new law to forest dwellers in Govindnagar and elsewhere. The movement of people did not end with the passage of the FRA: people from Ramnagar were in constant motion, not only for work in distant cities and farms, but to meet with other villagers, to attend rallies or court cases in the district headquarters, in the state capital Lucknow, or in distant Delhi. If the law's meaning was worked out through collective action, then the constant movement of people was necessary to produce the collectives that would act.

My research was in motion as well, along with the villagers, lawyers, activists, and the law, and it was clear to me from early in my fieldwork that I would not be producing either an urban ethnography or a village ethnography in the tradition of McKim Marriott and M. N. Srinivas. My fieldwork was meant to be divided between Delhi—where I spent time with activists, interviewed bureaucrats and politicians, and put together an archive of the many bills and memos that led up to the FRA—and Ramnagar. Yet even before their village was destroyed, the Ramnagaris were on the move. More than once I would arrive in the village after the thirty-six hours of travel from Delhi only to be told that we would be boarding a bus to catch another train for Allahabad, or Robertsganj, or Lucknow. Following the making and remaking of the FRA and of Ramnagar

requires, then, movement along with the text and its many authors and inter-
preters, as new collectives and new futures of the forest are made, come together
and disperse, in the changing horizons of conditional futures. As my research
with the law required shifting sites frequently to keep up with the villagers and
activists as they moved, the book similarly moves sites and scales.

Providing a narrative of collective practices across shifting sites and scales
presents its own challenges: to introduce each of the hundreds of residents of
Ramnagar or the many activists, lawyers, and others not based in Ramnagar
would have made for an unwieldy book. I make the choice, therefore, to focus on
a relatively small number of Ramnagar's residents and activists for narrative
clarity and to make larger collective processes concrete and narratively legible,
while simultaneously striving to undermine through the narrative and analysis
the apparently individuated account of political practice that this choice implies.

Following the Text

In this book, I follow efforts to solve the problem of the forest, the efforts by
people who have been denied the ability to claim property to claim those rights.
To track the Forest Rights Act as it has been imagined, written, and brought
into social life, this book brings together a history of dispossession in Ramnagar and Duddhi with a history of the forest rights movement and the law that
it produced. The problem of the forest would not be resolved for the Ramnagaris
either through the direct implementation of the FRA or through efforts to circumvent the law by occupying the land without authorization, but through a
reworking of their relationship with state actors through collective action. The
book's first chapters trace the history of forest property and the forest rights
movement at multiple scales, establishing the conditions of possibility that led
to the law's passage and, ultimately, to the destruction of Ramnagar. The chapters examine first how the collectives through which the law came to be enacted
themselves became possible, how they came together to draft and pass the
FRA's contradictory text, and how that text arrived in Duddhi. The book pro-
ceeds chronologically: the first portion of the book follows the emergence of the
conditions of possibility that led to the attack, and its final two chapters follow
events in the aftermath of Ramnagar's destruction in order to examine the law's
ongoing effects, both in the region around Ramnagar and across India.

In chapter 1, I lay out processes beginning in the 1970s that led to forest
landlessness becoming a national political problematic and, thus, the emergence of the conditions of possibility that led to the attack on Ramnagar. As
forests were made into a national political issue, the many groups contending

for the forests also began to realign themselves around the law—rather than a corrupt and arbitrary state—as fixed, nonarbitrary, and just. These challenges to the legitimacy of Indira Gandhi's government led to a shared vision of a potential future in which a nonarbitrary law could be used to discipline an arbitrary government. The result was a broad reorientation of politics around law, setting the stage for both further dispossession of India's forest dwellers and mobilization for a legal solution to their dispossession: the FRA.

Chapter 2 reconstructs the contests over the FRA's drafting, tracing the shifts in the text of the draft bill as it was being written, rewritten, and argued over. I locate these shifts within the debates of the committees tasked with writing the bill as well as within the political struggles that the bill's wordings indexed and the imagined effects of these wordings. Through disputes in ministries and protests on the streets, the law's many authors created a text that could be interpreted through extralegal narratives that aligned with their own political projects through what a bureaucrat who was involved in the law's drafting called "word traps." In so doing, they deferred a resolution to the question of who would ultimately claim rights through the law, and what those rights would entail, to the moment of its implementation. It is because of this deferral that the resolution of the law's meaning in Ramnagar was so protracted and violent.

Chapter 3 follows the FRA as it was brought to Duddhi and Govindnagar and worked into the two political projects that both built and destroyed the village, focusing on how law functions as rumor. The act arrived in the village as a rumor before it arrived as a text: a promise of land and political authority for people who had little of either. But the law-as-rumor was understood through two political projects that were distinguished both in their caste constituencies and in their approaches to rural Indian landlessness. Geeta, a leftist activist from Delhi who encouraged the settlement of Ramnagar, situated the settlement of the village in a Dalit liberatory project and promised a future in which caste would be annihilated once property had been redistributed. Ramnagar's attackers, in contrast, drew on a political vision in which the caste hierarchy was preserved but remoralized, as land reform was limited to gifts from upper castes to lower castes. Political authority over the conservation of the surrounding environment was thus to be restricted to higher castes. Both projects would find a legal basis for their promised futures in the FRA's word traps.

With chapter 4, I move to the aftermath of Ramnagar's destruction in 2011. The collective action that established Ramnagar had been oriented toward a potential future of land rights and the transcendence of exploitative caste relations. This orientation was premised on a new caste affiliation, one that brought together members of the lowest castes, those classified as Scheduled Castes and

Scheduled Tribes, as "Dalit Adivasis." That future, premised on legal rights to the forest, did not arrive, however, and the political identification of Dalit Adivasi around which Ramnagar was established began to break down. In their place, collective action began to be reorganized around subcaste and gender. The chapter concludes with a coda describing a political opening: how a new, unaffiliated politician who appeared sympathetic to the Ramnagaris' cause allowed a tentative reaffiliation and return to the village, although still without formal land rights.

Chapter 5, the book's final chapter, shifts to a national scale of legal interpretation and collective action over the FRA's intertwined political and economic effects, showing how the act slowed accumulation dramatically enough that it came to be seen as a threat to Indian capital. The rearrangements of land and labor relations that were taking place in Ramnagar were being repeated across the quarter of India that is forest land. In restricting access to free or cheap land at that scale, forest-based collective action began to challenge the foundations of the country's political economy, particularly potential future profits—the anticipation of accumulation. In response, representatives of large companies pushed for further revisions to the act. In response to lobbying efforts, governments have continued to reinterpret, amend, and selectively ignore the FRA. The law's meaning, fifteen years after its passage, has yet to be resolved. In Ramnagar, however, the problem of the forest found a tentative solution: through collective action, a new relationship between the villagers and state actors has emerged, and the village remains in place, even without formal titles.

HOW THE FORESTS BECAME INDIAN

"The Emergency drove the Left into the forests," Amit told me. "They went there to escape the state's reach, but then they began to understand the political economy of the forests and they began to organize people." Amit, now a bearded activist in his sixties, usually clad in a kurta and trousers, was one of the leftists he was describing. He had been part of movements that had organized the landless in Uttar Pradesh's forests since the 1970s, since the twenty-two-month state of emergency declared by Prime Minister Indira Gandhi, popularly known simply as "the Emergency."

We were talking on a cool night in November 2010 while traveling by jeep to Ramnagar. In a typical hour, Amit drank two cups of sweet, milky tea and smoked four cigarettes. He could do neither inside the jeep, so every time we drove through a village or town, Amit would ask our driver to let us out by a tea stall so that he could get his regular fix of nicotine and caffeine. The drive had started in Robertsganj in the northern part of the district of Sonbhadra, the portion that falls in the agricultural plains of the Ganges River valley that make up most of the state of Uttar Pradesh. To reach the subdistrict of Duddhi and Ramnagar, we had to travel south, across the Kaimur hills to the forest valleys on the other side. The drive took four long and bumpy hours, with Amit's tea and cigarette stops helping to break up and punctuate our journey, providing a rhythm to our conversation.

During one of our stops, seated on a plastic stool by a roadside tea stall, Amit started to tell me about his arrival in the forests. Like many of his peers in Calcutta, as the city was then known, he had been politicized as a university student in the 1960s and had joined the Communist Party of India (Marxist), or CPI(M), which had split from the pro-Soviet Communist Party of India in 1966. The CPI(M) was at the time facing an internal challenge from its student wing, which argued that the party should align itself with a series of peasant uprisings in the Naxalbari district in West Bengal and that it should abandon parliamentary politics and work toward a Chinese-style peasant-led revolution. Amit agreed with the student wing that the party should strive to topple the Indian state, but he disagreed with those students who were arguing that their wing should break from the CPI(M) to pursue revolution on its own.

Ultimately, Amit was unable to stay in Calcutta to continue working with the CPI(M)'s trade union wing as he had planned. The ruling Congress government began a campaign to suppress the radicalized leadership of the student wing of the CPI(M), then known as the Naxalites, after the peasant revolt that had taken place in West Bengal's Naxalbari district. The leader of the Naxalites, Charu Majumdar, was killed by the police in 1972, and thousands of others were arrested or assassinated. The Naxalites were not the only movement challenging the government at the time. A wave of labor militancy was spreading through the country: the city of Bombay alone saw thirteen thousand strikes between October 1973 and June 1974 (Chandra 2003). A student movement with participants from the socialist left and the Hindu-nationalist right was gaining momentum across North India.

In June 1975, the president of India, Fakhruddin Ali Ahmad, declared a state of emergency at the request of Prime Minister Indira Gandhi. In a television broadcast to the country explaining the declaration, Gandhi cited the challenge posed to her government by the uprisings across the country: "Now we learn of new programmes challenging law and order throughout the country with a view to disrupting normal functioning. How can any government worth the name stand by and allow the country's stability to be imperiled?" (*Times of India* 1975). She had suspended the law and electoral democracy, Gandhi said, in order to protect both law and democracy. The Emergency, she insisted, would not affect "law-abiding citizens"; only those who were already outside the law in challenging the state would be affected.

The Emergency lasted for only twenty-two months, but during that period, the repression that had begun in Calcutta spread across the country. Elections were suspended, political rallies banned, newspapers censored, and activists and opposition leaders arrested. The Shah Commission, appointed in 1977 by the Janata government after the end of the Emergency, found that 110,806 people were detained under laws targeting political dissidents created during the Emergency. Gandhi arrested hundreds of politicians from opposition parties, including the CPI(M) and the Hindu-nationalist Jana Sangh, as well as members of the Islamic Jamaat-i-Islami and the Hindu-nationalist paramilitary Rashtriya Swayamsevak Sangh. Notably, Gandhi also ordered the arrest of Jayaprakash Narayan, the leader of the student movement in Bihar and Gujarat. She suspended state and national elections. She cut the electricity supply to Delhi-based newspapers and issued an order requiring that all news that was on matters that are "plainly dangerous" be passed by a censor. She considered closing all the country's High Courts. By the time elections were held and the Emergency had ended in March 1977, thousands had been arrested, hundreds had been tortured and killed, thousands had been forcibly sterilized, and working-class neighborhoods had been destroyed (Iyer 2000; Tarlo 2003).

Soon after the declaration of the Emergency, a police officer who was a close friend of Amit's father passed along a warning that the police had been keeping an eye on Amit. Amit, the officer advised, should leave the state or risk being arrested or killed. He left the next week for the forests of northern Uttar Pradesh. Radicals of various stripes had begun to flee to the forested hills to avoid arrest and torture. Amit was one of the many leftists who left the cities for the forests, "to keep the state at arm's length," in Scott's phrase (2009, 9). Once they arrived, many found in the forest dwellers an audience for Left analyses and programs. Indian Maoist and Marxist-Leninist militant groups had begun as urban proletariat and rural peasant-based movements, but they came to have their strongest base in the forests, where land rights were seldom settled facts and therefore, as Shankar Gopalakrishnan argues, all accumulation took place through dispossession (2010a). To the extent that the state had a presence in forests in the 1970s, it was as an agent of domination, not of hegemony: it appeared in the form of police and forest guards harassing and filing cases against forest residents for gathering firewood and grazing their animals. In the absence of settled land rights, the majority of residents lived in forests illegally, through the exception of the application of the law. These older legal exceptions of the forest would encounter the legal exceptions of the Emergency in the 1970s and would together initiate the processes that brought the Forest Rights Act to Duddhi, that resulted in Ramnagar's destruction in 2010.

The exceptional status of forests meant that forms of state surveillance available in Calcutta and Bombay were not available in Duddhi. Elders told me stories about meeting their first police officer or forest guard in their twenties. The region remained obscure in the country's capital and to popular politics in much of the nation: it was out of sight of the country's surveillance apparatus, and the demands of its residents were largely invisible to popular movements and electoral parties. Forms of collective action that took place in Duddhi had little impact on lawmaking in Delhi.

Duddhi's exceptional status had been produced over a longer history, however. The obscurity of the region, the lives of its people, and its landscape would mark Duddhi's incorporation into British India. Colonial officials, when they noticed Duddhi at all, struggled to create a property and legal regime to govern the relationship between its forests and the people who lived in them. In this chapter, I begin by tracing the incorporation of Duddhi into British India as an exception before turning to the years leading up to and following the Emergency. In those years the lingering question of land reform that had been promised by the nationalist movement, as it took political, economic, and legal shape, would produce further dispossession in Duddhi's exceptional forests.

I then move to a national scale, following in turn the struggle over the constitutionality of land reform that was among the precipitating events of the Emergency. The new jurisprudence around land and the Constitution that came out of the period of the Emergency would enable new claims by the state and capital upon land at exactly the moment at which the region was found to contain some of the largest quantities of coal in Asia, thus setting the stage both for intensified dispossession and a new form of left-wing militancy that would take hold in the area's forests.

The Emergency tied forests in India to national political and economic problematics, making elections, mass movements, and the accumulation of capital unthinkable without forests and their residents. If forests in India have been defined less by their ecology than by an absence of enforceable property claims, then the Emergency saw a critical redefinition of this absence. The reworking of the absence of enforceable property claims during the period of the Emergency went along with a new relationship between India's forests and the state. Although the problem of property in India's forests predated the Emergency, the 1970s set the stage both for an intensification of the problem through increased dispossession and for political mobilization against forest-dweller dispossession. These challenges would rework the legal terms of property in forests and set the stage for the movement for the Forest Rights Act.

For the Forest Rights Act to be passed by India's Parliament in 2006, the struggles over forest land in thousands of disconnected regions would have to be knit together, made into a common struggle, and the invisible demands of their residents would have to be made to matter to bureaucrats and politicians in Delhi. This process began with the Emergency, and the years following Indira Gandhi's television address would see increasing movement to and from the forests. Activists like Amit, seasonal migrants from the forests seeking work in the cities, and corporations pursuing forest land and resources all began to travel to and from places like Duddhi. The law kept pace with these movements, reshaping the relationship between people and the forests they lived in. A moment in which the liberal legal order was suspended counterintuitively led to a new legalization of politics and a new political orientation toward the Constitution.

This act of knitting together people, capital, and law would make the forests and the laws that applied to them into matters of national political concern. Elyachar (2010) has drawn on Malinowski's (1923) concept of the phatic—practices that create and maintain communicative channels—to show how such channels forged through everyday social practice can be made available for other purposes, such as the accumulation of capital. A similar production and reworking of phatic infrastructures was occurring between India's forests and cities, but these channels would ultimately do more than carry unexpected meanings; they would establish the possibility of collective action on a scale that had never before been possible. The channels were not neutral, however. They came into being through political projects of the left and right, through the circulation of capital via extraction, and through new ideologies about the law—the Constitution in particular—and its place in politics. By tracing the emergence of these channels and the capital, labor, and political-legal ideologies that would circulate through them, a new understanding of India's linked legal and environmental histories comes into view.

A number of anthropologists (e.g., Randeria 2007; Sundar 2011; Eckert et al. 2012), drawing on Habermas (1981), have in the last decades described a turn to the law in postcolonial politics, a process of "juridification" whereby politics has migrated to the languages and institutional sites of law and has thereby excluded the majority of people from the means of effective political practice. Yet the legalized conflicts that have played out in Duddhi and across India's forest belt have taken a form that can only be explained with reference to the political and economic history of the region. The law's meaning is indeterminate, and the law is available to be put to a range of contradictory political uses to an extent that it is not available in most of India and was not always available in Duddhi. The turn to the law in Duddhi can be understood as the result of a specific local conjuncture of three broader processes in India's post-Emergency political history: a spatial movement of left-wing political projects to India's forest belt, which tied forest politics into national politics for the first time; the increasing importance of forest resources to the accumulation of private and public capital made possible by a series of new laws; and a new role for the Indian judiciary, which claimed both increasing executive powers and the ability to represent a national public.

This turn to the law, however, would hold larger stakes than the simple interpretation or application of laws. In their struggles over land reform and the forests, multiple parties from the Supreme Court to Indira Gandhi to the Gandhian Banwasi Seva Ashram to, as we will see in chapter 3, the Ramnagaris would claim to speak on behalf of India's Constitution. This claim was buttressed by a set of claims about the time and space of politics that were drawn on by multiple parties to speak on behalf of a founding sovereign order. The gradual incorporation of Duddhi's forests into a set of national political and economic infrastructures would meet a new set of claims to speak on behalf of a national founding sovereign order via the Constitution.

As these infrastructures of social movements and capital were being assembled, the legal forms that the movement for forest rights would take were being set in place. In establishing a conflict between an elected prime minister and India's Constitution, the Emergency would set up a contest between popular sovereignty and the law that would persist long after elections resumed. Long debates and struggles about the promises of India's independence and the meaning of the rights it conferred on citizens were playing out in debates over the status of India's Constitution. Two key rights would form the axes of these debates—the right to property and the right to life—and each right would be refracted and rethought through the forest.

Dispossession in the Forest

The incorporation of Duddhi into British India and its forestry regime was a slow and uncertain process. In the name of preventing the dispossession of the region's poorest residents, the colonial state would pass a series of property laws that marked the residents and the land as exceptional and not subject to the legal and governmental order that prevailed in the rest of British India. The "tribal" inhabitants, officials would argue, were too naive to participate in the market in land, and they could too easily be tricked into giving up their holdings to members of caste Hindu society. These laws would run up against another imperative of the colonial state—that is, to find sources of revenue from the land. The contradiction between these two imperatives would be resolved by taking advantage of an ongoing uncertainty about legal meanings, jurisdictions, and boundaries that began with the first claims of the colonial state to the region.

In a note on the assessment of land revenues for Duddhi, H. C. A. Coneybeare, the assistant magistrate collector of the area, recalled the process through which the British East India Company claimed the area in 1849. To determine

Duddhi's boundaries, Coneybeare wrote that Mr. W. Roberts and Mr. Forbes, representatives of the East India Company, consulted a priestly member of the Baiga community:

> "He is supposed," writes Mr. Forbes, "to be better informed on all that concerns the village than anyone one else; *to have a thorough knowledge of its boundaries*, and to be able to point out each man's tenure. He is invariably the arbiter in all disputes as to land and rent." He takes in fact, the place sometimes taken elsewhere in these provinces by a village council (*panchayat*). On this occasion the baiga was conducted to the disputed land, where, to obtain inspiration, he sacrificed a cock. Cutting off the bird's head he streaked his forehead with its blood; and tying up the head in his turban, proceeded to walk along what he, or some guiding daemon, decided to be the boundary. That boundary was, however, far too long to be walked in one day: so, at evening, the augur secreted the cock's head in the jungle and went home. Returning next morning to the same spot, he replaced the unsavoury burden in his turban, and walked off the rest of the boundary. The Sirgujan chieftain "wished a probationary period of seven days, called *dank*, to be allowed ere the boundary was considered finally adjusted, and that if within that period sickness or death took place in the baiga's family or attacked his cattle, the decision should be set aside." But there being no provise to this effect in the agreement, the proposal was overruled. The frontier of a great province had been decided in a manner far less discontenting, and perhaps not more fortuitous, than if reams of paper had been filled with mendacious evidence. (1879, 9, 10; emphasis in original)

The Baiga resolved uncertainty over the British East India Company's jurisdiction in the same way that he resolved village property disputes: by walking a path following the sacrifice of a cock. His efforts succeeded in demarcating Duddhi, but they were only one episode in a longer history of doubt over jurisdiction and property. Laws would be declared and revised, and property boundaries would be declared and revised many times over between the nineteenth and the early twenty-first century. In Coneybeare's account, the story is presented as an amusing ethnological vignette: the boundaries of property, jurisdiction, and sovereignty were so murky that establishing them through the Baiga's walk was "far less disconcerting" than through "reams of paper" that could be filled with "mendacious evidence." The ethnographic primitive as a figure to be protected was to appear again and again in the struggles over Duddhi's land and forests, as logics of revenue and profits, labor and property repeatedly aligned with paternalistic logics of protection.

Duddhi fell on the border between two precolonial states, Bihar and Benares, making it difficult to determine whose control Duddhi ultimately fell under. Prior to its accession to the British, Duddhi was claimed by two different local rulers: the chief of Nagar-Untari whose territory fell within Bihar and the Raja of Singrauli whose territory fell within Benares. On British maps of the time, there was little clarity about which province it belonged to: Bihar or Benares. If it was Bihar, the British claim would have begun in 1764. In 1750, however, the kingdom of Singrauli was brought under the formal sovereignty of the Raja of Benares, and the Raja of Singrauli maintained his local authority with an annual tribute of Rs. 701 to Benares. The Nawab of Oudh, with a capital in Lucknow, was in turn the titular lord paramount to the Raja of Benares, making Singrauli formally part of Oudh. In 1775, to pay off debts the Nawab had accrued, Oudh ceded sovereignty of Benares and, therefore, also of Singrauli and possibly Duddhi, depending on whether Duddhi fell under Bihar or Benares, to the British East India Company. None of these states or kingdoms—Bihar, Benares, Singrauli, or Nagar-Untari—had ever held more than a minimal presence in Duddhi, however, which, with its dry soil, could not provide much revenue.

As the British East India Company took control of Bihar and Benares, its administrators paid little attention to Duddhi. The civil service officer D. L. Drake-Brockman (1911) reports that it was an "outbreak of violence" that finally attracted the attention of the British, who came to "inquire into the rights of the people" (326). The above-mentioned settlement officer, William Roberts, traveled to Duddhi in 1849. He determined the boundaries with the help of the Baiga priest, and he carried out a permanent settlement of the region and assigned occupancy rights. Duddhi was incorporated as the southern portion of a larger Mirzapur district and declared a government estate, in which property rights ultimately belonged to the government of India (Baden-Powell 1892). Cultivators, called *sapurdars*, and their tenants were given heritable but not transferable occupancy rights, which they could expand by cultivating uncultivated "waste" land. These cultivators were among the ancestors of the dominant-caste groups who own the largest holdings in Duddhi a century and a half later. The inhabitants of the so-called waste land who did not receive occupancy rights were among the ancestors of the Dalit and Adivasi residents of Ramnagar. This differential assignation of occupancy rights, and the differential ability to make claims against dispossession that would ensue, set up the problem of property in Duddhi's forests.

The assignment of property rights was worked out as the colonial government began to search for sources of revenue from Duddhi. The government of India had passed the Indian Forest Act in 1865, allowing the newly created Forest Department to claim forestland for timber to be sold for revenue. The forests of northern Duddhi were assumed from the earliest British surveys to be degraded because of the area's shallow and poor soil and thus were deemed not to be promising in terms of revenue. In the southern portion, however, there were more valuable sal and bamboo trees. Following a survey in 1870–1871, 40,048 acres of southern Duddhi that were not under cultivation were declared reserved forest (Singh 1966). This meant that residents of the area were no longer allowed access to the forests for cultivation or to hunt animals and gather forest products, like firewood and the leaves of the tendu tree. Northern parts of the district were home to profitable sandstone quarries, however, and an 1871 survey found fourteen outcroppings of coal in Duddhi, of which two or three had a "workable thickness of fair coal" (Geological Survey of India 1873, 2). That "workable thickness" would turn out to be India's largest bauxite seam, and it would lead to the emergence of a political economy premised upon the extraction of minerals and further dispossession seven decades later.

As the colonial state worked out its sources of revenue in Duddhi and the optimal distribution of occupancy and property rights between tenants, *sapurdars*, government forests, and coal fields, the dispossession of its original inhabitants became more common. Property rights were being framed in legal terms, and disputes over those rights were similarly turning away from local authorities (such as the Baiga priest) to the colonial court system. Within fifteen years of Roberts's settlement, however, the colonial state carved Duddhi out of the provincial laws of the United Provinces (UP) in the name of preventing dispossession. The legal system, Coneybeare (1879) claimed, was at the disposal of the higher castes of the area, and they had used it to trick and dispossess the area's poor, illegally transferring occupancy rights and claiming occupied land as waste from indebted "tribals." As a result, ostensibly to protect against the "defenselessness of the South Mirzapur peasantry against their astuter neighbors" (Coneybeare 1879, 31), the Governor-General of India passed Act XIX in 1864, which "remove[d] certain tracts of country in the District of Mirzapore [*sic*] from the jurisdiction exercised by the Civil, Criminal, and Revenue Courts and Officers of that District" and placed them under the direct jurisdiction of a provincial officer. Transferring the area into the direct jurisdiction of this officer did not allow the area's poor to escape their debts, however, or the property and labor relations to which those debts led. An 1869 account by a London Missionary Society missionary described the local official as a tyrant, "well versed in deceit and intrigue, with an unbounded love of power and wealth," who ruled over an extensive system of forced labor (Jones 1869, 55).

With the passage in 1874 of the Indian Scheduled Districts Act, Duddhi was made a "scheduled district," along with a range of other forest and hill areas that had been given exceptional status. Scheduled districts were exempted from

laws passed by the Indian legislature in Calcutta and placed outside of the jurisdiction of the courts. In many of these areas, the granting of exceptional status
was carried out in order to "pacify and keep contented these wild people"
(Ghurye 1980, 26) who had resisted the arrival of the colonial state. In Duddhi,
however, no sustained resistance to the colonial state had taken place. To the
contrary, as an article on Duddhi in the November 18, 1879, *Times of India* put
it, colonial officials classified Duddhi as a scheduled district because, as they
saw it, "the great bulk of the cultivators and village managers belong to the
aboriginal tribes, and are a simple ignorant people, easily overreached by astute
and grasping money-lenders" (3). Duddhi gained its scheduled status through
what Banerjee (2006) describes as a paternalistic economic exceptionalism, an
attempt by colonial administrators to maintain an economic boundary between
ostensibly modern caste Hindus who operated through relations of contracts
and primitive tribals who were governed by status relations. Duddhi's legal
exception was designed to recognize and incorporate these relations of status,
protecting residents from the predations of contracts and the market and the
predations of debt that followed.[1]

In establishing political and legal boundaries between caste Hindus and
Muslims on the one hand and ostensibly primitive tribals on the other, colonial
officials used property law to attempt to maintain a spatial separation between
the two groups. As P. Wyndham, the district collector in the early twentieth
century, put it, "It should be our policy to avoid the non-tribals like Brahmins,
Bunnia, Ahirs [Yadavs], etc., for they are interlopers and do not understand the
aboriginals" (see the "Report on Settlement of Dudhi Estate, Mirzapur District
1909–10," 13, quoted in Nayak 2001, 103). Critically, and in anticipation of provisions in the Forest Rights Act that would prohibit land from alienation or
transfer, tribal land in scheduled areas could not be sold or transferred to non-
tribals. These spatial distinctions between status and contract, between tribal
society and caste society, were difficult to maintain, however. Land transfers to
caste Hindus who migrated from neighboring Bihar and from the plains of
Uttar Pradesh were commonly used to settle debts. Debtors could transfer their
land to their *sapurdar*, who could then sell to outsiders. It was during this
period that members of the dominant Yadav caste began to arrive in Duddhi in
large numbers (see "Excluded and Partially Excluded Areas (Other than Assam)
Sub-Committee, 1947," quoted in Constituent Assembly 1976).[2]

As Duddhi was being carved out as an exception from provincial and Indian
law, more of its land was being claimed by the Forest Department. The Indian
government's 1878 Forest Act allowed the Forest Department to claim any
uncultivated waste land in the country that might eventually be managed as a
protected forest, in which a usufruct might be maintained, but those rights

could eventually be withdrawn if the forest were to be reclassified as reserved. By 1901, more than one-fifth of Duddhi's 388,983 acres had been claimed by the Forest Department. The colonial state was finding new sources of revenue from forests across the country and had begun to establish its own contracts in Duddhi. The Forest Department would lease protected forests to contractors to cut down timber, harvest lac, and gather tendu leaves for sale in the market. As land was claimed by the Forest Department, the department was required by the 1878 and the later 1927 Indian Forest Acts to survey and settle the existing property and use rights of the people who lived on and used the land. According to the department's working plans, however, such surveys were never fully carried out. As a result, as late as 1966, the state deputy chief of forests noted that "the state of boundaries of both protected as well as vested forests is far from satisfactory. There does not exist any boundary register describing the exact delineation of the forest boundaries" (Singh 1966, 35). The murkiness around boundaries had not changed in the century since the Baiga determined Duddhi's perimeter. Despite ostensible efforts to seal off Duddhi through the Scheduled Districts Act and its successors to protect its status-bound residents from the market, the market was arriving: a market in land and forest products, with participants from dominant-caste society and the Forest Department.

After India's independence in 1947, the contemporary political and property relations of Duddhi began to take shape. In most parts of the country, scheduled areas had been reclassified as either "excluded" or "partially excluded" areas by the 1935 Government of India Act, and then as Schedule Five or Six areas by the Indian Constitution in 1950. As scheduled areas, these areas would remain exempt from national laws and the prohibition on the transfer of Scheduled Tribe property would remain. Duddhi was to lose its scheduled status, however. The United Provinces that it belonged to would be renamed following Independence to Uttar Pradesh or the "Northern Province." Then as now, UP, home to a large Hindi-speaking majority and India's largest state by far, was often cast as standing in for a national Hindi-speaking mainstream. The state's early post-Independence leadership refused to set aside either regions or communities as falling outside of that mainstream, no areas were classified within Schedules Five or Six, and no communities in Duddhi were granted the protections of Scheduled Tribe status. The land that Duddhi's Adivasis and Dalits owned could now freely be sold on the market.

A new political economy would arrive with Independence: new state-led visions of agrarian improvement and industrial development took hold along with the triumphant Congress Party in power in the central government. Land reform would be central to these visions and would paradoxically result in further dispossession for Duddhi's Adivasis and Dalits, as an extractive economy took shape in the region. Bureaucrats and politicians in the region liked to proclaim to me that it is "the energy capital of India." With its dams and power plants, Sonbhadra, the larger district that Duddhi falls in, produces somewhere between twelve thousand and twenty thousand megawatts of power (Sirur 2019). The enormous amount of land owned by the Forest Department, the coal deposits under this land, and the ease of dispossessing people from it all set the stage for the region to take this role. The unsettled property relations of Duddhi, rather than posing an obstacle to private and state-led dispossession, in fact enabled it.

Promises of Independence

The years between India's independence in 1947 and the start of the Emergency in 1975 saw a reckoning with the demands and promises of the nationalist movement as they met the realities of independent government. Projects of agrarian reform and industrialization-led development helmed by India's first prime minister, Jawaharlal Nehru, aimed to feed the newly independent country and put a weak economy on its feet. Although the constituencies for agrarian reform and industrialization lay outside of the country's forests, in its vast river valleys and growing cities, the shifts underway would transform Duddhi's forests as well.

Rural exploitation and landlessness had fueled the growth of Left parties and peasant movements in the decades before Independence, and the leadership of the Indian National Congress spoke of an end to *zamindari*, or landlordism, as a political and economic necessity. The Congress manifesto for the 1945 Legislative Assembly election, the final election before Independence, outlined the party's plans for the new society to come. The manifesto laid out the basic form of a new constitution, and it promised land reform in order to "[remove] intermediaries between the peasant and the State" (Indian National Congress 1945, 6). A ceiling on landholdings not only would alleviate the poverty of landless workers and tenants but also was key to the Congress' industry-oriented development policy. Land reform would produce greater yields, feeding the nation, and monetize an agricultural economy that was in large parts of the country nonmonetary, providing tax revenues that could be invested into urban industry.

For such land reform to succeed in transforming India's economy, revenues and yields would need to improve. Water and electricity were needed for greater irrigation, and a source of both was found in Sonbhadra, with the construction of the Rihand Dam, which continues to be the largest dam by volume in the country. In July 2012, I met with a man who had once been an architect of the dam and of the Nehruvian developmental state. Sant Swami Saanand had renounced his possessions and his older name, G. D. Agrawal, a year earlier and moved to the city of Varanasi, a few hundred kilometers north of Duddhi, to take *sanyas*, or renounce his worldly life. The retired engineer now lived in an ashram a few hundred meters from the Ganges River, and he would die fasting in 2018 demanding that the government clean the river, which is holy to Hindus. Saanand began his career in Sonbhadra in 1952, after finishing his doctorate in environmental engineering at the University of California, Berkeley. He arrived in the district as the new post-Independence property regime and developmental agenda were beginning to transform it. In 1952, the year after UP's land reform law went into effect, construction began on a dam on the Rihand River, in the western part of the district.

When I met Saanand in his sparsely furnished ashram quarters, he was dressed in the saffron robes of a mendicant. Nothing about his appearance suggested his central role in planning one of the largest projects of the Nehruvian developmental state. Saanand described to me the Sonbhadra that he had first encountered in 1952, a region in which the state's presence was sparse enough that most residents had never encountered state-issued currency. The area had minimal commercial agriculture and no industry at all, and the dam was never intended to provide water or electricity to Duddhi. The water was intended for the more fertile agricultural terrain north of the Kaimur hills, where, as he put it, "the groundwater is so high that if you put a stick in the ground, water comes out." The plans that he and his team drafted for the new dam, he explained, were never intended to submerge a very large area. They had miscalculated, however. When the Rihand Dam was completed in 1960, its catchment area submerged 108 villages and displaced their fifty thousand inhabitants, none of whom were resettled or rehabilitated.

The destruction of 108 villages was not the only unintended consequence of the Rihand Dam's construction. Saanand explained to me that during the excavations that preceded the construction of the dam, the engineers stumbled on large coal deposits, part of a seam that was, by some accounts, the second largest in the world (Singh 1985). Colonial officials had been aware of small quantities of low-grade coal since the 1870s, but these were the first commercially viable deposits to be found and their presence would go on to transform Sonbhadra in the years after the Emergency. The dam could be built only because the people whose land it submerged had no enforceable claims to that land, and the coal could be made available only if the people living above it continued to be unable to enforce their land claims. The movements for land reform that would follow, however, would ultimately have the perverse effect of dispossessing even more of Sonbhadra's residents.

Neither rural poverty nor demands for land reform ended with India's independence in 1947. Jayaprakash Narayan, or JP, the leader and figurehead of the "JP movement" that was the immediate catalyst for the Emergency, was central to one effort at land reform that would leave a long legacy in Duddhi. In the early 1950s, along with Gandhian reformer Vinoba Bhave, JP founded the Sarvodaya Bhoodan or "land gift for the progress of all" movement, which used moral appeals to large landlords to gift their land to the landless. As the dam was going up on the Rihand River in 1952, a severe drought struck Duddhi. State presence was minimal at the time, and Uttar Pradesh Chief Minister Govind Vallabh Pant invited an organization associated with the Sarvodaya movement, the Gandhi Smarak Nidhi, to start drought relief and agricultural development work. He granted them 250 acres of forest land.

Following a second drought in 1967, which led to over a hundred deaths and over a hundred thousand people experiencing severe hunger, a sociology student named Prem Bhai from western Uttar Pradesh who had been inspired by JP's speeches joined the movement. Prem Bhai moved with his physician wife, Ragini Bahen, to Duddhi to join and lead the Gandhi Smarak Nidhi's operation, which he renamed the "Banwasi Seva Ashram," or "ashram in service of forest dwellers." Under Prem Bhai, the ashram dramatically expanded its governmental activities. It began a Gram Swaraj, or village self-rule program. The ashram managed the state government's Bhoodan Yajna, its gift of land to landless people in the region, identifying the small amount of land that had been granted and distributing it. They began to study the ecology of the area and tried to determine the agricultural techniques most suited for the region's dry climate and low water table. The ashram even brought a team from an Israeli kibbutz to UP to share technical knowledge about farming in arid regions during a period in which India did not have open diplomatic relations with the state of Israel.

Through the 1970s, the ashram played the role of surrogate government in the area, combining UP state funds with resources from Indian and European nongovernmental organizations. It began an employment scheme in the form of a center to make handloom cotton, *khadi*, and it started a series of interventions into local agriculture, including a dairy. Ragini Bahen started a clinic to treat yaws and malaria and began to teach local forest dwellers about ayurvedic forms of medicine. The ashram established a school for children and education centers for adults. The effects of these interventions were limited, however. In 1974, on the state government's behalf, the ashram conducted a socioeconomic survey of the villages in southern Mirzapur. They found that half of the population had less than five bighas of land, or three acres, and 87 percent lacked access to a year-round source of drinking water.

The Banwasi Seva Ashram represented one approach to poverty and land-lessness in Sonbhadra, one that emphasized moral appeals to landlords to encourage them to donate their land as a gift and technical solutions to improve crop yields. In UP's capital Lucknow and in New Delhi, however, legal struggles over land reform were taking place over the same decades. These struggles, the laws they would produce, and the legal ideologies that would emerge from them would reorganize Sonbhadra's landscape several times over, and they would provide the immediate pretext for the Emergency.

The Courts versus the Executive

If the Emergency can be seen as a response to challenges presented by social movements in India, it can also be seen as a bid in a long contest over power and over the meaning of India's Constitution between the executive and judicial branches of the government, which ended with a judiciary that was stronger than it had ever been before and the Supreme Court becoming "the most powerful court in the world." A contest over the source of legal authority had started almost the moment India gained its independence in 1947, even before the Constitution came into effect in 1950, and it was fought over state efforts at land reform. The resulting terms of the legal struggle over land would set the stage for the movement for the Forest Rights Act. As the Court began to claim to represent the popular will, it also began to claim greater authority over forest land.

In the years following Independence, the Uttar Pradesh land reform bill became an experimental testing ground for the debates over a constitutional right to property in the Constituent Assembly. Govind Ballabh Pant, the chief minister of UP, was a member of both the committee to draft UP's land reform legislation and the Constituent Assembly. His hope was to produce a constitutional right to property that would allow the land reform legislation he was in the process of drafting to pass and be implemented without interference either from the Union government or from the higher courts, which could rule on its constitutionality. The Constitution did not yet exist, nor did the constitutional courts that would evaluate legislation on its basis, but land reform legislation was being crafted preemptively in response to the Constitution and the higher judiciary.

The Constituent Assembly that wrote the Constitution weighed not writing into it any right to property at all, but members feared the capital flight that might result. Instead, they produced a weak right to property that was intended to protect land reform legislation from challenges in the courts. For Nehru, this was a question of Parliamentary sovereignty: "No Supreme Court and no

Judiciary can stand in judgement over the sovereign will of Parliament representing the will of the entire community" (9 C.A.D. 137). Parliament, as the sovereign representative of the community, would enact the land reform that it willed without judicial review. This limited right to property was established in two separate articles. The first read:

> 19(1)(f): All citizens shall have the right to acquire, hold and dispose property.

The second read:

> 31(2): No property, movable or immovable, including any interest in, or any company owning, any commercial or industrial undertaking, shall be taken possession of or acquired for public purposes under any law authorising the taking such possession or such acquisition, unless the law provides for compensation for the property taken possession of or acquired and either fixes the amount of compensation, or specifies the principles on which, and the manner in which, the compensation is to be determined and given.

The Constitution gave a right to acquire and hold property in section 19(1)(f), but in 31(2), it also allowed for that property to be acquired for a public purpose in exchange for compensation that would be fixed by law. Both clauses were placed under further restrictions, with an eye on enabling land reform. Article 19(6) made the right to property guaranteed in 19(1)(f) subject to "reasonable restrictions" in the public interest, and Article 31(4), inserted at the insistence of Govind Ballabh Pant with the UP legislation in mind, specifies that no bills pending in state legislatures before the commencement of the Constitution could be challenged in courts on the grounds that they were unconstitutional. In other words, the many pending land reform bills could not be challenged on the basis of a constitutional right to property or right to fair compensation for property (Report of the United Provinces Zamindari Abolition Committee 1948; Austin 1999).[3]

In the decades following Independence in 1947, every Indian state passed land reform or land ceiling legislation. UP's land reform was passed in 1951, in order to "[abolish] the Zamindari system which involves intermediaries between the tiller of the soil and the State" (Uttar Pradesh Zamindari Abolition and Land Reforms Act 1950). Yet the Uttar Pradesh Zamindari Abolition and Land Reforms Act, in abolishing such intermediaries, ended up transferring even more of Duddhi's forest land to the state. The holdings of the largest zamindars were transferred to their tenants, while uncultivated "waste," such as the forest lands around Duddhi, went to the state. Land reform in UP only increased the landlessness of Duddhi's lower castes.

UP's limited land reform legislation passed, but in a series of judgments starting with *State of Bihar v. Sir Kameshwar Singh* in 1952, the High Courts and the Supreme Court challenged the constitutionality of land reform laws. Attempts to amend the Constitution to allow land reform were similarly challenged by the court on the grounds that they violated not only the right to property guaranteed in the Constitution but also Article 14 of the Constitution, which guarantees equality before the law: "The State shall not deny to any person equality before the law or the equal protection of the laws within the territory of India." Even though Article 31(2) allowed for redistribution with compensation, the courts argued that, by redistributing land away from large landlords specifically, the government was violating their right to the equal protection of the law. In applying the right to property inconsistently, the government was violating Article 14, which guarantees legal equality, making the applicability of a right subject to exceptions on the basis of political or economic need. Any recognition of social or economic inequality, the Court was arguing, would violate the legal and political equality established by the Constitution.[4]

In his November 1949 speech before the Constituent Assembly, B. R. Ambedkar, a key leader of the twentieth-century Dalit movement and chair of the Constituent Assembly, anticipated the hold that a constitution written by an unelected and long-passed set of framers could have over future politics. "The Assembly," he said, "has not only refrained from putting a seal of finality and infallibility upon this Constitution by denying to the people the right to amend the Constitution as in Canada or by making the amendment of the Constitution subject to the fulfilment of extraordinary terms and conditions as in America or Australia, but has provided a most facile procedure for amending the Constitution" (11 C.A.D. 165). This was a vision of a flexible Constitution that was responsive to democratic politics, and not beholden to its original text, avoiding through a straightforward amendment process a "rigidity and legalism" that he feared (7 C.A.D. 48). In 1951, Parliament responded to the Court's challenge to land reform's constitutionality by using this "most facile procedure" to pass the First Amendment to the Constitution. The First Amendment exempted laws that enabled the state to acquire what it called "estates," the holdings of large landlords, from judicial review, leading a chief justice to have allegedly quipped, "the Indian Constitution became the only one that contained a provision providing for protection against itself" (quoted in Bhuwania 2017, 21).

In 1955, Parliament passed the Fourth Amendment, which further restricted property rights. In 1961, however, the Supreme Court struck down Kerala and Madras' land reform legislation, arguing that the *ryotwari* holdings, a land tenure arrangement in which land is held by the cultivator, that were being redistributed by the states were not in fact "estates" as defined by the First Amendment. In response, Parliament passed the Seventeenth Amendment to the Constitution, which expanded the definition of "estates" that were exempt from judicial review under the First Amendment to include *ryotwari* land in order to make laws such as Kerala's land reform constitutional according to the standards established by the Supreme Court.

Soon after Indira Gandhi became prime minister in 1966, however, the Supreme Court overturned the amendments that had made land reforms constitutional in the 1967 case *Golaknath v. State of Punjab.* The amendments, the court argued, violated fundamental rights guaranteed in the Constitution. The courts would go on to announce that several other of Indira Gandhi's supposedly "socialist" measures were unconstitutional, such as bank nationalization and the withdrawal of princely states' privy purses. In 1971, in response, Parliament, led by Indira Gandhi, passed the Twenty-Fourth and Twenty-Fifth Amendments. The Twenty-Fourth Amendment explicitly claimed constituent power for Parliament, allowing it to revise the Constitution, including the fundamental rights. The Twenty-Fifth exempted all land reform laws from judicial review under the fundamental rights. The Supreme Court struck back with a ruling in the 1973 case *Kesavananda Bharati v. State of Kerala* that brought the ongoing contest between the courts and the judiciary over the constitutionality of the amendment of fundamental rights guaranteed in the Constitution out of the terrain of legal textual interpretation.

To make this argument, the Supreme Court reached back to arguments that had been formulated in Germany's Weimar period over the scope of parliamentary power in relation to a constitution. Carl Schmitt ([1928] 2008) had distinguished between constitutions, which were produced by the sovereign constituent power that established political orders, and laws, which were rules established by accidental legislative majorities. Because a constitution, for Schmitt, was an expression of a political order, the passing majorities that allow parliaments to amend constitutions cannot impinge on its essence, what he called its "basic structure."

Drawing on Schmitt's arguments, the Court argued that the Indian Constitution in fact possessed a consistent and nonarbitrary basic structure that could not be altered by Parliament.[5] These arguments arrived in the Supreme Court through the work of German legal scholar Dietrich Conrad, whose 1970 article "Limitation of Amendment Procedures and the Constituent Power" was cited repeatedly in the case, both by the lawyer for the petitioner, Nani Palkhivala, and by the justices. In his article, Conrad responded to the question of whether the Indian Constitution could be amended by referring his readers to the experience of Weimar Germany and Schmitt's arguments in support of the notion of basic structure: "To take an example, Schmitt argues, the oath of allegiance to the constitution which a civil servant or a soldier swears must have as its real object the fundamental structure of the constitution as described. If it were otherwise, the oath would practically mean but allegiance to the amending procedure" (391).

In his influential opinion supporting the majority view, Justice H. R. Khanna quoted Conrad's Schmittian argument directly: "Although there are some observations in 'Limitation of Amendment Procedures and the Constituent Power' by Conrad to which it is not possible to subscribe, the following observations, in my opinion, represent the position in a substantially correct manner: Any amending body organized within the statutory scheme, howsoever verbally unlimited its power, cannot by its very structure change the fundamental pillars supporting its Constitutional authority" (*Kesavananda Bharati Sripadagalvaru v. State of Kerala* 1973, 1485).

In his summary of the majority's opinion, Chief Justice S. M. Sikri argued on similar lines that central to the Constitution's basic structure were "the federal character of the state and the rights of citizens vis-à-vis the state," the negative liberties codified in the fundamental rights. Notably, the Court removed the right to property from the Constitution's basic structure while still insisting on the unconstitutionality of that right's arbitrary suspension. Sikri wrote that the fundamental right to property implied that in cases in which property was claimed by the state: "one, the property shall be acquired by or under a valid law; secondly, it shall be acquired only for a public purpose; and, thirdly, the person whose property has been acquired shall be given an amount in lieu thereof, which, as I have already said, is not arbitrary, illusory or shocking to the judicial conscience or the conscience of mankind" (*Kesavananda Bharati Sripadagalvaru v. State of Kerala* 1973, 438).

The Court thus described a constitution that lay outside of the text itself, a fantasy Constitution, with two characteristics: it possessed a basic structure, including fundamental rights and the arrangement of the state, and it possessed a logical character of nonarbitrariness. These characteristics, being the expression of a now-past constituent order, could not be altered by Parliament or by state legislatures. This nonarbitrary fantasy Constitution, which notably was distinct from the intentions of the Constitution's framers, many of whom were still alive and had been party to the debates over land reform, did not allow for the arbitrary suspension of the right to property. The Constitution, in other words, was to be interpreted not in terms of the text as it existed—contradictions, amendments, and all—but rather in terms of an ideal and nonarbitrary set of rules that could be discerned to underpin it. These rules were laid down by a sovereign, constituent power that had existed in the Constituent Assembly, that did not live on in any existing institutions, but on behalf of which the Supreme Court could speak and rule.

The right to property guaranteed in the Constitution was itself ambiguous and contradictory, having emerged through a Constituent Assembly and a political party, the Congress, that was concerned about capital flight without a right to property but was under pressure to end landlordism. Through its assertion of the existence of a nonarbitrary essence that was distinct from the Constitution's text, the Court was attempting to sever a portion of the law from politics, by making those parts of it that emerged from the Constitution's basic structure superordinate to politics and by post facto erasing the political contradictions that had produced the Constitution. Because redistribution would withhold the right to property on an arbitrary basis, the Court was condemning not just the Constitution but the Indian state as a whole to a role in upholding economic inequality as it existed.

The struggle between the courts and the executive began to play out on other grounds beside land reform, and it was ultimately one of these skirmishes that precipitated the Emergency. In 1975, the Allahabad High Court ruled that Indira Gandhi had won her reelection in 1971 illegally, that she had used state resources in campaigning. The court ruled that her election was invalid and removed her from her seat in Parliament. Gandhi challenged the ruling in the Supreme Court, which upheld the removal, invalidating her reelection but allowing her to continue to serve as prime minister. Gandhi refused to resign from her seat, and two weeks after the court's ruling, she declared the state of Emergency, beginning a period of twenty-two months in which elections would be suspended, political opponents would be imprisoned, and the press would be censored.

Demands to complete the unfinished project of land reform resonated throughout Indian popular and electoral politics in the decades after Independence, from Dadasaheb Gaikwad's extension of the Ambedkarite movement toward land redistribution to Dalits in the 1950s and 1960s to the election of a Communist-led government in West Bengal in 1977 with land reform central to its agenda. The conflict in Delhi between Indira Gandhi and the courts reflected and refracted these land conflicts across the country. In 1976, during the Emergency, Gandhi passed the Forty-Second Amendment to the Constitution, which both made her reelection legal once again and allowed her to continue the executive's struggle against the judiciary. The Forty-Second Amendment restricted the High and Supreme Courts' ability to rule on the constitutionality of constitutional amendments and made land reform the sole prerogative of the executive and legislative branches. If, for Schmitt, the state of emergency revealed the reality of a sovereign behind the law, revealing that the law itself was a fantasy, then Gandhi was doing away with the fantasy of political equality and through her own sovereignty addressing social and economic inequality.

The state of Emergency ended in 1977, when Gandhi called and lost a general election. The parties and organizations that had coalesced around the JP movement, from the social democratic Samajwadi Party to the Hindu-nationalist Jana Sangh, along with defectors from the Congress Party and with outside support from the Communist Party, organized themselves into the new Janata or People's Party and won the elections easily. The Janata government struggled both to contain the ideological variety it represented and to prosecute the abuses committed by the previous government during the Emergency, and it soon began to lose popularity.

Before it was voted out in favor of Indira Gandhi and the Congress in 1980, however, the Janata Party managed to pass the Forty-Fourth Amendment to the Constitution. This amendment repudiated the Emergency, restricting severely the conditions under which emergency rule could be declared in the future. It also demoted the right to property from a fundamental right to a legal right, taking it out of the special purview of the Supreme Court and ending the doctrine of basic structure:

1. Recent experience has shown that the fundamental rights, including those of life and liberty, granted to citizens by the Constitution are capable of being taken away by a transient majority. It is, therefore, necessary to provide adequate safeguards against the recurrence of such a contingency in the future and to ensure to the people themselves an effective voice in determining the form of government under which they are to live. This is one of the primary objects of this Bill.

2. It is, therefore, proposed to provide that certain changes in the Constitution which would have the effect of impairing its secular or democratic character, abridging or taking away fundamental rights prejudicing or impeding free and fair elections on the basis of adult suffrage and compromising the independence of judiciary, can be made only if they are approved by the people of India by a majority of votes at a referendum in which at least fifty-one per cent of the electorate participate. Article 368 is being amended to ensure this.

3. In view of the special position sought to be given to fundamental rights, the right to property, which has been the occasion for more than one amendment of the Constitution, would cease to be a fundamental right and become only a legal right. Necessary amendments for this purpose are being made to article 19 and article 31 is being deleted. It would, however, be ensured that the removal of property from the list of fundamental rights would not affect the right of minorities to establish and administer educational institutions of their choice. (Forty-Fourth Amendment to the Constitution of India 1978)

In addition to amending the Constitution to limit executive power and prevent the declaration of future emergencies, the Janata Party sought to strengthen the courts and give them the autonomy necessary to protect against abuses of arbitrary executive power. The Supreme Court responded by developing a number of precedents that expanded its mandate and enabled it to speak on behalf of a broader public; this claim to represent the public, rather than simply to interpret the law, had previously been made only by the executive and legislature. The Supreme Court began to exercise the writ of mandamus more and more frequently, prescribing action to the executive and often framing it in the language of rights.

Most crucially, the Supreme Court claimed a new role with respect to the public, creating a new jurisdiction called "public interest litigation" (PIL). The Court began to encourage petitioners to file PILs: existing rules of *locus standi* or standing were dropped on the grounds that the majority of Indians lacked access to the language and procedures of the law and were thereby excluded from its protection. The courts, instead, began to accept litigation filed by anyone, including judges who were to hear a case, on behalf of publics to which they might not belong. The courts could then use a writ of mandamus to compel executive action on the basis of their rulings. The higher courts were claiming not only a greater share of executive power, but also, in PIL, a new ability to act on and on behalf of a larger, often national, public. Bhuwania (2017) has argued that the court, in doing so, was echoing Indira Gandhi's populism: it weakened formal procedures to act on behalf of a national public. PILs formed a new link between the law and social movements, as the court, in effect, invited them to represent their publics in the language of the law and, in particular, through the fundamental rights guaranteed in the Constitution. Although PILs would be used first to uphold the property rights of forest dwellers, by the 1990s, PILs and the higher judiciary would be the means for the dispossession of hundreds of thousands of forest dwellers.

Forests as a New Site of Capital Accumulation

The coal found by Saanand and the team that built the Rihand Dam in the 1950s was not yet available, either to the Forest Department or to the public and private capital that would build mines, dams, and factories in Sonbhadra. To make that coal available would require a further set of legal shifts, shifts that would bring forests under greater Union government control and would establish a set of political positions toward the law itself among those contending for the land, including the forest rights movement.

With the end of the Emergency, land reform slowly shuffled off the stage of Indian politics. After the short interregnum of the Janata Party government between 1977 and 1979, Indira Gandhi's Congress was reelected. On her return, the social democratic tendencies of Gandhi's previous terms were rejected in favor of a neoliberal orientation. As a *Times of India* editorial noted, "A change of considerable significance is taking place in India . . . the emphasis has shifted from distributive justice to growth" (February 22, 1981; quoted in Kohli 2006a). Gandhi sought a higher rate of economic growth: she distanced herself from the efforts at land reform that she had staked her pre-Emergency career upon, she passed legislation discouraging strikes and labor activism, and she began to encourage private investment.

This new orientation took on a paradoxically conservationist tone in the forests. Under the 1952 Indian Constitution, the 23 percent of India's land area that had been claimed by the Forest Department was subject to the authority of state governments. With Gandhi's return to power, this land would be brought under the authority of the central government and, in the name of conservation, made available to state and private capital. Soon after Amit made his way to the forests, the central government and private capital followed.

The more social democratic Indira Gandhi of the pre-Emergency period had been opposed to an environmentalism that she characterized as an ideology for the privileged. In 1972, she asked an audience at the first United Nations Conference on the Human Environment in Stockholm, "Are not poverty and need the greatest polluters? The environment cannot be improved in conditions of poverty. Nor can poverty be eradicated without the use of science and technology. For instance, unless we are in a position to provide for the daily necessities of tribal people and those who live in and around our jungles, we cannot keep them from combing the forests for their livelihood, from poaching and despoiling the vegetation. When they themselves feel deprived, how can we urge the preservation of animals?" (Gandhi 1972; quoted in Rangarajan 2009). In 1976 however, Indira Gandhi passed the Forty-Second Amendment to the Constitution, placing forests on the "concurrent list" to give both the central and state governments authority over them. The amendment added a new, environmentalist directive principle to state policy: "The State shall endeavor to protect and improve the environment and to safeguard the forests and wildlife of the country." It also added a new fundamental duty, for citizens: "It shall be the duty of every citizen of India . . . to protect and improve the national environment and forests, lakes, rivers, wildlife and to have compassion for living creatures." Gandhi, influenced by naturalists and environmentalists she had known socially her entire life, began to implement a stronger preservationist policy during the Emergency (see Rangarajan 2009).

The first law Gandhi passed on her return to power in 1980 followed the Forty-Second Amendment in its environmentalist orientation. The 1980 Forest Conservation Act placed forests exclusively under Union government control: under the act, no area of forest land greater than ten hectares could be diverted for any other use without Union government authorization.

But the Forest Conservation Act had effects in Sonbhadra and across India's forests that were diametrically opposed to the goals of conservation. The act ushered in a new phase of private and public capital accumulation at the exact moment that Gandhi was seeking to shore up Union government finances to be eligible for a $5 billion loan from the International Monetary Fund. One sticking point for the increased rate of gross domestic product (GDP) growth Gandhi sought was India's energy consumption. India's oil resources have always been minimal, and oil imports only grew dearer in the wake of the late-1970s oil shock. A report by the Government of India's Planning Commission's Working Group on Energy Policy in November 1979, two months before Gandhi would return to power, suggested that coal was the solution to the "energy crunch" faced by the country as well as its economic problems. Indian coal had always been plentiful and cheap, and its uses extended beyond electricity production to transport, industry, and agriculture. "Coal," the commission stated, "in the years to come, will find its true value not as a fuel but as a reductant in metallurgical industry and as a feed stock for liquid fuels and a wide variety of synthetic products including fertilizers" (Planning Commission 1979, iv).

This growth in public and private capital was enabled in part through the Forest Conservation Act; in the 23 percent of India's land area that was forest land, accumulation through dispossession increased in pace and extent: according to Wani and Kothari (2008), 1,140,177 hectares of forestland were cleared between the passage of the Forest Conservation Act in 1980 and 2006 for dams, mines, roads, factories, and other projects. With approval for such projects under the control of the Union government, rather than under state governments, clearances could be given quickly and easily. The act had the added benefit of making the country's coal reserves more easily available. By 1990, three of the country's four largest coal-powered power plants in India in 1990 had been built on forest land using the provisions of the 1980 Forest Conservation Act. The fourth, the Chandrapur Super Thermal Power Station in Maharashtra, continues to rely on coal mined from the surrounding area under the provisions of the 1980 act. The government's revenues from power generation similarly grew rapidly, from Rs. 589 million (US$74 million in the exchange rates of the time) in 1978–1979 to Rs. 1.8 billion (US$228 in the exchange rates of the time) by 1984–1985. India quickly achieved an annual growth in GDP of 6 percent, the highest in independent Indian history to that point.[6]

The 1980 law, then, marked a major redistribution of both property and authority, with a quarter of India's land area coming under the control of the Union government. Like the land reform legislation of the 1950s and 1960s, the Forest Conservation Act worked to strengthen state finances, but instead of doing so through redistribution and increased production by those cultivating the land, the Forest Conservation Act operated by displacing the already land-less. Public and private forestry, mining, and dam projects proliferated. Millions were displaced at the same moment that forest residents were drawn into left- and right-wing infrastructures of collective mobilization. As the leftist People's Union for Democratic Rights put it in a 1982 publication criticizing the new law, the Forest Conservation Act represented "a unilateral declaration of war by the Government" (People's Union for Democratic Rights 1982, 23). By consolidating control over forests in central government hands, it paved the way for dis-possession by state and private capital as well as the criminalization of forest dwellers for continuing to live in forests and draw upon forest produce.

The forests of Duddhi were not excluded from this new regime of accumula-tion. Ramshakal, a resident of Ramnagar who cannot remember his age but thought he was around sixty-five years old, explained to me that everything changed in the area in 1980. One day in early 2010 we were sitting on a cot outside his house in Ramnagar. Gesturing at the hills and forests around us, he told me:

> See, Anand *bhaiya*, this land was all ours before. My father used to gather sticks and fruit here, and we even did some farming here. But then in 1980 Umesh Company came here. It's a Yadav company, owned by Umesh Yadav in Duddhi, but they were on the side of the Forest Department. Umesh Company started sending big trucks into the forests and cutting down all the trees. The officers would come here and blame us Adivasis, saying that we were cutting down the trees, but they knew it was Umesh Company because they had given them permission. So one day we got together and captured an Umesh Company truck as it was coming down the hill with logs. We caught the driver and wouldn't let him go. Then we called the Forest Depart-ment officers to show them who had been cutting down the trees. Do you know what they did? They started beating us up with big sticks! Then we heard that Umesh Yadav said that he would kill us if we went to Duddhi, so we didn't go there for a whole year.

Govindnagar's forest dwellers lost the land that they had used for years to the Umesh Company as this wave of forest-based private accumulation arrived in Duddhi, further impoverishing the community. The conditions for the landless to contest their displacement were arriving in Sonbhadra's forests during the same period in which they were being displaced: activist networks were extending to the forests, bringing a range of tactics with them. Some of those tactics, as I discuss in the next section, were legal: it was a law that was being used to displace forest dwellers, and a law was used to challenge that displacement.

Dispossession would begin on a larger scale than just the Umesh Company and the forests near Duddhi, however. As it did so, it would continue to weave Duddhi's forests into larger political and legal infrastructures. In 1982, the National Thermal Power Corporation (NTPC), the public corporation that runs many of India's coal power plants, announced plans to draw on both the enormous bauxite reserves that Saanand's team stumbled upon in the construction of the Rihand Dam as well as water from the dam to start the Singrauli Super Thermal Power Station, which would ultimately produce two thousand megawatts of electricity. Over the decade, the public coal mining company Northern Coalfields Limited would establish its headquarters in the area and six thermal power plants would be built in Sonbhadra, leading to the popular claim that the district was the "energy capital of India." More mines would follow, as would aluminum factories, chemical factories, and the cement factories that thicken and cloud Sonbhadra's air. These mines and factories would be built on forest land, much of it occupied by forest dwellers.

The Banwasi Seva Ashram, which started life as a de facto welfare state sanctioned by the Uttar Pradesh state government in an area where the state government had little presence, began to challenge the state more frequently in the 1980s, in response to the increase in dispossession. In response to the post-Emergency shift in the locus of state control over forests to the Union government and the corresponding new, more confrontational relationship between the Forest Department and landless forest dwellers, the Banwasi Seva Ashram, faced with a Forest Department that was no longer under local or state control, began a series of confrontations with the department on legal grounds.

To do so, the Banwasi Seva Ashram took advantage of the new jurisdiction claimed by the post-Emergency Supreme Court, known as public interest litigation, or PIL. The poor and marginal were central to the "public" of the early years of Indian PILs, and the court worked to expand the right to livelihood promised to them in Article 21—although this was to change over the course of the 1980s and 1990s with devastating effects on forest dwellers, as I discuss in chapter 3. The ashram took advantage of the jurisdiction of PILs and the Court's reading of Article 21 to challenge the evictions the NTPC was carrying out for its power station. Arguing that the Forest Department had not followed the provisions of the Indian Forest Act of 1927 in acquiring the land by failing to survey and settle land rights in 433 villages in the area, in 1980, the ashram initiated a campaign to educate forest dwellers about their legal rights so that they could resist eviction. In 1982, the ashram drew on the emergent precedent of public interest litigation to challenge the evictions in the Supreme Court. In 1983, the Court issued a writ of mandamus creating a three-member committee headed by the ashram's founder, Prem Bhai, to survey and settle land rights.

The committee failed, however, to align legal land rights with settlement patterns for Sonbhadra's forest dwellers. Ragini Bahen, Prem Bhai's widow, acknowledged to me in a 2011 interview that the other two members of the committee had frequently given titles to people in exchange for money, with the result that many of the area's poorest residents were left landless and members of the dominant Yadav community extended their holdings. As I discuss in chapter 3, the failures of this committee to achieve land rights for the area's landless in 1983 would be remembered by the Ramnagaris. These failures would be recalled to indict the Banwasi Seva Ashram and to explain the more militant methods that they would adopt in their work with the Sangathan.

And yet, all these projects required land. The NTPC's Super Thermal Project claimed an area of forest land within the Banwasi Seva Ashram's committee's jurisdiction on which 1,500 families lived without formal title. Prem Bhai and the ashram began a "*bhoomi haqdari morcha,*" a movement for land rights that entailed a week of protests and road blockages in 1986. In 1987, they turned to the law, as Prem Bhai and the ashram filed a second PIL to challenge the NTPC's plans in the Supreme Court, citing Article 21, one of the fundamental rights promised by the Indian Constitution, which read, "No person shall be deprived of his life or personal liberty except according to procedure established by law." The Court ruled in favor of the ashram, arguing that despite their lack of property rights, displacing forest dwellers without resettling them deprived them of their livelihoods and was therefore illegal. The Court had ruled, in other words, that forest dwellers had rights to occupancy without property. The Court ordered the NTPC to resettle the displaced forest dwellers in the area, and plans were prepared for the resettlement.

By the time the Supreme Court ruled in favor of the Banwasi Seva Ashram in 1987, the Supreme Court had already redefined the right to life promised in Article 21, making it central to post-Emergency politics. In 1985, the journalist Olga Tellis filed a PIL against the Bombay Municipal Council on behalf of pavement dwellers whom the council had evicted. The Supreme Court ruled that the evictions were not arbitrary, because the pavement dwellers were violating the law by living on the pavement. In evicting the pavement dwellers, however, the city municipal council had violated their right to life and livelihood: there was no affordable housing available within a reasonable commuting distance of the pavement dwellers' places of employment, and so in evicting them, the council was depriving them of their ability to have a livelihood. With the Olga Tellis case, the Supreme Court dramatically expanded the meaning of the right to life promised in the Indian Constitution: a right to life was not a simple right not to be killed, it was now a right to the material preconditions for life, including a livelihood and place of residence. The Court brought this expanded meaning of the right to life promised in Article 21 into service again in the Banwasi Seva Ashram case, arguing that evictions, even in the case of unlawful occupation of property, were illegal if the evicted were in the process deprived of their livelihoods.

J. C. Seth, who was the lawyer for the NTPC in the trial, explained to me in an August 2012 interview that the NTPC never had any plans to implement the resettlement plan, and the majority of the displaced were never resettled. The court-ordered settlement was considered by many, including Prem Bhai, the founder of the Banwasi Seva Ashram, to be a failure. Members of the agency had in many cases settled land rights, and Dalits and Adivasis like those who eventually settled Ramnagar were left without title deeds. The forms of legal struggle that the ashram had engaged in had succeeded in distributing land rights to a portion of Duddhi's landless forest dwellers, but that portion had repeatedly been limited by competing demands for the land, both by private capital and by wealthier farmers, that were also working through legal and state mechanisms.

The growing value of the minerals contained under Sonbhadra's land from the late 1960s on brought a wave of new mines, factories, and power plants, along with workers to work in them and merchants to sell goods to the growing population. The transformation was stark. Saanand had told me in my July 2012 interview that local forest dwellers did not recognize Indian rupee notes when he first arrived in the area in the early 1950s. By the post-Emergency period in the 1980s, Duddhi had been integrated into the national economy, and the caste and occupational makeup of its residents diversified alongside this integration.

These movements of capital were accompanied by movements of activists and of ideals of the Indian state. One of these activists was a young doctor named Vinayan. He had joined the JP movement as a student and traveled to the rural areas and forests where the Sarvodaya land gift movement had an organizational infrastructure. He came to accept the Naxalite position on agrarian politics, however, that, given the repressive nature of the Indian state, land reform would not be possible except through armed struggle. When the Emergency was declared in 1975, Vinayan, like Amit, left the city for the forests of Bihar and Sonbhadra and split from the JP movement, which he had found was becoming dominated by Hindu-nationalist groups.

Vinayan's arrival in Sonbhadra was a critical early step in the establishment of a far-left political infrastructure in the region. He founded the Communist Party of India (Marxist-Leninist) Party Unity (CPI(M-L) Party Unity), the predecessor of the organization that ultimately organized Ramnagar's landless forest dwellers. Following the Emergency, the CPI(M-L) Party Unity began a militant struggle: organizing landless Dalits and Adivasis in order to redistribute local political authority away from dominant-caste-dominated village councils, thus ending bonded labor among Dalits and Adivasis, ending sexual violence against Dalit and Adivasi women committed by dominant-caste men, and redistributing property. Party Unity's methods were mixed: in a move away from the early Naxalite goal of the "annihilation" of landlord and capitalist classes that had practiced the "selective annihilation" of particularly oppressive landlords, moneylenders, and state agents, Vinayan's party leveraged wage strikes, economic blockades, and people's courts. The 1980s saw a period of intense violent confrontation between Party Unity and other Naxalite groups, on the one hand, and armies organized by dominant-caste landlords in the region, on the other.

M-L groups began to take shape around Sonbhadra's many new mines and factories as well. Shubha worked closely with Geeta, one of the conveners of the Sangathan and the person who had first brought me to Sonbhadra. Shubha had been born in West Bengal, but her husband was hired as a technician by the UP Cement Corporation in the mid-1980s. There, he joined a CPI(M-L)-affiliated union that represented workers in the factory. In 1991, when the factory was privatized and sold to the Dalmia Corporation, his union went on strike preemptively, fearing that staff reductions would follow. Shubha joined the protests outside the factory, was fired on by police with the other protestors, and went to jail with them. It was in that struggle, she told me, that she was drawn into the social world of left politics in the district. She had lived in Hindi-speaking UP for six years, but she only learned Hindi outside the factory gates and in jail with the union organizers. It was in these protests that Shubha met Vinayan, Amit, and Geeta and was introduced to the antidispossession struggles of forest dwellers through the new organization that they had started, the Sangathan.

Forest dwellers were also brought into left politics through work in the factories. As Govind, a Bhuiya man in Ramnagar in his late forties told me in 2011, it was through the M-L union that he met Geeta and Amit. When he left the factory, he joined the Sangathan and became involved in the struggle for land rights. The emergence of an economy based on dispossession and extraction as well as an industrial working class followed on the heels of the arrival of left activists to Sonbhadra. A world of left sociality took form, with ties to national political parties and unions, and struggles as far away as Delhi and Calcutta. M-L organizing picked up in other forest areas, and around other forest-based coal plants: Chandrapur, in Maharashtra, and Singrauli in neighboring Madhya Pradesh saw M-L unions gain strength in their new thermal power plants as M-L organizations gained strength in the surrounding forests.

In the early 1990s, Vinayan left the CPI(M-L) Party Unity in the face of intense police repression and a split within the party over whether to emphasize violent or nonviolent tactics. He founded the Jan Mukti Andolan, or the People's Liberation Movement, which worked for land reform through mass actions, such as strikes and demonstrations, rather than through violent confrontation with the police or landlords. As Kunnath (2012) points out, however, the nonviolent Jan Mukti Andolan was in fact dependent on militant groups for its efficacy: the threat of violence provided by militant groups strengthened the nonviolent Jan Mukti Andolan's position in negotiations. The implicit threat presented by the andolan was that violent groups or means would enter the political field if the negotiations failed.

The hills and the trees of the forest belt that had long prevented the arrival of a centralizing state had enabled the sedimentation of layers of infrastructure of collective action in the forests and among the forest dwellers. Far-left movements fled to the forests to escape state repression, but in the process, they tied forest politics into national politics for the first time. The absence of formal property rights that resulted from the long absence of a centralizing state, in turn, made the 23 percent of India's land area that is forest land easily available to private and public capital for dams, mines, and factories. The late arrival of the centralizing state, then, brought both a left-wing political infrastructure and the increasing immiseration of forest dwellers that produced a population for this infrastructure to organize.

The Sarvodaya Bhoodan movement had arrived in the form of the Banwasi Seva Ashram with the goal of bringing about land reform through moral persuasion. The ashram was drawn into the conflict over the forest. The same Emergency that had sent left activists to the forests, however, had simultaneously inaugurated a new tightening of Union government control over them, and forest dwellers who lacked legal rights faced active dispossession by the Forest Department. The Banwasi Seva Ashram's response was to turn to the legal remedies of legal education and PIL in defense of the forest dwellers' right to forest land, not as property but as a necessity for their livelihood. Vinayan and the CPI(M-L) Party Unity responded first through violent confrontation with the same Forest Department with similar demands—an end to bonded labor and the distribution of Bhoodan land—and later through nonviolent collective actions.

An Outbreak of Violence

There is a long history of violent conflict over land in Duddhi and in central India's forest belt: it was after all an "outbreak of violence" that brought Roberts, the settlement officer, to Duddhi in 1849 to assign property and use rights. Legal conflicts over land date back nearly as long. The attack on Ramnagar, however, was a conflict over the meaning of a law. The means of its interpretation and violent enforcement had been claimed not by police officers, judges, or bureaucrats, but to members of a dominant caste as they destroyed a village.

The turn to the law and the multiplication of the agents who would implement and violently enforce the law represent the long legacy of the Emergency years in India's forests. The Emergency brought about a realignment of insurgent and counterinsurgent political forces in the forests over the same period that forests were emerging as a site of extractive capital accumulation. This legalization of politics in Duddhi can be seen as the legalization of counterinsurgency, of state actors struggling for hegemony in the face of multiple powerful alternative projects of hegemony. Counterinsurgency in India's forests is then a variety of Benjamin's ([1921] 2009) lawmaking violence, violence that inaugurates sovereignty and the rule of law. If this is so, then what are we to make of a law such as the Forest Rights Act, itself intended as a counterinsurgency measure, that legalizes a limited number of the ends of these insurgent groups? In such a case, the insurgent violence itself is lawmaking, but only partially. Its goals of land redistribution are partially met, but only through an ambiguous law. The Forest Rights Act, as the next few chapters outline, would become the contested ground of this bid for hegemony, accessible to all sides but unfixed in its meaning.

In Duddhi, this was not a mere formal or institutional shift in politics. The contestants over Ramnagar's land would make concrete claims to territory and sovereignty that extended beyond a small patch of forest. The turn to the law was inseparable from a turn to the Constitution, and the Ramnagaris would build on the claims made by the Supreme Court, Indira Gandhi, and the Banwasi Seva Ashram to claim the legacy of the country's founding sovereign constituent order. For Habermas (2011), constitutions are a key stage in the process of juridification; they formalize political victories, but only by eroding the space of pluralistic contention. In the forest belt, however, the turn to the Constitution did not mark the end of contention but instead a deepening of the stakes and claims of existing conflicts. Claims to speak on behalf of the Constitution were brought into the logic of insurgency and counterinsurgency. As Duddhi was incorporated within national political economic infrastructures, its contentious politics would claim the inheritance of a national founding sovereign order through the Constitution. Radical visions of the redistribution of land and political authority would take the shape of a document written decades earlier.

In the aftermath of the Emergency, the law acquired a centrality to state-led dispossession in forest areas that made it into the ground for struggles against that dispossession. In the next chapter, I move to the drafting of the Forest Rights Act to look at how competing political projects came together to produce its text. The infrastructure of collective action produced after the Emergency met a Supreme Court and Forest Department that claimed much greater powers over the forest. In response, the insurgency turned to the law. In the next chapter, I ask what sort of law insurgency and counterinsurgency produce, when they become lawmaking. Put differently, when projects of radical redistribution are enacted through the same law as other, contradictory projects, including counterinsurgency and environmental conservation, what sort of text do they produce?

HISTORICAL INJUSTICES AND THE MOVEMENT TO CREATE THE FOREST RIGHTS ACT

The eviction of Kalla and his family in Rajasthan that was discussed at the start of this book's introduction was one of roughly three hundred thousand carried out by India's Forest Department starting in October 2002 (Drèze 2005). Across the country, guards forced forest-dwelling families from their homes, and in many cases like Kalla's, they ignored the pattas or deeds that these families possessed as they did so. The guards who carried out the evictions were acting on orders from their superiors, who were in turn acting on orders found in a circular that had been issued by the Ministry of Environment and Forests (MoEF) in New Delhi. The circular ordered that "encroachments which are not eligible for regularization . . . should be summarily evicted in a time bound manner" (MoEF 2002, quoted in Campaign for Survival and Dignity 2003, 226).

In the four years that followed Kalla's family's eviction, however, the eviction drive would come to a halt and a new law would be passed, the Forest Rights Act, that attempted to solve the problem of the forest and recognize the rights of forest dwellers. But for the evictions to be halted and the law to be passed would require a new status for the records of lives lived in the forests. This chapter tracks the political forms through which records of settlement on the land would become translatable into legally enforceable property rights: a new politics of proof that aimed to give legal force to pattas like Kalla's.

Even following the passage of the Forest Rights Act, the status of proof of residence in the forest was contingent, however. The possibility of obtaining forest rights through the FRA depended on the way the law was read, as the Ramnagaris were to learn when their village was destroyed in 2010. The Forest

Rights Act that was passed in December 2006 had emerged over months of conflict between distinct organizations, politicians, bureaucrats, and lobbyists, all seeking to create a legal text that would produce distinct arrangements of people, property, and forests. These visions coexist in the legal text, as contradictory possible readings enabled through what one bureaucrat who was involved in the process called "word traps" (Gopalakrishnan 2005, 5), apparently innocuous words and phrases that allow readers to read the law within various extralegal narratives, fitting it back into diverse and conflicting political projects. Specific contexts and readings reappear, then, in potential form in the Forest Rights Act, through these word traps.

A law like the Forest Rights Act purports to be universal, to apply evenhandedly and nonarbitrarily to events that have not yet taken place. The act emerged, however, out of specific events that had to be fit within nonspecific categories in order to build the larger coalition that could exert collective action on a scale that would force Parliament to pass a law. The politics of proof and the Forest Rights Act's word traps are means of narratively connecting pasts and futures, fitting events to generalizable concepts that can travel across time and space and enable collective action at a scale that can pass a law to rearrange forest property across India. This capacity of concepts to abstract from and tie together events and to create potential futures was identified by political theorist Reinhart Koselleck. As he puts it, "every concept entering into a narrative or representation . . . renders relations discernible by a refusal to take on their uniqueness. Concepts not only teach us of the singularity (for us) of past meanings, but also contain structural potential, dealing with the contemporaneous in the noncontemporary, which cannot be reduced to the pure temporal succession of history. Concepts that comprehend past states, relations, and processes become for the historian who employs them formal categories which are the conditions of possible histories" (2004, 112).

Legal concepts, however, do not only comprehend multiples states and processes but also carry with them compulsion, the ability to act on those states and processes. Law's concepts are contingent on future events, and they carry the threat of force if certain other future events do not follow. Such rules, another name for contingent and forceful concepts, can be brought into social life attached to conditions and with threats attached to them, such as police violence, arrest, or fines. Rules travel like concepts and, like concepts, they are malleable, subject to interpretation and reinterpretation as they are brought into social life. No rule must be followed, but a rule implies the possibility of compulsion or coercion—and, in the case of legal rules, coercion by state actors. As laws are interpreted through other concepts and are fit within other narratives that travel separately from them, the range of rules that they can be drawn on to impose expands, and the range of political projects that laws can be used for widens. The task that faced the Campaign for Survival and Dignity's activists, then, was first to establish concepts out of events and then to draft the law in such a way that it would be useful to particular political projects, to create a law that appeared even-handed but that also could be read to enable certain rules and not others. If the Campaign for Survival and Dignity sought to adhere text and context through a politics of proof to put an end to the evictions, then the task of the drafting of the bill was to reverse this adhesion, to allow cotexts that were already in circulation—that is, narratives about a just relationship between people and forests—to be inserted between the law and its possible contexts.

The 2002 Eviction Drive

In 2011, I met with Uma, a Delhi-based lawyer who had been involved with left-ist forest groups for several years to discuss the evictions and the movement to halt them. Over email, Uma explained to me that the Supreme Court had been central to the evictions, and she invited me to join her the next week at the Supreme Court's forest bench, which met weekly to hear forest-related cases. It was an appropriate place to begin to understand both the evictions and the movement to pass the Forest Rights Act: since the 1990s, the Supreme Court has become the key institution in Indian forest policy.

The Supreme Court's increasing influence over forest policy has tracked its increasing political influence more generally. As I discussed in chapter 1, in the years following the end of the Emergency in 1977, the Supreme Court began to claim a larger political role and a new relationship to the Indian public. The threat of an authoritarian executive that had been gestured to in the *Kesavananda* decision had been realized in the Emergency, which the Supreme Court used to justify a stronger role for itself. The Court began to encourage petition-ers to file public interest litigation (PIL), dropping rules of standing to allow anyone to file a case on behalf of a public to which they need not belong. In the early years of public interest litigation, the "public" consisted largely of the poor and marginal. As Gauri (2014) has shown, however, this changed in the 1990s. Through the late 1980s, PIL claimants from the state categories of Scheduled Caste, Scheduled Tribe, and Other Backwards Classes had a higher rate of win-ning cases than claimants from forward castes. From the 1990s on, however, claimants from forward castes began to win PILs at a higher rate than those from lower castes.

As we saw in chapter 1, the shift in the public on whose behalf PILs were decided was accompanied by a jurisprudential shift that centered on a changing interpretation to the right to life and livelihood promised in Article 21 of the Indian Constitution as it began to read the right to a "healthy environment" into the right to livelihood, bringing the Court in line with India's conservationist lobby. It was this new, environmentalist reading of Article 21 that motivated the creation of the Supreme Court's forest bench. The case *T. N. Godavarman v. Union of India* was filed by a member of an erstwhile royal family in South India whose land had been claimed by the Forest Department in Tamil Nadu. Godavarman was protesting the logging that continued on what had been his family's land and the failure of the Forest Department to put a stop to it. The PIL made its way to the Supreme Court, which never closed the case: the Court filed a writ of continuing mandamus, claiming indefinite executive powers over India's forests. In its first ruling, the Court ruled that the 1980 Forest Conservation Act applied to all land in the country with dense forest cover. The case is now the single largest in Indian legal history, with more than two thousand subcases, all of them heard by the forest bench.

Uma invited me to visit the Supreme Court on a Friday, the day that the forest bench meets. The bench met in the chief justice's courtroom. One of thirty-two courtrooms in the Supreme Court, it was a large room with high, arched ceilings, wooden walls on which were hung paintings of distinguished jurists, and eleven ceiling fans that struggled to circulate the thick July air. Uma and I sat in the visitor's area in the back of the room, an area that was fenced off by shelves carrying leather-bound legal tomes. Forty or so people, mostly men middle-age and older, sat with us. In the center of the visitor's area, ran a corridor that led to a lawyer's gallery and, beyond it, the bench. Some thirty lawyers were packed into the corridor, almost all of them men and all wearing heavy black robes. Facing the room from behind the bench were three high-backed chairs for three justices. On the wall above the chairs was hung the seal of the Republic of India.

I was alerted to the arrival of the three justices by a commotion and a rush by the gathered lawyers and visitors to stand. We sat down. After a brief introduction by one of the judges, one amicus curiae who advises the bench as a "friend of the court," Siddharth Chaudhury, began to discuss the case at hand. The forest bench's case load is so great that the amicus helps in deciding which cases will be heard and in advising the justices on how to rule. Sitting in the back of the room, I struggled to hear the three judges, the lawyers, and the petitioners above the sound of the fans hanging from the ceiling.

That day's case concerned the spurs of the Aravalli range that runs through Delhi, most of which are reserved or fall within a wildlife sanctuary. Outside of Delhi, in the state of Haryana, the spurs are not protected forest land, and mining there had drawn down the water level in the protected areas that fall within

Delhi. As a result, in 2002 the Court banned mining in the entire range. Mining companies appealed the ban, but that day, the amicus was speaking in favor of keeping the ban in place. Speaking loudly, and entirely in English, he recited a list of every mineral found in the Aravallis. Damage to the environment and human health both harmed the public interest, he said. Development was necessary, but it must be sustainable. "The hills must not be damaged at any cost." The justices listened to the amicus's concerns and, after consultation with one another and the petitioners, they elected to maintain the mining ban in the Aravallis.

After the session had ended, Uma and I went to the Court's library. Trying to speak softly to minimize the inconvenience to people reading at the tables arranged in the library, Uma and I discussed her work and the events that led to the push to pass the Forest Rights Act, events in which the forest bench and the amicus Siddharth Chaudhury had played a key role. Soon after the 2002 eviction drive began, Uma explained, she and a group of activists had asked Forest Department officials for a copy of the eviction order, and it was given to them. The order had been written in March 2002 by V. K. Bahuguna, who was at the time the inspector general of forests. Bahuguna's order directed all state-level conservators of forests to summarily evict all "encroachments which are not eligible for regularization," citing as justification Supreme Court IA No. 703 in Writ Petition 202/95. An IA, or Interlocutory Application, is an appeal that is made to a ruling before the ruling has itself been ordered. Bahuguna's directions had been echoed and approved by a report published in September 2002 by the Central Empowered Committee, which is made up of retired forest officers and Supreme Court lawyers established by the Supreme Court to hear and recommend actions on forest cases. The Forest Department had cited a Supreme Court order in order to evict hundreds of thousands of people, and, through the Central Empowered Committee, the Court had appeared to endorse the Forest Department's actions.

Uma told me that she had tried to find a copy of IA No. 703, but the order had not been published. To find the IA, Uma went to the office of Harish Salve, an amicus curiae to the forest bench. Because of the amicus curiae's key role in handling the bench's large volume of cases, his private office contained, in effect, a second archive of the forest bench's decisions.

Uma told me that Salve had not been in his office when she visited. She knew, however, that Salve would be unlikely to give her a copy of the order. It was Salve who had filed IA No. 703, and it had presumably remained unpublished precisely to avoid any strict accounting of the legal decisions that led to the evictions. Uma told me, though, that she managed to trick the junior amicus curiae, who was in the office that day, into giving her the order. She had simply demanded it, acting as if she were within her rights to do so.

The junior amicus complied and gave Uma the order, which read, "An application has been filed by the ld. Amicus Curiae in Court against the illegal encroachment of forest land in various States and Union Territories is taken on board. Let the same be registered and numbered. Issue notice to the respondents returnable after six weeks. There will be an interim order in terms of prayer (a)" (Vide order dated 11/23/2001, unreported, quoted in Khanna and Naveen 2005). The Supreme Court order cited by Bahuguna's order, then, did not in fact contain explicit instructions to the MoEF, but rather a citation of a second unpublished document. The Court's order directed the MoEF to follow the instructions provided by "prayer (a)." A prayer is that portion of a complaint in which a plaintiff or amicus asks a court for specific remedies. Prayer (a) was unpublished, like IA No. 703, so the specific remedies directed by the Court were unpublished.

Uma told me that she asked the junior amicus for a copy of "prayer (a)," which he also provided. Prayer (a) in the Interlocutory Application read, "(a) Restrain the Union of India from permitting regularization of any encroachments whatsoever without the leave of this Hon'ble Court" (Vide order dated 11/23/2011, unreported, quoted in Khanna and Naveen 2005). Prayer (a), which outlined the specific measures that Inspector General of Forests Bahuguna cited in IA No. 703 when ordering the eviction of all unauthorized encroachments in India, did not in fact ask for any evictions. The prayer, instead, asked the Court to restrain the government from "permitting regularization of any encroachments": no further unauthorized settlements in forests were to be made legal.

The eviction drive that led to three hundred thousand families being rendered homeless was authorized by a chain of legal citations, from individual foresters to the Forest Department to the MoEF to the unpublished Supreme Court order IA No. 703 to the unpublished prayer (a) of Harish Salve, the amicus curiae. Because the last two documents cited were never published, the authority and agency that lay behind the evictions was obscured. For Callon (1984), chains of translation allow scientists and politicians in certain settings to align the interests of diverse constituencies and claim new sources of power. In the eviction drive, *claims* of translation were being used to assert an authority that ultimately could not be grounded in any one constituency, institution, or set of individual actors.

Such a claim of translation—grounded as it was upon a chain of *mis*translations—was open, however, to a counterclaim and to a contest over the authority claimed in the original translation. The initial chain of translations claimed authority through an existing set of institutions, the Supreme Court and the MoEF, which in turn claimed their authority through a claim to democratic representation of the Indian people. Uma's work to challenge the legality of the eviction drive was the beginning of a contest over a much larger set of claims and relationships: the authority of the Ministry and the Court over forest matters, property relations in India's forests, and even political authority in India's forests.

Uma was not simply revealing a mistranslation and making a negative claim. Rather, she was setting in motion a political contest through counternarratives and counteranalyses that were grounded in the evidence that she had produced of the mistranslation. This evidence proved what hundreds of thousands of forest dwellers already knew: that many had never received legal rights to the land that they lived on, that others like Kalla had received legal rights that could be ignored by the Forest Department, and that all of them could be evicted at any time.

The Campaign for Survival and Dignity

The scraps of proof produced by Kalla, Uma, and others began to cohere over the subsequent months into both a politically powerful narrative of the eviction drive's injustice and a powerful movement to put an end to forest evictions. The political infrastructures discussed in chapter 1 that took shape in the years following the Emergency helped to circulate stories of eviction out of individual forests to activists across the country. Two individuals who had been involved in forest politics since the 1970s would play key roles in turning the narratives around the eviction drive into a bill and law: Pradip Prabhu and Madhu Sarin.

Pradip Prabhu is an animated man with a shock of white hair, overflowing with stories and analyses. Prabhu was a Jesuit priest until the mid-1970s, when he left the priesthood and became involved in forest rights movements in Maharashtra. Since then, he had been involved in a number of efforts to regularize forest rights in the state, including a 1978 government order regularizing forest dwellers' rights, and had helped to draft a 2002 law that would recognize forest rights. When I first met him in 2009, in a Chinese restaurant in Delhi's outskirts, Prabhu explained that he started hearing stories of the evictions, of elephants being used to evict people in forests in Maharashtra in May 2002. Soon he received an email with the leaked proof that Uma had uncovered of the Forest Department's mistranslation of the Court order. Prabhu and a small group began to contact friends in order to hold a public hearing about the evictions. Among that group was Madhu Sarin.

Sarin had been trained as an architect in the United Kingdom, but on returning to India in the 1970s, she became involved in women's forest organizations and participatory forest management efforts. This work, which, as Sarin put it to me, had put her more on the development side of things than the civil disobedience side, had nonetheless brought her into forest rights circles, and she had known Prabhu for several years. When I first met Sarin at her home in Chandigarh in 2010, she was sixty-five. Dressed in a cotton *salwaar kameez*, she rolled a series of cigarettes as she explained the events that led to her involvement in the push for the Forest Rights Act. Like Prabhu, she had started receiving emails in early 2002 about the violent evictions that were taking place and began hearing rumors about the MoEF's order. "No one had quite seen it," she told me. "Even on the email groups, you heard about it. Then one started finding out and hearing about these absolutely atrocious evictions. There was absolute outrage. I think that outrage brought some conservation, development groups together also with groups which were out there, already fighting."

Through a series of emails, phone calls, meetings, and hearings, the discrete and local events of dispossession were turned into concepts that could travel, take in longer histories, and rally hundreds of millions of people into a campaign. The stories that circulated produced outrage, and the rumors that someone had found proof that the evictions were being carried out without court sanction produced the possibility that they could be stopped. In response to the stories, Prabhu told me, "We formed this small group, called the Campaign for Survival and Dignity and started contacting friends, a small group of friends." Prabhu and Sarin were the Campaign's first conveners.

By October, protests had slowed or put a stop to the evictions in most of the country. In July 2003, Uma, Pradip, Madhu, and delegates from more than two hundred organizations that represented landless forest dwellers held a public hearing, a *jan sunwai*, in Delhi to discuss the evictions and Uma's findings. The meetings ratified what their participants already knew: hundreds of thousands of people had been forced from their homes over the preceding months, these evictions followed decades of more localized evictions and harassment of forest residents, and the claims and proof of residence of enormous numbers of forest dwellers had never been recognized. Through the mistranslation identified by Uma, however, they had proof that the evictions had been carried out unlawfully, which they drew together with an analysis of the role of the state and capital in forest dwellers' dispossession and a project to end such dispossession through a new law.

In the hearing, representatives spoke of their evictions and the violence that accompanied them. Verifying what Prabhu had heard, one man from Maharashtra described elephants being sent into his village to destroy its homes. In their accounts, the evictions were also set into a longer history of state-led dispossession that was understood in loosely Marxist terms, as an ongoing process of what Harvey (2003, 67) has called "accumulation by dispossession." In testimony after testimony, activists and forest dwellers argued that the drive had been intended to clear the forest of its inhabitants to make land, minerals, water, and timber available for state and private accumulation in the name of conservation.

In our first meeting in 2009, Prabhu explained to me that a common narrative among left forest movements from the 1970s on was that such dispossession of forest dwellers had resulted in a "historic injustice": their right to the forests had never been recognized by either the British colonial state or the independent Indian state, and that evictions, harassment, and underdevelopment had followed.

In their depositions in the public hearing, Prabhu and others repeated this narrative. "For centuries," he told the gathered representatives, "the tribals were considered to belong to the forest and were called that way. Ensconced in the lap of nature, they built up a civilization centered around nature's bounty. The tribal people themselves believed they belonged to the forest, much like a child belongs to its mother. The tribal ethos and spirituality was built around the principle that 'the forest is the only power in the known universe that converts the energy of the sun into food,' a truth only recently understood by most others" (Prabhu 2003, quoted in Campaign for Survival and Dignity 2003, 106). Here, this narrative of historic injustice was fit into what Greenough (2001) has called the "Standard Environmental Narrative" of the South Asian environment, which posits the existence of a precolonial forest order in which land was held in common and people stewarded their natural surroundings.

Prabhu however filled out this standard narrative historically in relation to successive projects of state formation:

> This history of tribals and the forest spans four epochs; a) the precolonial phase stretching over centuries during when the tribals withdrew into the forest habitat as their last bastion for survival; b) the colonial period spanning two centuries, which witnessed the colonization of the tribal's forest habitat, disruptions of their society, resistance to colonial encroachment and a partial re-ordering of survival strategies; c) the post-colonial phase where internal colonization of the forest-tribal realm by the timber lobby in connivance with the state spelt doom for tribal communities and d) the contemporary phase of contesting ideologies, one that seeks integration as a means of tribal development, while the other argues for their eviction in the name of conservation. (Prabhu 2003, quoted in Campaign for Survival and Dignity 2003, 106–107)

He tied this narrative into both an analysis of the contemporary state's work to dispossess forest dwellers and a program to end this dispossession. He explained recent dispossession as the result of the failure of recognition of tribals' rights by the forest bureaucracy and the Supreme Court.

The recent wave of evictions, however, could be explained only through the collusion that Uma found between the Court and the Forest Department. Uma's proof was incorporated into a larger condemnation of the relationship between the judiciary, the executive states, and India's forests:

> As we can see, through the numerous Supreme Court directives in the hundreds of interventions in the Godavarman case, the history of forest conflict is being written anew. The forest department is rewriting the Indian Forest Act (1927) through the orders of an "environmentally sensitive" and activist Supreme Court. The Godavarman case, in effect, has created a frame through which the executive (forest department) has taken on the mantle of the legislature (Parliament) via the hundreds of interventions that have been admitted and the directions issued by the judiciary in these cases (Supreme Court). This frame has also allowed these two institutions of the state, i.e., the executive and the judiciary, which are largely insulated from the public, to write a new law in the public realm, effectively bypassing the elected representatives. The process of law making has thereby lost its democratic character. In a surreal twist of fate, India's largest landholder has metamorphosed overnight into prosecutor, jury and judge. (Prabhu 2003, quoted in Campaign for Survival and Dignity 2003, 4, 5)

Because of the nexus between the Forest Department and the Supreme Court, the two were able to set forest policy and evict hundreds of thousands, each deflecting responsibility onto the other through the mistranslated orders. To end such dispossession in the future, Prabhu called for "the recognition of rights and concessions," "the ownership of minor produce and majority share in forest income," and "the restoration of stewardship for the future of both the tribals and the forest" (Prabhu 2003, quoted in Campaign for Survival and Dignity 2003, 106–107).

Prabhu's narrative and program were largely repeated in the public hearing, as speaker after speaker fit the recent eviction drive into the long historic injustice against forest dwellers and signed on to a loosely shared set of legal demands to end the injustice. Many of those who spoke were, like Kalla, forest dwellers who had recently lost their homes. Many were lawyers and activists, like Uma and Prabhu. The shared conceptual work that they were doing, however, hinged on the proof that Uma had been able to furnish: the chain of documents, each mistranslating and misciting the other, which established the legal illegitimacy of the eviction drive.

Following the jan sunwai, the umbrella organization, the Campaign for Survival and Dignity (CSD), would both coordinate the collective efforts of its constituent members and represent them in national political matters. The CSD's proposed path to arrive at the recognition of forest dwellers' rights, which emerged in the conversations of the jan sunwai, was to wrest forest policy away from the unelected justices in the Supreme Court and the bureaucrats of the MoEF. The campaign, drawing on Uma's analysis, published a report in 2004 that demanded a restoration of parliamentary sovereignty over forests: "Restore forest law and policy making to the legislature" (139). Restoring forest policy to the legislature, activists decided during the jan sunwai, could be accomplished through the passage of a new law that would recognize forest dwellers' rights. Through further hearings, sit-ins, rallies, and meetings across the country, the CSD began to campaign for the creation of a law that would check the judiciary's control over forests and bypass the forest bureaucracy.

In February 2004, just months before a general election, the MoEF issued two orders that were apparent concessions to the CSD's demands. The first was titled "Stepping Up of Process for Conversion of Forest Villages into Revenue Villages," which asked state governments to begin to regularize forest settlements that had existed before 1980. The second, titled "Regularisation of the Rights of the Tribals on the Forest Lands," began a process to recognize "the traditional rights of the tribal population on the forest lands" for all tribal people who could prove continuous occupation of forest land since December 1993 (Campaign for Survival and Dignity 2003, 123).

Before the MoEF's orders could be implemented, however, amicus curiae Siddharth Chaudhury filed a petition with the Supreme Court asking for them to be stayed, and the petition was granted. Having conceded to some of the CSD's demands and having distanced itself from the Supreme Court, the MoEF now found it was unable to act because of the Supreme Court. It, too, would require a new law to bring forest policy out of the hands of the Court.

The Forest Department's evictions had begun before Uma had made the court orders public, and the injustice of the mass dispossession had been clear to the activists and forest dwellers gathered at the jan sunwai before they saw Uma's documents and before they had received some national publicity. How was it that knowledge and experience of an injustice did not catalyze the formation of a national movement for forest rights, but a public hearing around a series of mistranslated documents did? What role did these documents play in particular? Uma's work can be seen as a politics of proving what is already widely known, a verification of a Gramscian ([1926] 2005) "common sense."[1] The act of proof, however, allowed the common sense to travel and crystalize. As it traveled, new audiences heard what was already known, allowing the common sense to become a claim upon the state and the people who knew it to become a mass movement.

Uma had been able to acquire from the junior amicus curiae the textual objects that she then spoke on behalf of. She circulated them and published them and spoke about them to growing numbers of people, first to a small network of activists and then to a new national campaign. Uma, and subsequently the CSD, successfully narrated the event of the eviction campaign to produce a mass movement. In the second portion of this chapter, I show how the narratives produced through this mobilization found their way into the law and how, as they were written in and between the lines of the new law, they enabled further mobilizations.

Word Traps and the Forest Rights Act

The drafting of the bill that was to become the Forest Rights Act was a long and contentious process, with forceful debates, quiet maneuvers, and public protests not only over who exactly would be eligible for rights, how they would establish their eligibility, and what the rights would entail. It was also a contest fought over the language through which these new rights would be granted, over what ideologies and histories words called up, how those words were imagined to be picked up and used by forest-dwelling constituencies and foresters in the future, and how those words could be isolated and advertised by politicians involved in present-day bids for new constituencies. Visions of specific injustices and possible justices, possible arrangements of people and the forests around them, would jostle together as they made their way into a legal text that was necessarily acceptable to many constituencies: a law that could give Kalla's family their land back without naming Kalla or his family's story.

By the time India's United Progressive Alliance formed a government in May 2004, conditions were in place for India's landless forest dwellers to be finally granted legal rights to the forests, but it was unclear how those rights would arrive. The CSD, which had grown to be the most visible and politically powerful representative of landless forest dwellers, had demanded that a law be passed that would guarantee rights, and every major party had promised some resolution to the problem of forest dwellers' landlessness. Forest dwellers, who had consistently voted for the Congress for decades, seemed to be defecting to the Bharatiya Janata Party (BJP) in key states: they were a constituency that was up for grabs. The Congress Member of Parliament (MP) Mani Shankar Aiyar argued in a 2003 article that members of Scheduled Tribes could easily be won back to the party, however, with measures to address forest landlessness: "A Congress which imaginatively examines the problem [of tribal landlessness] and provides a constructive, detailed solution in time to reach it to far-flung tribal communities would snatch back the tribal vote." The BJP had been making its own overtures to forest dwellers, advertising its efforts to regularize forest dwellers' rights in newspapers and in rallies. The national political parties contesting the 2004 general election began to align around a similar position: the evictions should end, and those forest dwellers whose land rights had yet to be recognized should be granted rights.

In the forest belt that stretches across central India, however, other forms of politics were taking root. As discussed in chapter 1, diverse Maoist and Marxist-Leninist parties that had emerged in the wake of the 1967 peasant uprising in the Naxalbari district, in West Bengal, had fought through social movements, electoral politics, and armed struggle. A number of these parties that were committed to armed struggle merged in 2004 into the Communist Party of India (Maoist), which both coordinated guerrilla warfare against landlords, capitalists, and the Indian state and, in its strongholds, established its own governing structures. By 2003, fifty-five districts in India were classified by the Union government as "Maoist affected," stretching across a "red corridor" from Andhra Pradesh to Bihar and West Bengal, bisecting the Central Indian forest belt. By 2009, Prime Minister Manmohan Singh would announce that the Maoist movement represented "India's greatest internal security threat." A politics of extralegal violence was taking shape in the forests, and the proposed law was intended as a counterinsurgency measure among others. Tribal Affairs Minister K. C. Deo explained to me in a 2012 interview that the government's hope had been to defuse Maoist political movements by offering rights to the forest dwellers who were their potential constituents. This effort to defuse the Maoist threat through legal concessions proceeded in parallel with the government's support for an intensified conventional and paramilitary counterinsurgency war against the movement, however, with an "all-out paramilitary offensive" named Operation Green Hunt launched in 2009.

The May 2004 elections put in power a coalition of parties across the center and left of the political spectrum, anchored by the Congress Party and led by the new prime minister, Manmohan Singh. In forming what they called the United Progressive Alliance (UPA) government, the coalition agreed to a common minimum program for their government that included the following promises, echoing the demands made at the CSD's public hearing: "The UPA will urge the states to make legislation for conferring ownership rights in respect of minor forest produce, including tendu patta (leaves of the tendu plant), on all those people from the weaker sections who work in the forests"

(United Progressive Alliance 2004, 9–10). This was still an inchoate promise. The program did not promise that the new government would pass a law that would confer ownership rights over forest produce to forest dwellers, only that the government would urge states to do so. It was also unclear whether ownership and use rights to minor forest produce would be extended to forest land, whether all forest dwellers or only members of Scheduled Tribes would be eligible, who would draft the law that granted these rights, or what language they would use in doing so.

In June, the new Congress-led government established the National Advisory Committee (NAC), a group of well-known academics, activists, and bureaucrats who were charged with drafting legislation that would fulfill the Common Minimum Programme, including the promise to urge states to give forest dwellers rights to forest produce. The NAC would go on to shepherd a number of laws that would guarantee rights to information, to food, and to government-provided employment, recasting welfare measures as rights to be claimed rather than rights provided by the governmental state.

Inviting the conveners of the CSD to a meeting with Prime Minister Singh, the NAC initiated a process through which the activists who had lobbied for the law would play a key role in shaping it and through which older political conflicts over India's forests would be refracted through a struggle over a bill's text. The leadership of the CSD were not only representatives of a mass campaign of forest dwellers for rights; they also had close social ties with many of the intellectuals, activists, and bureaucrats who were initiating the drafting process. On November 5, a bureaucrat and activist named Aruna Roy, who was a friend of both Prabhu and Sarin and a member of the newly created NAC, set up a meeting between the two CSD activists and Prime Minister Singh to discuss evictions in forest areas. The meeting ended with the prime minister pledging to send letters to individual states ending evictions. Also present at the meeting was R. Gopalakrishnan, whom Prabhu knew from classes he had taught at the civil service academy in past years. Gopalakrishnan, who would go on to play an important role in shepherding the bill through Parliament, was a joint secretary in the Prime Minister's Office and a bureaucrat who had a long record of aligning himself with left forest activists.

In December, the economist Jean Drèze, also a member of the NAC and, like Roy, a friend of Prabhu and Sarin, asked Prabhu, who had been involved in drafting a 2002 Maharashtra law recognizing forest rights, to write a draft of a bill that would grant forest dwellers land rights that could be sent to Parliament. On the morning of January 15, 2005, Gopalakrishnan reached out to Prabhu, asking him to attend a meeting that evening to discuss the creation of a committee to draft a bill and to give a presentation on the history of Adivasi dispossession, but "not to sound like an activist." In the meeting, Prabhu managed to convince the prime minister that the Ministry of Tribal Affairs (MoTA) and CSD representatives—rather than the conservation-minded MoEF, which had ordered the 2002 eviction drive—would be the appropriate authors of the bill, because they had the trust of forest-dwelling communities.

The prime minister created a new Technical Support Group with twelve members, six of them unofficial members to be chosen by Prabhu, and asked them to draft a bill that would not only grant ownership rights over forest produce as promised in the Common Minimum Programme but also "recognize the land rights of scheduled tribes and forest dwellers." In asking Prabhu to choose half of the committee's members, the prime minister gave him considerable discretion to put together a committee that reflected his concerns and the concerns of his constituency. Theirs was by no means the only potential constituency that could be interested in the ultimate text of the law that they were drafting, however. A well-organized group of conservationists, who had long held that India's forests could be protected only by removing forest dwellers, would soon find their way into the rooms and committees that were shaping the bill's text. The contours of the CSD's constituency too would soon be debated. Within the coalition, there would be controversies over whether the CSD represented all forest dwellers or only those who belonged to Scheduled Tribes. Forest dwellers who did not belong to any of the coalition's member organizations would begin to contest the CSD's claim to represent everyone who lived in the country's forests.

The day after Prabhu's meeting with the prime minister, Gopalakrishnan wrote a brief to the new Technical Support Group. In it, Gopalakrishnan examined the reasons why a new law was necessary and considered potential problems the law might face in its implementation. In outlining a vision of what the new law would do to grant rights to the country's forest dwellers, Gopalakrishnan was also concerned with identifying the reasons why those rights had not previously been granted. He wrote, "If the Government formulates an order worded sensibly to give independence to a group of people denied so far after India became independent in 1947, no court in its right mind can oppose it. The word traps that officials in the Ministry have consciously constructed to complicate this issue has been the problem. Here again the real solution lies in a new Act to be introduced called Scheduled Tribes and Forest Dwellers (Recognition of Forest Rights) Act" (Gopalakrishnan 2005, 2).

Land rights, in other words, had so far not been granted because of the MoEF, which was responsible for India's forest areas and was required by the

Indian Forest Act of 1927 to survey existing rights in areas that were notified as Reserved Forests. "The Ministry" had worked to prevent such a survey, Gopalakrishnan argued, and had avoided court pressure to fulfill its obligation through the use of "word traps," which he explained and illustrated later in the memo:

> What may be considered a minor issue but with significant ramifications needs to be mentioned. These are about the "word traps" created by the Ministry of Environment and Forests (perhaps consciously woven into [sic] deny the genuine demands of tribal communities). To give an example, while the PMO [Prime Minister's Office] refers to the first issue as regularization of occupation of pre-1980 settlements, the communication from the Ministry of Environment and Forests (including the reply to the Prime Minister by the Minister) refers to this as regularizing encroachments. The battle is lost even before it begins in neutral spaces like courts. It is this kind of wrong use of language that has brought the Government into this protracted legal wrangle. (Gopalakrishnan 2005, 5)

Gopalakrishnan was concerned that the use of the word "encroachments" to describe India's unauthorized forest settlements had set a trap for the interpretation of existing laws that do or could grant land rights to those settlements. The word might have the same referent that phrases like "unauthorized forest settlements" do, but it allowed for the invocation of a theory and history of forest settlement as illicit movement onto preexisting forest land, just as the word had in the chain of mistranslated Supreme Court orders that had led to the 2002 eviction drive. This implicit theory and history, which did not need to be spelled out in order to shape interpretations, had affected who was able to receive land rights through existing laws.

Any new law that successfully gave "independence to a group of people denied so far" (Gopalakrishnan 2005, 2), India's forest dwellers, would have to explicitly grant those rights. It would also have to avoid word traps, phrases that would implicitly allow rights claims to be denied. To avoid these word traps—or, more accurately, to set traps that would successfully grant rights to forest dwellers—it would be necessary to use different words in the new law, words that cued up a different theory and history of forests and their relationship to the people who lived in them. It was in order to set these new traps that Gopalakrishnan invited Pradip Prabhu to the meeting with the prime minister and pushed for the new bill to be drafted by Prabhu and his fellow forest rights activists, along with representatives not from the MoEF but from the MoTA.

Word Traps and Potential Chronotopes

Contexts and absence of context would be fit together like a jigsaw puzzle, via Gopalakrishnan's word traps. The work of the CSD in their public meetings could be seen as fixing the relationship between text and context, ensuring that many families like Kalla's would have the proof of their forest residence recognized by state actors. The task that lay ahead of the CSD's representatives now was to loosen the relationship between text and context, however, to ensure that texts that might not make their way through Parliamentary legislative processes could nonetheless travel with the Forest Rights Act as plausible cotexts, that the chronotopes—the configuration of people and places and time—in the law's text could be fit into other extratextual political chronotopes.

In some sections of a law, past and future chronotopes are kept separate, as in preambles in which past problems are described, discussions of existing laws, or discussions of future potentialities. Preambles are not formally enforceable, but they frame the law's enforceable provisions in a narrative that explains the problems that exist and the ways in which the law addresses them. Often, however, as with the word "encroacher," a chronotope that narrates the past can exist as a potential within a sentence prescribing some future action, a moralized narrative of the past that is available to be drawn on in the moment of the law's interpretation. Through abstraction, however, past and future chronotopes are often joined in laws' texts, which both diagnose and resolve problems. In other words, laws, whether explicitly or implicitly through words like "encroachments," both invoke histories that the law is seeking to remedy and anticipate future particular uses of the abstract and general procedures and principles laid out within them.

The Forest Rights Act was written by one such small group of people—activists, lawyers, politicians, and bureaucrats—who were engaged in a political and ecological struggle on the terrain of a text, channeling constituencies and struggles through chronotopes into legal abstractions that would become available, as the law was passed by Parliament and traveled across India's forests, to new constituencies and struggles. The law's many word traps functioned as covert chronotopes, whose literal meanings could in fact conceal the theories about the history and future of India's forests that they implied, as Gopalakrishnan lamented. The formal content of the law was shaped by the analysis of the cause of forest dwellers' dispossession produced through the CSD's mobilization against the 2002 evictions. The word traps, in contrast, were ways to smuggle the narratives around which the mobilization formed into the law covertly, to enable further future mobilizations.

The Drafting Process

Pradip Prabhu found himself representing a much longer and larger movement of forest dwellers, hundreds of organizations, including leftist movements and NGOs, groups representing only Adivasis, and groups representing larger caste alliances. For the Technical Support Group, Prabhu chose six friends and political allies from his years working for forest rights, including his CSD coconvener Madhu Sarin, the environmentalist Vandana Shiva, and the lawyer Sanjay Upadhyay, to join the group. The remaining six members were chosen from the MoTA.

The committee was intended to bring together a group of individuals who could stand in for ideological positions regarding forests—for land rights for forest dwellers, for example, or for a strict conservationist stand—that aligned with larger constituencies, whether forest dwellers or the nation's environment itself. Prime Minister Singh had already accepted Gopalakrishnan and Prabhu's argument that the ideology of the MoEF was known to be hostile to the goal of the bill and its intended beneficiaries, India's forest dwellers. As he proposed the other five members of the committee, however, Prabhu was claiming that the various drafters would represent a range of views that he, in fact, knew that they would not. Sarin and Shiva, for instance, were appointed to the committee as environmentalists, but Prabhu explained to me that he knew that they would approach the resolution of forest dwellers' rights more or less in the same way that he would. The committee was therefore configured by Gopalakrishnan, Prabhu, and others to create a legal text whose implementation would align with their understanding of a just forest order and would benefit the constituencies that they represented.

The drafting process began with a meeting on February 5, 2005, between the six representatives of the MoTA and the six unofficial members. Prabhu presented a draft bill that he had written for the occasion, drawing on his experience attempting to implement a forest regularization drive in Maharashtra in 1990. Prabhu's draft, which would become the foundation of the bill that was ultimately sent to Parliament, explained the necessity for a new law in its preamble: "because these rights were not verified, recognized or recorded during the declaration of many tribal and other areas as state forests during the colonial period as well as in Independent India either due to faulty and incomplete settlements or settlements not being undertaken. This has resulted in historical injustice to these communities, rendering them as 'encroachers' on their ancestral lands in the eyes of the law" (Prabhu 2004, 1). Forest dwellers, the preamble asserted, had always had rights to forest land, but these rights had never been recognized, either by the colonial state or the independent Indian state.

The result of this failure of recognition was the "historical injustice" of forest dwellers being framed by the law as "encroachers." The goal of the new law, then, would not be to create a new legal right or even to bring the state to recognize existing legal rights, but to bring the law in alignment with existing, unrecognized forest rights. The rights of forest dwellers to forests, in other words, exist outside the law, and predate the law. Prabhu's aim, which he intended to make the explicit aim of the law as well, was simply to have Indian laws recognize the existing rights of forest dwellers to forests.

Prabhu's draft cited the word "encroachers" that the 2002 eviction order had used and that Gopalakrishnan's January memo had cited as a legal word trap. Prabhu thereby brought an existing legal framework into the bill's draft in order to distinguish its potential to bring about justice through the law from the existing legal precedents that were preventing that justice. Prabhu spelled out exactly the chronotope of forest history through which forest dwellers were the victims of a historical injustice, "either due to faulty and incomplete settlements or settlements not being undertaken" (Prabhu 2004, 1). Naming unauthorized forest dwellers "encroachers," the preamble implies, not only denies this history of injustice; it is also the means through which the injustice took place, a chronotope through which forest dwellers are cast as recent arrivals to the forests and as themselves *agents* of an injustice against India's forest ecosystem.

This new law was not being built on the basis of existing laws, although they were cited frequently, and not simply on the basis of electoral necessities, although they played a role. Instead, the law was being built on competing notions of justice that were tied through activists and politicians to constituencies: forest-dwelling Scheduled Tribes, forest-dwelling non–Scheduled Tribes, conservationists, and the broader public who shared an interest in conservation. Older conflicts between castes and tribes, between forest dwellers and the Forest Department, and between competing representatives of forest dwellers were now playing out in the struggle to draft the text, and the new textual and political logics of the conflicts ended up transforming them. Notions of justice, electoral calculation, and the interpersonal dynamics of the drafting committee, in other words, all articulated to produce the Forest Rights Act by creating a text that was full of competing and contradictory chronotopes and potential chronotopes.

An MoTA bureaucrat who was a member of the Technical Support Group told the journalist M. Rajshekhar that at the point that Prabhu presented his draft bill, "everything looked like a fait accompli. A draft was ready. All one would have to do is comment on that draft, suggestions would be considered, and the Bill would be finalised well within that two month deadline of the PMO [Prime Minister's Office]" (cited in Rajshekhar 2011). But consensus was not reached within the Technical Support Group over who exactly should be eligible for the rights recognized by the bill. Prabhu's draft provided rights for all forest dwellers who could demonstrate forest residence prior to 1980, but representatives from the MoTA in the group argued that the only victims of the historic injustice of forest dispossession were the members of Scheduled Tribes and that, therefore, only members of Scheduled Tribes should be eligible for rights under the new law. In arguing their case, the representatives made explicit the chronotope of forest history that grounded it, in which only members of Scheduled Tribes had been dispossessed in the forests and all non–Scheduled Tribes were complicit in their dispossession. The first draft bill that the group prepared, therefore, would immediately recognize all land rights for members of Scheduled Tribes in forest areas, but not the many millions of non–Scheduled Tribes who lived in forests. Non–Scheduled Tribe residents of forest areas would still be eligible for rights, but they would be required to prove that they had lived in the area since before 1993, a compromise that would make it harder for non–Scheduled Tribes to claim eligibility.

Opposition to the first draft came from outside of the committee, from conservationists who had ties to senior Congress leaders. Following a meeting with the prominent conservationists Valmik Thapar and Malvika Singh in February, the Prime Minister's Office changed its position on the draft bill. It sent comments asking for the cutoff date to be moved back to 1980, which would decrease the number of forest dwellers eligible for rights and establish a burden of proof that many would not be able to meet. The Prime Minister's Office also reversed its position on the eligibility of non–Scheduled Tribes for forest rights and asked the Technical Support Group to revise the bill accordingly. Sonia Gandhi, the head of the National Advisory Council and president of the Congress Party, herself wrote a note to the group a few days later that cited the opposition from the same conservationists, Valmik Thapar and Malvika Singh, and asked for the cutoff date to be moved back to 1980 "to discourage continuous encroachment" (Gandhi 2005).

The conservationists were not contesting the narrative established by the draft bill's chronotopes, only its chronology and the date after which legitimate occupants of the forests had been joined by illegitimate encroachers. According to this narrative, there were legitimate occupants of the forests who lacked rights, but they were all members of Scheduled Tribes and had all lived in their current habitations before 1980. Drawing on their social access to the Prime Minister's Office and to Sonia Gandhi, the conservationists deployed exactly the word traps that Prabhu, Gopalakrishnan, and the CSD had been battling: the cutoff date should be moved back to prevent "encroachments."

The Technical Support Group conceded. They moved the cutoff date to 1980 and excluded non–Scheduled Tribes from eligibility for forest rights. Despite their formal exclusion from the Technical Support Group, conservationists were managing to shape the draft bill and deploy their own word traps. They were shaping it by adding traps that were far more overt than the choice between "encroachers" and "forest dwellers" by explicitly restricting non–Scheduled Tribes from eligibility.

On April 14, 2005, the *Indian Express* published an article that quoted a leaked MoEF memo that accused the proposed bill of destroying India's forests by distributing 2.5 hectares of land to all of India's Adivasis and undermining Forest Department authority over forests (Ganapathy 2005). The leaked memo made the bill and its supposed provisions public and opened them up to scrutiny. Thapar, Malvika Singh, and H. S. Panwar, the former director of the government's Project Tiger conservation program, began to argue through the English-language press to an English-reading audience that the law was both unnecessary and dangerous. By making the supposed contents of the bill public, the authors and addressees of the bill shifted dramatically. No longer was it only subject to contestations between forest rights activists and the MoTA. Instead, the group of conservationists who had been lobbying the government were now able to mobilize a constituency for themselves not through a crowd on the streets of New Delhi but through a series of indignant newspaper and magazine opinion pieces.

Now that the debates over the bill had moved into the newspapers and had become public, members of the constituencies the drafters claimed to represent began to contest the drafters' ability to represent them, and fissures began to develop among organizations representing Adivasis. On July 27, 2005, the *Hindu* reported that twenty-eight civil society groups complained that the draft bill failed to "comprehensively address the historical injustice and the collective rights of the tribal and indigenous people and forest dwellers" that it claimed to be addressing. The letter sent to the Union Cabinet further complained that the representatives of forest dwellers from the MoTA and the CSD who were drafting the bill did not in fact represent them and that the bill had been written in a "restricted and hurried manner" (*The Hindu* 2005) without consultation with forest dwellers who did not have access to Delhi-based government and activist networks. The letter inaugurated a series of challenges to the CSD's position, which argued that the bill was invoking the chronotope of historical injustice without producing a law that would actually redress the historical injustice and challenged the CSD's claim to speak on behalf of the entire forest-dwelling constituency.

Fissures began to develop within the ruling UPA coalition as well. On August 5, 2005, the *Hindu* reported that the Left parties within the coalition attacked the government in the Rajya Sabha, the upper house of Parliament, for failing to introduce the bill. Leaders of the Communist Party of India (Marxist), the

CPI(M), told the newspaper that conservationists were coming in the way of the bill and that "'some unseemly controversies' were being created by certain sections by 'counterposing' the right to forest-dwelling scheduled tribes against that of other forest inhabitants, including wildlife." Brinda Karat, a member of the CPI(M) Politburo, accused the government of acting on behalf of another constituency, the timber mafia and contractors. As the number of potential constituencies of the bill multiplied, both the CSD leadership and the Congress leadership struggled to maintain their monopolies on representing the groups they claimed to represent. The drafting process was being slowed down by conservationists, making the government vulnerable to attacks from its coalition partners who claimed that it was not fulfilling the promise made in the Common Minimum Programme to pass a law giving rights to forest dwellers. The bill's future was now in question. There was no indication that it would be tabled in Parliament in the near future, and as the bill languished, the constituencies of India's forests were rapidly fracturing and resisting representation.

The Forest Bureaucracy Responds

R. Gopalakrishnan was not alone in his attention to laws' word traps. Controlling and directing the ways in which seemingly neutral words and phrases could be used to trap the uses of the law was a priority for Dr. Ramvir Singh of the Indian Forest Service, the special secretary to the Government of Orissa Planning and Coordination Department. On September 6, 2005, while the protests and political maneuvering over the bill continued in Delhi, he submitted his own criticism of the draft bill to the prime minister and to the MoTA:

> The proposed forest rights 3(a) i.e., "right to hold and live in the forest land . . . for habitation and cultivation . . ." are clearly inconsistent with forestry land use. We need to understand that habitation and cultivation as land uses are generally in conflict with forestry land use. They cannot coexist over a long period. Even after the existing encroachments up to the cut off date are regularized, any one may invoke this right to further occupy forests for habitation and cultivation. Given that we poorly respect property rights and have weak governance in tribal pockets, this provision has great potential to create chaos and open up new avenues for increasing conflicts between forest dwellers and forest managers. As population grows with time, there is more likelihood of this happening and then again the bogey of "historical injustice" may be used to settle new encroachments. (Singh 2005, 1)

Invoking the nation's natural patrimony in order to rally a conservationist constituency within the government, Singh argued that the framing of the law as a response to the "historical injustice" of India's forest dwellers' dispossession was itself a word trap, one that cued up an entirely false chronotope that had already been used many times to regularize illegal forest settlements. The proposed Forest Rights Act, he argued, was not the remedy to a historical injustice but was instead a simple political capitulation to a political process. As a result, Singh declared, "we may perhaps find a better solution to this serious problem if we accept the fact that these are recent encroachments, which cannot be easily evicted in view of the socio-political dimensions, and law and order aspects, of this serious problem" (2005, 9). The law would be passed, in other words, because of the Maoist revolt in forest areas and because of the increased electoral relevance of Scheduled Tribe votes. To the extent that its effects could be kept precisely technical, its harmful effects on the environment could be limited. Conversely, framing the Forest Rights Act as a moral action to reverse a historical injustice done to India's forest dwellers would moralize the spirit of the law, and it would legitimate claims that could extend well beyond the specific procedures and requirements of the law's text.

The MoEF had been sidelined from the drafting process, as Pradip Prabhu and others had argued that a ministry that had carried out years of forest evictions could not be trusted to reverse those evictions. Nonetheless, the MoEF submitted two unsolicited draft bills of its own to the government, both of which would have granted ownership rights over Minor Forest Produce rather than land rights to forest dwellers and would have pushed back the bill's cutoff date from 2005 to 1980, restricting the number of forest dwellers who would be eligible. Both bills would also have expanded eligibility for claims to all forest dwellers, not only members of Scheduled Tribes. The MoEF argued that the distinction between Scheduled Tribes and non–Scheduled Tribes is often an arbitrary one. One draft explained in its preamble that "there is a large population of tribal and non tribal landless and economically backward communities in the state who derive their livelihood security from the forests of the state" for whom "minor forest produce is the main source of livelihood," telling a narrative not of historical injustice, but of poverty among forest dwellers that could be alleviated by providing them with ownership over minor forest produce ("State/Union Territory Minor Forest Produce (Ownership of Forest Dependent Community) Act" 2005).

The MoEF's bills were not accepted by the Prime Minister's Office, and Gopalakrishnan wrote a memo to the prime minister accusing the MoEF of attempting to sabotage the bill entirely. They did, however, prompt the Prime Minister's Office to organize a meeting on November 4, 2005, between the

MoTA and the MoEF to reconcile the differences between their bills. Despite its early exclusion, the MoEF had succeeded in entering the discussions around the creation of the draft bill, both through internal government lobbying and by invoking a larger public as a constituency through its leaked comments on the draft bill. The two ministries reached a compromise in a draft bill that set the cutoff date at 1980, restricted eligibility to individual members of Scheduled Tribes rather than communities or non–Scheduled Tribe forest dwellers, excluded forest dwellers in core areas of parks from receiving anything more than provisional rights, and granted only 2.5 hectares of land per family. The CSD had been excluded from the meeting between the two ministries. Sarin explained to me in 2011 that they had lost the government access that they had enjoyed earlier, and they had "crossed their limits." The CSD went on to write a critical memo about the new bill, arguing that it gave dangerously weak rights to forest residents in parks and ignored a history of collective land tenure among forest dwellers.

The bill was sent to Parliament in December 2005 and was reviewed from December to May by a Joint Parliamentary Committee (JPC) composed of thirty MPs and led by the Congress MP Kishore Chandra Deo. Most of these ministers were themselves members of Scheduled Tribes, and they were drawn from a variety of political parties, including a strong presence of Left parties. The JPC held hearings with both the MoEF and MoTA, heard testimonies from forty-three experts, and read 109 commentaries on the draft bill. The committee ultimately produced a revised bill that conceded to many of the demands of the CSD and the Left parties. The revised bill provided land rights for all forest dwellers, not only members of Scheduled Tribes and it allowed for communities to claim rights and set a new cutoff date of 2005 rather than 1980, lowering the standard of proof required to claim forest rights.

Madhu Sarin explained to me in a 2009 interview that during this time, she and the CSD drew on their ties to the Left parties and to Brinda Karat of the CPI(M) in particular to influence the committee's work on the bill. The CSD was no longer formally involved with the bill, but Shankar Gopalakrishnan, Madhu Sarin, and Pradip Prabhu from the CSD were all able to testify before the JPC. In a 2009 interview with the historian and CPI(M) Politburo member Archana Prasad, she told me that the Left parties themselves had serious disagreements with the draft bill and its exclusion of non–Scheduled Tribe forest dwellers. Ashok Chowdhury, convener of the National Forum of Forest People and Forest Workers (NFFPFW), a key member organization of the CSD that represented a large number of non–Scheduled Tribe forest dwellers, explained to me in a 2009 interview that the National Forum pushed the CSD and threatened to pull out of the campaign entirely if they were not able to include non–Scheduled Tribe forest dwellers in the bill, demands that were ultimately reflected in the committee's changes. In response to these changes and to the CSD's success in working with the JPC to achieve them, Rajshekhar (2011) writes that Gopalakrishnan, who had been responsible for bringing Pradip Prabhu to the initial meeting with the prime minister, broke off communication with Prabhu and the CSD.

The JPC's revised bill faced heavy opposition from the MoTA, however, and it was never tabled in Parliament. On September 28, 2006, a meeting was held at the Prime Minister's Office with Brinda Karat from the CPI(M), the secretary of the MoTA Meena Gupta, and Gopalakrishnan in an attempt to reconcile the positions of the MoTA and the JPC. Gupta proposed that the bill be passed without granting rights to non–Scheduled Tribe forest dwellers and that a second law could be passed later to grant rights to non–Scheduled Tribes. Karat argued that this would establish a new legal distinction that did not correspond with the true history of India's forests. The notes from the meeting record that

> [Karat], however, mentioned that there are large number of forest dwellers other than the STs also in the forest areas for a long time and their rights also need to be simultaneously recognized by the same Bill. According to her, it would be a great injustice to the other forest dwellers if their rights were not recognized. She further stated that the cut off date of 25.10.1980 as proposed in the Bill "as introduced" is meaningless because it does not recognize rights of those who have settled in 25 years. This would amount to injustice to almost an entire generation. (Prime Minister's Office 2006, 1–2)

The position of Karat and the Left parties mirrored that of Ashok Chowdhury: not all forest dwellers belonged to the Scheduled Tribes, which was a colonial sociological category that had been applied in inconsistent and uneven ways across India's forests. To deny those forest dwellers who happened not to be members of Scheduled Tribes rights would only perpetuate the injustices that the draft bill purported to undo.

Despite Karat's arguments, consensus on the bill was not reached, and the government continued to delay introducing the bill to Parliament. The MoTA was not placated by the meeting, and it submitted a critical memo to the Prime Minister's Office, arguing that if they followed the recommendations of the JPC to move the cutoff date to 2004 and to give forest rights to non–Scheduled Tribe forest dwellers, the law "would, perhaps, be doing great injustice to the forest dwelling STs instead of undoing the historic injustice done to them over the centuries, as was the original objective of the legislation"

(Ministry of Tribal Affairs 2006, 25). Not only were the non–Scheduled Tribe forest dwellers and people who could not prove residence before 1980 not the victims of the historical injustice that the law was intended to reverse, the Ministry argued, but to grant land rights to them would be to compound the injustice that was already done to members of Scheduled Tribes. On November 13, 2006, a group of five Congress ministers examining the proposed bill came to the same conclusion, arguing that "inclusion of the non-ST forest dwellers within the scope of the proposed bill would dilute the tribal character of the Bill and the purpose of the proposed legislation would be defeated" (Group of Ministers 2006, 4).

At this point, in a series of rallies and published articles, the Left parties and the CSD began to criticize the government publicly for its delay in introducing the bill in Parliament. On November 13, 2006, a meeting was held between the UPA and its Left allies, and later in the day, the government met and agreed to concede to a number of the demands made by the CSD along with the Left and the JPC. They would raise the limit on claimed land to four hectares and would accept 2005 as a cutoff date, but only members of Scheduled Tribes would be eligible for land.

Once the revised bill was sent to the cabinet, however, new electoral and political concerns gained relevance, and they would accomplish the inclusion of non–Scheduled Tribe forest dwellers that the CSD and the Left parties had so far failed to achieve. Rajshekhar (2011) reports that cabinet members began to worry about the potential for social conflict in forests if only Scheduled Tribes were given land rights. Laloo Prasad Yadav and Ram Vilas Paswan, representing the Rashtriya Janata Dal and Lok Janshakti parties that respectively relied heavily on Other Backward Caste and Scheduled Caste votes, wanted the law to provide some benefits to their constituents. The cabinet, therefore, revised the bill before introducing it to Parliament, allowing what it termed "Other Traditional Forest Dwellers" to claim land rights, saying that "the non-tribal forest dwellers with a minimum stay of three generations in forest areas, as on the cutoff date, be also vested with rights" (Cabinet Secretariat 2006). Karat's threats within the Parliamentary alliance and the NFFP-FW's threats within the CSD coalition had failed on their own, but a new political calculation—the need for parties representing Other Backward Caste and Scheduled Caste voters to support the bill—found its way into the law not simply as an extension of rights to non–Scheduled Tribe forest dwellers but through a phrase that implied that non–Scheduled Tribe forest dwellers too could be "traditional," once again enabling the law to be read through a narrative of the historical relationship between people and forests without providing that narrative.

The Passage of the Law

The session of Parliament was due to end on December 19, 2006, and in order to have the law passed by both the Lok Sabha and Rajya Sabha before that date, the government brought the bill to Parliament on December 15. Ministers reportedly did not have time to read and discuss the many recent changes to the bill, but they passed it anyway (Rajshekhar 2011). The day the bill passed, the CSD organized a *jail bharo andolan*, a movement to fill the jails in eleven states, with roughly seventy-five thousand people protesting and courting arrest. They argued that the bill had been "diluted and undermined in a fashion that severely threatens forest rights" (Campaign for Survival and Dignity 2005) by restricting forest rights in protected forest areas and by requiring that non–Scheduled Tribes forest dwellers prove seventy-five years of residence. The CSD's protests notwithstanding, when the *Scheduled Tribes and Other Traditional Forest Dwellers (Recognition of Forest Rights) Act* was finally passed in December 2006, its preamble contained a passage that framed the law in exactly the moral terms that Ramvir Singh feared: "AND WHEREAS the forest rights on ancestral lands and their habitat were not adequately recognized in the consolidation of State forests during the colonial period as well as in independent India resulting in historical injustice to the forest dwelling Scheduled Tribes and other traditional forest dwellers who are integral to the very survival and sustainability of the forest ecosystems."

The body and rules of the act spell out the qualifications for eligibility for land and the exact amount of land that claimants are entitled to. Scheduled Tribes must demonstrate residence in the forest before December 26, 2005, and non–Scheduled Tribe forest dwellers must demonstrate seventy-five years of residence in the forest to claim up to four hectares of land. In a concession to the CSD, claimants are defined in the law as either individuals or groups, and the law allows for "community rights" to be claimed for both forest use and tenure. The preamble, however, spells out a moralized narrative of the history of the relationship between India's forests and forest dwellers. In it, forest dwellers have been integral to the survival of forests, but their existing rights to ancestral lands were not recognized by the colonial and independent Indian governments, resulting in the historical injustice of their dispossession.

In Ramnagar, the law's preamble, and its claim to be reversing the historic injustice that had left them landless, was the portion that villagers cited most frequently: "The law is to end the historical injustice (*etihasik anyay*)," I would hear, "and we are the victims of the historical injustice." When faced with technical objections to their land claim, the villagers and the activists who worked with them held the objections up to the test of whether or not the proposed interpretation of the act met the test of reversing the historical injustice done to the villagers. If it did not, then they rejected it. By including the phrase "historic injustice" in the Forest Rights Act's preamble, Prabhu and Sarin had succeeded in inserting one of the word traps that Gopalakrishnan had described. The battle over the law's meaning had not been won, but to the extent that courts did not intervene, the phrase enabled the law to be embedded within an extralegal chronotope, a historical narrative that contained its own moralized rules through which the law could be interpreted. This chronotope, in turn, kept the struggle to implement the law in places like Ramnagar alive, placing it within a much longer and larger struggle for land rights for landless Adivasis.

Prabhu explained to me in a 2012 interview that he "firmly believe[s] that the final implementation of the Forest Rights Act will only be through struggle, it will not be through the state." Shankar Gopalakrishnan, one of the conveners of the CSD, argued similarly in an essay on the law that "these rights will not in fact be recognized or respected just because of the law alone. To believe that is to believe in the trap that this law also contains: an imagination that the law can create social change. Such a belief becomes a way of upholding domination rather than challenging it" (2010b, 22). Soon after the law's passage, the NFF-PFW published a pamphlet explaining the Forest Rights Act's tactical uses, titled "Forest Rights Act: A Weapon of Struggle," which located the law in the longer struggle for forest rights: "We must use the tools the Forest Rights Act offers, and we must fight for amendments in it to make it stronger" (NFFPFW 2008, 42). No law can implement itself and no law interprets itself. Those, for the NFFPFW, will take place through continuing contestation and struggle. The tools for those extralegal contestations and struggles are present within the law's text, however, through its word traps.

These word traps enable speech communities (Silverstein 2010)—polities that are ready with the moralized chronotopes through which the Forest Rights Act's many potential chronotopes can be read—to make the case for the inevitability of one reading and one just and legal future. The push for the law emerged out of one such mobilization around a narrative of injustice against forest dwellers. This narrative was produced and ratified through the forensic work of Uma but also through the collective action of the growing CSD. As we will see in chapter 3, the CSD's narratives were not the only narratives through which the Forest Rights Act would be interpreted and used. Other infrastructures of collective action existed across the country, and they would draw on the law in unexpected and contradictory ways.

In the jan sunwai and public meetings of its early days, the task of the CSD was to produce a new political efficacy of proof, allowing for signed deeds like those of Kalla's family in Rajasthan or of oral testimony from village elders to prevent dispossession. In the drafting process of the Forest Rights Act, the CSD's leadership found itself seeking to extend the efficacy of that proof away from preventing dispossession and toward formal property and use rights for the largest number of forest dwellers possible—and, for some of its constituent groups, toward a larger and more revolutionary redistribution of forest property. The Forest Rights Act became one text among many circulating in and out of India's forests, interpreted through those other texts into a set of rules to be read and enacted toward envisioned futures.

It was the collective action of these groups—of Maoist insurgents and NGOs across India, refracted and represented by the constituent organizations of the CSD and once again refracted and represented by Prabhu and Sarin, the CSD's conveners—that produced the law's first draft. The demands and representatives of forest dwellers as a constituency were never settled once and for all, however, as Prabhu and Sarin's claims to represent them were challenged both from within and without the CSD. Futures made their way in and out of the law's text, leaving traces as word traps and enabling hooks that allowed other narratives and efforts at rulemaking to incorporate the FRA as it traveled. In chapter 3, I follow the law as it traveled to Ramnagar and was picked up and drawn into older histories and narratives of struggle. The law had been passed by Parliament: the question that remained was if and how it could be used to solve the problem of the forest and enable low-caste forest dwellers to claim property rights against dispossession.

THE LAW AS RUMOR

Raju paused. He finished his cup of tea and tossed the small plastic cup out onto the ground for effect. "Ramnagar is nothing," he said. "Forget Ramnagar. It's a creation of the NGOs [nongovernmental organizations]." Raju, a journalist with a national news agency, and Alok, a local correspondent for a national Hindi newspaper, were warming up—and they were enjoying disabusing me, the naive young anthropologist, of my illusions. We were seated on benches behind the front counter of a small newspaper and book stand. The counter faced the large, dusty parking lot of the public bus terminal in Robertsganj, the district headquarters of Sonbhadra. The newspaper stand had few customers, but buses were groaning past us as we talked, kicking up dust and roaring exhaust as they arrived and departed for towns near and far. To be understood above the din, Raju was forced to speak louder and gesture more dramatically.

"Those people who live in Ramnagar, they only arrived three years ago from Bihar and Jharkhand," he said, referring to two neighboring states. "They won't get titles through the Forest Rights Act. You should go to another village, one that isn't full of liars and cheats." He snapped his fingers for more tea, and a young boy who worked at the station's tea stall arrived with three more cups, their plastic softening from the heat of the liquid inside. Alok took over as we collected our cups and took first, hesitant sips. "The people in Ramnagar are liars and cheats," he agreed. "Forget about Ramnagar. Go talk with the Banwasi Seva Ashram instead."

Raju and Alok may have been dismissive of Ramnagar's villagers, but the two journalists were right that the village was, in some sense, a creation of groups that had arrived from outside the region; they were only mistaken in thinking that this was unusual or exceptional. In fact, everywhere the Forest Rights Act (FRA) traveled, it was being carried by political movements like the Sangathan and by bureaucrats and NGOs. It was circulating as a printed text and by word of mouth, text message, and email. The law never contained a single, coherent meaning, as I showed in chapter 2: the legal text was always a compromise, a composite of distinct visions of the forests' futures sitting together as what R. Gopalakrishnan called "word traps" (2005, 5). And yet this composite, contradictory law was being made and remade once more as it traveled. It was being inserted into other political narratives that had existed before its drafting and that were nowhere formalized in law: resolutions to the problem of property in the forest that took the shape of visions of a just arrangement between people and the land they lived on that circulated independently. As the law moved, it picked up multiple meanings, and with them, it gained multiple standards of proof and multiple claims to the authority to adjudicate such proof.

The FRA took shape against the political currents and problematics set up in the aftermath of the Emergency, but the law had to be brought to Duddhi. The act arrived here circuitously, packaged with other stories, spread through small meetings and casual rumor. In this chapter, I track the arrival of the FRA through two organizations, the Banwasi Seva Ashram and the Sangathan, that are associated with two distinct caste coalitions and political visions. In so doing, I examine how two radically different interpretations of a single law came to be attached to their organizations and their constituencies. The law, I show, has arrived in Duddhi as the most recent iteration of a longer series of attempts to rework the relationship between caste and property in the region. For each, the FRA was to be brought to life through collective action oriented toward a possible future that was read into the law. These possible futures of new arrangements of forest land knit together, however tenuously, two coalitions across differences of caste and gender.

It was in my conversation with the two journalists that I learned about a second interpretation of the FRA that was distinct from what I had been hearing in Ramnagar and that an organization existed, the Banwasi Seva Ashram, that was working to implement the FRA along these lines. For the Banwasi Seva Ashram, the FRA did not allow landless forest dwellers like the Ramnagaris to claim land; instead, it expanded the landholdings of members of Scheduled Tribes who already had received land rights in earlier settlements. These interpretations were circulating with political projects, latching onto pieces of land and proof that might expand their constituencies and widen the circle of their collective action. But proof opens up the possibility of dispute, of counterclaims to authority. It is to the currents of circulating legal interpretations and possible proofs that we now turn, on a trip from the bus station where I met with Raju and Alok: first to Ramnagar and then to the Banwasi Seva Ashram.

When we left Duddhi at the end of chapter 1, its property relations were up in the air, but patterns had emerged. Duddhi's land and rights to it had been apportioned and reapportioned among sapurdars, zamindars, and tenants, and between the Forest Department and its contractors, but boundaries between properties had a way of being blurred and revised over time. The FRA and its meaning were similarly unresolved: Who should be able to claim property through the law, and what should those property rights mean? What rights did forest dwellers who were not members of Scheduled Tribes have to forests? What land was available to be settled on, and when should it have been settled? How would these rights be settled and enforced? Answers to these questions would take the form of stories and rumors that would travel independently of the legal text and the rights that it promised.

The Road to Ramnagar

The day after my conversation with Raju and Alok, I returned to Ramnagar, where I had been doing fieldwork for three months at that point, in February 2011. The trip was by bus, and I left in the morning from the same bus stand where I had met the two journalists the previous day. We bounced over and down the Kaimur hills, past cement factories and mines, and into Duddhi, where I caught a shared jeep taxi to arrive in Govindnagar in the early afternoon. Lalti, a Dalit woman who lived in Ramnagar who had taken a position of leadership within the Sangathan, was going to meet me at Kumar's store on the main road, and she would walk with me to Ramnagar, but she seemed to be running late. Seeing a stranger standing alone, an older man seated on a cot adjacent to the store buttonholed me. What was I doing in Govindnagar? Who was I meeting? Lalti? How did I know Lalti? How could a prosperous-looking city person like me know Lalti?

When I explained that we had first met in Delhi, at a rally, Lalti's political work and the large circuits it had taken her on clicked. "Oh, you met her through *Geeta*. Through the Naxalites!" he replied. The word "Naxalite," referring to the guerilla Maoist movement, was a convenient term of disparagement, not only between dominant castes and leftist activists like Geeta but also within the left-oriented forest rights movement. It marked tactics and individuals who were more militant and less committed to liberal legal norms than the speaker, associating them with the armed tactics of the Communist Party of India (Maoist), more frequently than it named members of the Maoist movement themselves.

"Those are dangerous people. Do you know that they're cutting down the forest to build houses?" the old man said. I offered a defense of Lalti and the Ramnagaris, and their attempts to gain land rights. "Can I just build my house on the road here?" the man jumped in, before answering his own question: "No, it belongs to the *public*," he said, using the English word. "The same goes for the forest. It belongs to the public. How can those people just take it?"

Lalti arrived after a few minutes. She exchanged cursory greetings with my interlocutor, and the two of us set off toward Ramnagar. Our path took us down Govindnagar's main street, past groups of dominant-caste men sitting in chairs and on cots arranged in the sun. Several called out questions as we passed, wondering, like the man I had met in front of Kumar's store had, what someone like me was doing in Govindnagar, with an Adivasi woman. Lalti explained the questioning as we proceeded: the Ramnagaris had once worked for these men's families, on their fields and in their homes. The Yadavs and dominant castes owned the village's prime land, like the plots neighboring the small stream we crossed to get to Ramnagar, which had a supply of water guaranteed throughout the year.

The landscape grew drier as we crossed the stream and began to climb the hills beyond. This land was not irrigated, but it provided grazing land for the dominant-caste families' goats and cattle. The departure of the Ramnagaris from Govindnagar had upset this arrangement of land and labor, Lalti explained, depriving the dominant castes of both labor and access to some of their grazing land. As we climbed the five kilometers to Ramnagar, we passed women carrying bundles of firewood, the occasional grazing cow or goat, and scattered trees and small fields. These fields, growing lentils, wheat, and potatoes, managed one crop per year, following the monsoons, rather than the two crops the irrigated Yadav fields close to the river could yield.

"Water is our biggest problem," Lalti explained, as would many villagers. The Son River, the only river in the area, was two kilometers away, and without electricity in the village, there was no way to pump its water up the hills to irrigate the fields. A small stream ran a kilometer from the village, but it flowed only during the rains, leaving greenish puddles the rest of the year that constituted the villagers' only source of drinking water. The water table in the arid area had never been very high, but mining operations and the borewells of the wealthier farmers had made it even lower. The only way the village could get wells, either for irrigation or for drinking water, would be for the local government to build them. But like Raju and Alok, the local government had not recognized Ramnagar as a legal village, and therefore had not provided it with the infrastructure that it provided to legal villages.

In the absence of land rights and the government provisions that would come along with them and allow two annual harvests, Ramnagar's residents continued to carry out *mazdoori*, paid labor. Young men and women from the Ramnagaris' families migrated to cities as far away as Kerala in south India, joining India's estimated 140 million domestic migrants from Uttar Pradesh and neighboring Bihar (Office of the Registrar General and Census Commissioner 2011). Those who did not migrate supplemented their income however they could. They collected *tendu* leaves and firewood from the forest for sale in towns. They worked in nearby factories or built infrastructure for the government at Rs. 120 (approximately US$2.40) per day through the 2005 Mahatma Gandhi National Rural Employment Guarantee Act or, as a last resort, on the fields of the Yadavs at Rs. 100 (US$2.00) per day.

Ramnagar consisted of three clusters of earthen homes—the largest settled by members of the Agaria community, the other two mixed, with Ghasiyas, Chamars, Bhuiyas, and others—surrounded by fields. A few homes had small enclosures for cows, chickens, and goats, but most either had no cattle or allowed their animals to roam. In the center of each cluster was a clearing, a central gathering point. When we arrived, children were playing in this area, with one mother keeping an eye on them. This was far from the "nothing" described by Raju at the bus stand: this was a bustling village of hundreds.

I would stay in Ram Lakhan's home for the next several days, with his wife Baldeva and their two children. Neither Ram Lakhan nor Baldeva knew their exact age, but they believed they were in their early forties. The hut was perched on the site of one of the ravines that run through Ramnagar, and adjacent to the hut was a small field. One warm evening we discussed Alok and Raju's claims about the village over a meal of rice and *dal*, with raw onions as a condiment. His children were outside playing with friends while they waited for us to finish eating.

"We used to go to the Banwasi Seva Ashram for school when we were children," Ram Lakhan explained. "But when the settlement happened, we didn't get anything," he said, referring to the settlement of land rights in Duddhi that was carried out by the Banswasi Seva Ashram in 1983. Ram Lakhan, like most of the residents of Ramnagar, had grown up in Govindnagar, in which the ashram had been active from the 1960s on. But his family did not have the money to pay the ashram-affiliated official who visited in 1983 in exchange for a land title. Instead, they had made do with *mazdoori*, and worked on the farms of dominant-caste locals with large holdings.

This dependence on a limited number of higher-caste employers had once gone along with a set of ritual obligations toward the higher castes, known as *jajmani* (Raheja 1988; Saksena and Sen 1999).[1] Low castes were required to perform agricultural and domestic work for higher castes in exchange for payment in kind. Social ostracism, economic deprivation, and physical and sexual violence against low castes were commonly used to maintain the hierarchical relationships (Raheja 1988; Gupta 2000).

Such structural and everyday forms of caste violence are common to large parts of South Asia, but the struggles against this violence in Duddhi were shaped by the political history of the state of Uttar Pradesh, and Uttar Pradesh's belated legal recognition of Scheduled Tribes. In the majority of India's forest belt, Adivasis are categorized not as caste groups but as members of Scheduled Tribes. Scheduled Tribes (or STs) are groups that are asserted by states to be outside of the cultural mainstream of caste-Hindu society and therefore requiring state protection, including the restrictions on the sale or alienation of ST property discussed in chapter 1. Unlike in the rest of India's forest belt, however, most Adivasi communities in Uttar Pradesh were not listed as members of Scheduled Tribes until 2002. The state, India's largest, is frequently framed as representative of the national cultural mainstream, and its post-Independence government refused to legally recognize the state's forest dwellers as culturally and socially distinct to the extent that they would require legal recognition or protection. Five communities that mostly live in northern districts of the state were classified as Scheduled Tribes in 1967. In contrast, communities in Sonbhadra that were defined as Scheduled Tribes in other states, such as Agarias and Gonds, were classified as Scheduled Castes until 2002, when they were reclassified as Scheduled Tribes. The political category of "Dalit," therefore, which in most parts of the country applies only to members of the lowest or Scheduled Castes, is readily adopted by many members of Scheduled Tribes in Duddhi. The category "Adivasi," similarly, or "indigenous," has come to be used, in turn, by many members of Scheduled Castes in Duddhi. Claims of indigeneity common to forest-dweller politics across India alternate in Ramnagar with the rhetoric of Dalit empowerment that found a powerful political expression in the Dalit-aligned Bahujan Samaj Party (BSP).[2]

Some days later, after we had finished our dal, rice, and potatoes, we were sitting around a fire outside Ram Lakhan's home. Raju's criticisms were on my mind, and I asked Ram Lakhan about Ramnagar and the FRA, specifically about how they had learned about the law. Ram Lakhan explained to me that it was a left activist named Dr. Vinayan who had first told him about the FRA. As discussed previously, Vinayan had arrived in the region through the student movement of the 1970s and had become associated with Marxist-Leninist groups in the area. He had played a role in organizing armed Dalit groups in the region in the 1980s, groups that had gone on to successfully redistribute both property and village political authority away from dominant-caste groups (Kunnath 2012). In the late 1980s, however, Vinayan rejected armed struggle and began organizing land occupations among agricultural workers and, from the mid-1990s, forest dwellers.

It was Dr. Vinayan who first told Ram Lakhan and the others about the new law, Ram Lakhan said. "In 2006 he came to Govindnagar and told us that a new law had been passed in Delhi that gave this land back to the Agarias," one of the several jatis or subcastes who lived in Ramnagar.

"Only to the Agarias?" I asked. "Not to the other Adivasis?"

"To all of us, I mean. And he said that we should go and build a village on it."

Ram Lakhan and two hundred other Agarias left Govindnagar and other nearby villages and started to clear trees to build some eighty huts, each of which had roughly eight hectares of farmland, and a central clearing and shelter for the new community to gather. As the settlement grew, other communities began to join them: Gonds, Chamars, Ghasiyas, and Bhuiyas. The newcomers started building some distance away from the Agaria settlement: just west of the Agarias but across a ravine some fifteen meters deep.

As the evening went on and the group around Ram Lakhan's fire grew, he placed the story of Dr. Vinayan's arrival into a larger, more expansive political narrative. Ram Lakhan had emerged as one of Ramnagar's leaders, and it was clear why. He is charismatic and a good speaker, with a voice that carries over the hills. Ram Lakhan's narrative fit the law into the movement for Dalit equality, starting from Dr. Bhimrao Ramji Ambedkar, the mid-twentieth-century Dalit leader and drafter of India's constitution, and bringing it into recent state-level Dalit and leftist politics. Uttar Pradesh had, at the time, its first Dalit chief minister, Mayawati. Her party, the BSP, claimed Ambedkar's legacy in advocating for Dalit equality. The BSP had formed a series of coalition governments in the 1990s and, from 2007 to 2012, held a majority of the seats in the state legislature and governed the state independently.

Mahua liquor, made from the flowers of the mahua tree, was brought out in a jug, and it warmed the company up, complementing the fire. Ram Lakhan was playing with a plastic bag while we talked, and he threw bits of it into the fire, where they sizzled and released a sharp smell. Ram Lakhan began to expound on the law and its true meaning, and a small audience gathered, standing and squatting around, to listen:

> You see, Anand brother, this Forest Rights that is now going on, it starts much earlier. When India became independent from the English, they needed someone to write the Constitution. In those days, most of the educated people were foreigners [*videshi log*], Brahmins and Thakurs

and people from the forward castes. But they asked Bhimraoji Ambed-kar, who was a Dalit, if he would write the Constitution. He said, "Yes, I will do it. But I will need time. Give me twenty-four hours and twenty-four minutes." In twenty-four hours and twenty-four minutes, he gave them the Constitution, which said what the law was, which way the country would be run, who the country belongs to, who the water, jungle, and land [*jal, jangal, aur jameen*] belong to. Then they asked Bhimraoji Ambedkar if he would be India's first prime minister. He said he would, but then Nehru, because he was a Brahmin, prevented him from being the prime minister, and hid the law. Bhimraoji said, "Fine, you are prime minister. But our Adivasi people will not stay quiet. Today they won't talk. Tomorrow they won't talk. But the day after tomorrow, they will talk."

This Forest Rights Act was written by Bhimraoji himself. But Pandit Nehru hid it. But now our Chief Minister Mayawati and her comrade Vinayan Doctor have given this law to us. They have said that all the property is ours. If we give up the struggle, we will remain slaves, because all of these foreigners [referring to the Yadavs and upper castes in the area] have taken all of the property from us. Because as long as the property is with the foreigners, the profits will go to them. We work, and the foreigners eat. The struggle is old, but we did not have the knowledge until now. As our people have slowly learned to read and write and traveled around the country and abroad [*desh videsh ghumne lage*], we have learned about the law, we have learned that the law is true, and we have begun to struggle.

The FRA, in Ram Lakhan's account, was placed entirely within a narrative of Dalit liberatory politics. The law was written by the movement's iconic leader, Ambedkar. It was suppressed by the Brahmin Jawaharlal Nehru, India's first prime minister, only to be recovered by the Dalit movement's most visible contemporary representative, Mayawati. Critically, Mayawati then gave the law to Dr. Vinayan, an activist of the nonparliamentary Left, and entrusted him with its implementation.

In Ram Lakhan's account, Nehru not only suppressed the FRA but also hid it and the Constitution, the true law, by stealing the entire state apparatus that would implement them. The true law, according to Ram Lakhan, lays out the proper distribution of property in the country, recognizing the property rights of Adivasis. But the people accepted their dispossession and their ongoing economic exploitation, Ram Lakhan adds, because they did not have knowledge of the true law. That knowledge requires both that people become educated and that mediators like Dr. Vinayan bring the law to them. In this account, Marx's original sin of primitive accumulation, the separation of labor from land, is made possible by the dispossession of the state itself. Ambedkar lost the prime ministership to Nehru, and as a result, Dalits have been kept down by a state that did not implement the true and just laws that Ambedkar wrote.

In chapter 2, I argue that forest rights activists embedded word traps in the text of the FRA that enable the law to be hooked to narratives not contained in the text of the law itself. Forest rights activists won a contest with officials from the Ministry of Environment and Forests in framing the law in its preamble as a response to the "historic injustice" of forest dwellers. In so doing, they succeeded in enabling further mobilization around a narrative propagated by the Campaign for Survival and Dignity (CSD) in which indigenous forest dwellers have been dispossessed and evicted from their land by the colonial and independent Indian governments.

Ram Lakhan's account does not contradict the CSD's, but builds on it, expanding its categories and adding new actors. For Ram Lakhan, the victims of the historic injustice are not only Adivasis but include Dalits. Or, more accurately, for Ram Lakhan, the categories "Dalit" and "Adivasi" become joined. The FRA, further, is not a recent legal recognition of forest dwellers' land rights but is instead a much older law, written by Ambedkar as part of the Constitution, which only recently has been made public and brought to forest dwellers' attention. The water, forest, and land are Dalit-Adivasi patrimony, but knowledge of that patrimony in the form of Ambedkar's true Constitution was hidden from them. Not only does the denotational content of the FRA not define its ultimate interpretations, then, but even the narratives embedded within it as word traps are susceptible to further embeddings within the narratives attached to political projects distinct from the CSD's.

Dalit politics, centered around a largely urban and agrarian community, do not always intersect with Adivasi, or "tribal," politics, which are based in largely forest-dwelling communities. In Ramnagar and in Ram Lakhan's account, however, Adivasi politics were being articulated in the idiom of Dalit politics, and a national law was being given a new meaning in the process. The law's chronotopes and its participant roles were being aligned with the chronotopes and participants of Dalit-Adivasi liberatory movements. Far from being the misguided and disingenuous claimants of Raju's account, then, Ram Lakhan cast Ramnagar's villagers as the agents of the implementation of the true FRA, which had been hidden through successive upper-caste-led governments. By occupying the land, they were undoing the injustice of their economic and political dispossession.

Ambedkarite Politics and Land

For Ram Lakhan, Ramnagar was not only real; it was a step toward the realization of a much older political project, a reclamation of the Dalit-Adivasi sovereignty promised in the Constitution that Ambedkar helped to write. His narrative drew the FRA into a range of political narratives and visions, legacies of fifty years of shifting alliances in Ambedkarite land struggles.

This history of Ambedkarite land struggles follows a reevaluation of Ambedkar's own arguments about the relative priority of struggles against caste and class. In *Annihilation of Caste* (1936), Ambedkar argued that caste-based social hierarchy had to be removed before the class-equalizing goals of socialist and communist movements could be realized. Caste, Ambedkar argued, was an inherited, endogamous form of class; it was, in his famous phrase, "not merely a division of labour" but "*also a division of labourers*" (233, emphasis in original). With the working class divided into castes, the forms of solidarity necessary to bring about a socialist order—or even a liberal one—were missing in India, and an uprooting of caste had to precede efforts to bring about economic equality.

The Ambedkarite political tradition has deep roots in Uttar Pradesh, and the leadership of the BSP, from its founder Kanshi Ram to its current leader and then-state Chief Minister Mayawati, claim to be contemporary heirs of Ambedkar's movement. It was this tradition that informed accounts of the FRA in Ramnagar. The party claims a constituency that is larger than only Dalits—that is, the bahujan samaj, or "majority society," first identified by Jyotirao Phule as the non-Brahmin castes who were subjugated by the Aryan Brahmin invasion of India (Pai 2002; Omvedt 2008; Rao 2009). Such a group, for Ambedkar as well as for the BSP's founder Kanshi Ram, could comprise an electoral majority as well, and Kanshi Ram now redefined the bahujan samaj as an alliance of Dalits and Adivasis with the Other Backwards Classes who account for nearly half of the country's population, as well as Muslims and the country's other religious minorities. Along with an expanded constituency, Kanshi Ram departed from Ambedkar's position on the relationship between caste and class inequalities.

The party's program, laid out by its president Daryam Pal and Kanshi Ram,[3] was first to capture state power through elections, and then to use state power to allow Dalits to restrict their contact with upper castes and allow them to perform free, waged labor. In a 1993 booklet titled *Concept of Bahujan Samaj Party*, Kanshi Ram wrote that the party would simultaneously address social and economic inequality both through land redistribution and by encouraging migration for work in industry: "BSP seeks to put the interest of the lowest of low, the landless peasant as high on its economic agenda as that of the farmers who are the victims of our prevented policies. A vast majority of these people will need to be helped to move away from a dependence on the land to primary industries and related business" (1997, 159). Kanshi Ram went on to explain the party's slogan, "*Jo zameen sarkari hai, woh zameen hamari hai*" (The land which is the government's, that land is ours).

The slogan was coined to encourage landless Dalits to occupy residential and agricultural land: "Baba Saheb Dr. Bhim Rao Ambedkar gave to every Indian, through our constitution, the fundamental right to property. . . . Four decades have passed, in spite of many land reform schemes, the vast majority of the Bahujan Samaj is still without any property. BSP now refuses to tolerate the conspiracy which made our people who till the land to feed us are prevented from owning the land, our people who labour to build magnificent mansions in our cosmopolitan cities are not helped to own a roof over their own heads" (Ram 1997, 159–63).

As discussed in chapter 1, the right to property outlined in India's constitution is a limited one that was intended to enable the land reforms envisioned by many members of the Constituent Assembly: it was not a right of every citizen to own property, but a right of every citizen to acquire and hold property unless public purposes required that the property be taken from them. Like Ram Lakhan, however, Kanshi Ram here read into the Constitution a larger vision of redistribution of property, in line with the redistributionist visions of the Ambedkarite movement. For Kanshi Ram, the oppression of Dalits was the outcome of personalized and ritualized economic dependence on upper castes. The BSP's emphasis on land redistribution opened the door to tacit alliances with class-based leftist organizations like the Sangathan to reorganize property relations, both legally and extralegally. This was part of a larger reorganization of the relationship between leftist and Ambedkarite movements in Uttar Pradesh following the rise of the BSP in the state in the 1990s, a convergence around both what Jaoul (2006) calls Dalit "symbolic politics" as the Communist Party of India Marxist-Leninist [CPI(M-L)] began to build statues of Dalit leaders and martyrs and around the material politics of land rights. As Lerche (1999) documents, land-rights movements that had been encouraged by the BSP under the banner of its slogan "jo zameen sarkari hai, woh zameen hamari hai" had opened new space for CPI(M-L) groups in eastern UP that were already involved in such struggles.

The Sangathan has transposed the tactics of Marxist-Leninist Dalit politics from the rest of Uttar Pradesh to the very different political and legal landscape of Duddhi's forests. Geeta arrived in Duddhi in 2002. She grew up in Delhi in a Brahmin Punjabi family, but as a university student studying psychology in the 1990s, she became involved in left-wing groups that worked with forest dwellers. Geeta first traveled to Duddhi at Dr. Vinayan's invitation. In 2004, she began putting posters up in towns and cities across Sonbhadra with a photo of Ambedkar and with the BSP's slogan "Jo zameen sarkari hai, woh zameen hamari hai" alongside a new slogan: "Jo jangal sarkari hai, woh jangal hamari hai": the government's *forest* is ours. By deploying a slogan that had become associated with the ruling party, Geeta attempted to encourage land redistribution far beyond what the government had attempted, calling on landless forest dwellers to occupy the forest land that the state government had been unable to redistribute. Geeta was arrested by the police for the posters and charged under the National Security Act. Chief Minister Mayawati heard about the case, however, and Geeta told me that Mayawati personally instructed the police to release her, saying that "no one should be put in jail for putting up posters of Ambedkar." The Sangathan continued to maintain close ties to the BSP after Geeta's release; it helped with campaigns for BSP candidates, and one of its leaders was even appointed to Mayawati's cabinet.

The new political formations of the 1990s had produced new temporal arrangements of the possible futures for landless Dalits and Adivasis in Uttar Pradesh, an intercalation of the symbolic and the material, each opening up new possibilities for the other. The narratives and analyses associated with Marxist-Leninist and the BSP's Ambedkarite politics had, in turn, made their way to and been brought to the forests through Dr. Vinayan and Geeta, as Ram Lakhan explained to me that day. For Ram Lakhan and other Ramnagaris, this meant reading the FRA as a reversal of the failure of the Indian state to realize Ambedkar's vision as well as a reversal to years of indigenous dispossession. These futures became possible alongside new collectives that would claim them. The forests, the land, the water—the state—belonged to Dalit Adivasis, and with the FRA in hand, they were going to take it all back.

"We Women Are Saving the Forest for All of Our Lives"

The FRA arrived in Ramnagar through a reworking of Ambedkarite struggles and analyses in the terms of existing struggles over land and caste relations in Sonbhadra. The collective action that continued to produce the law, however, was not defined by the narratives that they drew upon. The shape of the movement—those who participated and those who did not, and the social world that it produced—emerged through the futures created by collective action. The social relations of Govindnagar had taken shape through a long history of low-caste dispossession, but relations of caste and gender were to be made and remade through the movement for forest rights. As temporal horizons of possibility shifted, so too did the terms of sociality. The terms of caste sociality shifted with these new futures: sociality and commensality across Ramnagar's jatis, its caste communities, followed the shared identification as Dalit Adivasis.

It was clear that the movement had not only challenged social relations between Ramnagaris and higher-caste landlords; relations among the Ramnagaris too began to be understood and contested through the future-oriented terms of the movement. For many of the women in Ramnagar, the Sangathan had allowed them to challenge the distribution of political power in the village. They continued to perform the bulk of domestic labor, but they were brought into conversations over the fate of the village, and both Geeta and Shubha went out of their way to solicit the views of Ramnagar's women. Geeta explained to me in an interview that when she first became involved in Sonbhadra she felt more comfortable working with women than with men and that she saw the project of gaining land rights for landless forest dwellers as particularly critical for women's empowerment.

> Very important thing was that my coming into this whole movement, I could make easily inroads into women's space. And I was very comfortable doing that, because I had this experience in Rajaji [Rajaji National Park, where Geeta had begun her political work] also that women were very powerful and they could really take the organization ahead and they could really dig deep into those issues sharply which men will not be able to do, because their issues are totally related to land and their livelihood security and their future security. So I felt very comfortable working with women, and women also responded very well. They would come in collective manner, they were not individually focused. So whenever they have a meeting they are in collective manner. Where ever they go they will go collectively, they will respond collectively.
>
> So I started teaching them and empowering them with small small things, you know small small skills like, sitting in a meeting how do you talk? How do you sit? How do you relate your issues? How do you keep papers? Any document which is coming to you, though you don't read, how do you keep it properly? They know also that documents are important, but they keep it under the roof somewhere or in some dabba [box] somewhere and it gets destroyed. So then I started teaching them, even though you don't read, you keep all these documents. . . . We also taught them how to measure the land with a measuring chain so that nobody misleads you, and all these small small things.

We started taking them out for exposures, we started taking them to meetings, and giving them importance. Delhi, Lucknow, Nagpur, Bombay. This empowered them a lot and they could see that their issue was not an isolated one. Everywhere, you know, the issue of poor is the same. And the unity of poor is important. . . . Whenever they went out, they would come and they would occupy land. They got so empowered.

To empower the women she was working with, Geeta saw, she would need to share some skills with them: the bodily habitus most effective in meetings with officials, how to maintain and use documents even if they could not read them, and how to measure their land themselves to avoid being cheated out of land either by men in the village or by people from outside the village. Like the Mumbai settlement residents described by Anand (2017), Geeta saw legibility to the apparatus of governmentality through a politics of proof achieved via land surveys and documents as enabling the possibility of new claims on the state. Also central to their empowerment, Geeta argued, was travel, which allowed the women to form a new identification with poor people from other parts of the country and world, to develop a new analysis of poverty, and to translate that analysis into new land occupations. Such travel created the possibility of producing new scales of politics and enacting new scales of collective action.

Ratna, a slight women of about thirty-five years old with a big smile who favored red saris, had grown close to Geeta and had begun to play a role in the village leadership. She explained to me what the movement had done for women in Ramnagar and the area in terms similar to Geeta's:

> We women are now awake. We are now united. Before, people thought they could do anything to us. When we were walking down the street, people would do all sorts of thuggery [*gundagiri*] to women, especially Adivasi women, and say all sorts of dirty things to us. Now we are awake and we know our rights. A Dalit girl who was only fifteen years old in a nearby village was raped by a Brahmin boy. Then he killed her. Before, people would have kept quiet. Now women from all over the area came together and took him to the Police. We know our rights. We know that the water, forest, and land [*jal, jangal, aur jameen*] are ours. We are awake and united.

Such politics shifted the terms of sociality as they remade temporal horizons of possibility. Adivasi and Dalit women, alone or in small groups, now indexed in their persons the larger collective political forces that the Sangathan had aligned. In their persons they pointed to possible futures of retribution for harassment.

Their indexing of the larger collective's possible futures became, in itself, a claim against the caste- and gender-based practices of humiliation described by Guru (2011).

One long evening around the fire in October 2011 began quietly, as I joined Gopal and four other men to eat the rice and dal that Baldeva and two other women had prepared and were serving us. The women joined us after they had finished serving the food, and Gopal brought out some strong *mahua* liquor in a plastic jug, pouring us all cups. Settled by the fire, Baldeva brought up the harassment from higher-caste men that Ratna mentioned women faced while traveling through Govindnagar. One of the men by the fire interrupted, telling Baldeva to go help with the cooking: "Go cut onions instead of talking."

Baldeva grew angry and explained why she would stay:

> Look at this movement that we have made. It's a women's movement. Look at the road ahead. We have a law and the land will be ours. But this is because of women's strength and women's intelligence—that's what Geeta is saying. We women are saving the forest for all of our lives. In this no one will allow men to lead. Whatever has been done, women have done it. Before this, women were just following the men, but that's not going to happen anymore. Before this, there were all sorts of tricks and all sorts of nonsense against us. Not anymore. We have our rights and we know them.

Women had been key in the movement for forest rights: in decision-making, in facing down forest guards and landed higher castes, and in the cooking, cleaning, and other forms of labor that had kept the movement in motion. Baldeva was projecting this strengthened role for women forward: women knew their rights now, and they were not going to follow the men on the road ahead. She would stay by the fire and finish telling her story. The future-oriented terms of the collective action that produced the FRA in Ramnagar allowed for a knitting together of a collective across differences of caste and gender. That same dependence on collective action allowed for new claims to be made, as Baledeva in this case leveraged the centrality of women to the movement to demand a shift in divisions of labor and sociality.

The Banwasi Seva Ashram and Bhoodan Politics

Before I set off from Robertsganj for Ramnagar, Alok and Raju put me in touch with Ragini Bahen, who led the Banwasi Seva Ashram. The ashram had been working in parallel with the Sangathan to establish land rights in the area, although it operated through more formal institutional channels and emerged from a distinctive Gandhian political tradition. The Banwasi Seva Ashram had played a key role in Duddhi's land struggles: it initiated the 1982 and 1987 Supreme Court cases that led to a limited settlement of land rights in the area (as discussed in chapter 1), and starting in 2008 had been active in helping forest dwellers claim rights through the FRA. The Banwasi Seva Ashram, Alok and Raju told me, was doing a good job of implementing the FRA. Unlike the Ramnagaris, they were not cheating or lying. Over the phone, Ragini Bahen invited me to visit the ashram and told me that she would arrange for a visit to some of the villages the ashram was helping to claim rights for through the FRA.

After a few days in Ramnagar, I set off for the ashram, taking a bus twenty kilometers west until I arrived in front of its large, tidy compound. Inside the gate, irrigated fields circled the complex's periphery, with a complex of airy modernist buildings from the 1960s and 1970s in their center. Ragini, a small woman in her seventies wearing a green cotton sari, met me at the door to her small cottage and invited me in. She asked a young woman to bring us some tea and snacks, and we sat down to talk.

Ragini was from a Brahmin Marathi-speaking family from the South Indian city of Hyderabad. She had trained as a doctor before she met her late husband Prem Bhai in the early 1960s. While at university, both Ragini and Prem Bhai became involved in the Sarvodaya Bhoodan (land gift) movement, the Gandhian movement for village autonomy and land redistribution that had been Dr. Vinayan's first entry to politics. As discussed in chapter 1, the Sarvodaya movement, which was started by Gandhian reformer and the socialist leader Jayaprakash Narayan, who would go on to be the figurehead for the student movement in the years leading to the Emergency, aimed to resolve the deprivation caused by landlessness while reforming village political and cultural institutions without destroying them. The Sarvodaya movement sought to bring about the land redistribution that other political formations demanded, but they would do so neither through state policy nor through forced redistribution but rather through moral appeals to large landowners, who were asked to voluntarily gift land to the landless.

The Sarvodaya Bhoodan movement emerged in response to the Telangana movement for land reform in the late 1940s and early 1950s, in what is now Andhra Pradesh and the state of Telangana. Geeta and the leadership of the Sangathan also cite the Telangana movement as a central inspiration for their movement but claim to be heirs of its tradition rather than claiming, as the Sarvodaya Bhoodan movement did, to be critics of that tradition. In the Telangana movement, organized by the Communist Party of India, hundreds of thousands of landless Dalits forcefully occupied *zamindari* land, which they ran as autonomous collectives from 1946 to 1951 (see Roosa 2001).

The Gandhian leader Vinobha Bhave visited Telangana in 1951 and, in response to the militant methods of the Communist movement, began the Sarvodaya Bhoodan movement to encourage landed members of upper castes to gift their land to landless Dalits (see Sherman 2016). The movement spread quickly across the country through local Bhoodan committees, including to Duddhi through Prem Bhai, Ragini Behen, and the Banwasi Seva Ashram. Several states, including Uttar Pradesh, passed laws in the 1950s to coordinate the distribution of Bhoodan land. But the movement's frequent failure to successfully redistribute the land that had been promised—or its success in redistributing only poor-quality land—led to a series of countermovements. By the early 1970s, the Bhoodan movement faced considerable criticism for its failures, and even Jayaprakash Narayan distanced himself from the movement in 1972 when he was presented with evidence that it had failed to distribute viable agricultural land to landless Dalits in Bihar (see Bhattacharjea 1978).

When the BSP took up the slogan "Jo zameen sarkari hai, who zameen hamari hai" (the government's land is ours) and when M-L groups and the Sangathan echoed it, they had the same intent: a critique of the Bhoodan movement and a demand for Bhoodan (and all the other) land that had never been equitably distributed. What had been offered as a gift but never delivered, these Dalit and leftist movements asserted, was in fact their right: they would take it. The Sangathan and the Banwasi Seva Ashram thus emerged from political traditions that have, in a sense, been in a sixty-year dialogical relation with each other, with critiques and countercritiques of each other's programs of land and social reform. The slogans and narratives around which each tradition has built constituencies, including visions of past injustice and future justice, thus both draw on each other and refute each other. The redistribution of land and the end of caste oppression are promised by movements in both traditions. The way they understand the nature of caste oppression differs, however, with the Gandhian tradition seeking to end the violence associated with caste hierarchy without ending either the hierarchy or the caste categories, as both Marxist and Ambedkarite visions seek to. The means to achieve these ends similarly vary, as does the role of the state in these means. The Sarvodaya Bhoodan movement has worked, as its leaders say, "nonviolently," through moral appeals and gifts and with the support of state agencies. Leftist and Ambedkarite projects, in contrast, have occupied land with and without state sanction.

Ragini Bahen explained to me that the Banwasi Seva Ashram had been established following a severe drought in southern Sonbhadra in 1952. As discussed in chapter 1, apart from the Forest Department, the local state's presence there was thin, and Chief Minister Govind Vallabh Pant granted 250 acres to the Sarvodaya movement to establish an ashram to provide drought relief. Over time, the government entrusted the Banwasi Seva Ashram to provide a variety of welfare services in an area that the infrastructure of the welfare state did not reach. The state Forest Department offered an area of land to landless forest dwellers as Bhoodan and asked the ashram to administer its distribution. The ashram opened a school and medical clinic, and it began to teach local forest dwellers how to farm with the limited water supplies available in the area. It began a campaign against what it called the "liquor merchant-moneylender nexus," which it alleged kept Adivasi men both alcoholic and indebted. The campaign successfully closed the twenty-five liquor stores in southern Sonbhadra. Land reform efforts in the area through moral appeals were largely unsuccessful, however, because the majority of the land had been granted to the Forest Department with the abolition of *zamindari* in 1951 (Shourie 1984).

Govindnagar

Kishore Yadav, a worker for the Banwasi Seva Ashram, took me one day in 2010 on his motorcycle to Govindnagar, which was only two kilometers south of Ramnagar. Despite their physical proximity, the two villages could not have been more different. Here the signs of hunger that were everywhere in Ramnagar were not visible. Govindnagar has three paved roads running through it and brightly painted brick and cement village council, primary, and middle-school buildings. Around this central area are three more brick buildings: the homes of the village headman and his two brothers. The other homes in the village are the mud huts with thatched roofs that are standard in southern Sonbhadra, including in Ramnagar. Small hand pumps appeared along the roads every three hundred meters, providing access to relatively clean water for drinking and bathing, and the electric wires strung through the village allow those residents with fields close to the river to pump water to irrigate their fields. The river, in turn, has two small dams across it as it passes through the village, to trap water for use during the dry season. Legal land rights, and the claims on the state that they make possible, had transformed the material conditions of the village.

Yadav took me to meet Gopal Gond, the village headman, who had also been the head of the Forest Rights Committee. Gond called to a young boy who had been sitting across the road by a hand pump and watching us, ordering him to bring some chairs and tea. The boy scurried to arrange plastic chairs around a wooden table and came back after five minutes with hot, sweet tea in small metal cups and a plate arranged with salty *namkeen* and tea biscuits. Things worked well in Govindnagar, Gond explained: most children are able to attend primary and middle school, alcoholism is not the problem that he said it is in most of the area, and through the Banwasi Seva Ashram they had received development funds from the Japan International Cooperation Agency (JICA) in exchange for starting a community forest management program. Water was still a problem, though, as was landlessness. Relatively clean water for drinking was available from covered wells with mechanical "hand pumps" attached. But anyone whose fields were not adjacent to the river was not able to irrigate them, and so they could manage only one harvest per year. And two-thirds of the villagers, almost all of them members of Scheduled Tribes and Castes, had no land at all.

With Yadav's help, the members of Scheduled Tribes in Govindnagar who had obtained land rights in the Supreme Court–led settlements in the 1980s (or in earlier settlements) had been able to expand their holdings. Almost all of the five hundred or so families in the village had applied for land rights under the FRA in 2009, but only one-third—all members of Scheduled Tribes who already owned land—had their rights recognized. Even among the members of Scheduled Tribes who had applied, the majority had received only two or three of the four hectares they had applied for. In one case, two neighbors had applied for rights to the same plot of land, each claiming that he had been farming it for years. Neither had received rights to it.

A number of those who had not received land or had received only a few hectares through the FRA complained to me that only the relatives of Gopal Gond had received the full four hectares. The same relatives who had received land, I was told, had been the beneficiaries of a range of other government schemes. It was the relatives of the headman who had been able to acquire the Below Poverty Level (BPL) card required to receive subsidized food from government stores, for example. The job cards that entitled people to one hundred days of paid work per year through the United Progressive Alliance's Mahatma Gandhi National Rural Employment Guarantee Act, similarly, had preferentially gone to Gond's relatives. Conversely, in Ramnagar, I met only four people who had job cards and twenty who had BPL cards.

In effect, a law that had been framed as ending the dispossession of landless forest dwellers in India had, in Govindnagar, allowed only the small number of members of Scheduled Tribes who already had land rights to further expand their holdings. The members of Scheduled Tribes who had expanded their holdings the most, moreover, were the relatives of headman Gopal Gond. Gond had drawn on his political position as headman to act as a political patron, expanding the landholdings of his relatives and funneling the benefits of state welfare schemes toward them.

The FRA, as interpreted by the Banwasi Seva Ashram in Govindnagar, had in fact reshuffled caste-class relations. A group of small Scheduled Tribe landholders now had slightly larger holdings, although none of them, apart from Gopal Gond, had very profitable farms. In Govindnagar, the law had not resolved the problem of property for the landless; it had simply allowed those who already owned property to claim more.

Making Ramnagar

At the Robertsganj bus station, Raju and Alok had told me that Ramnagar is a creation of the NGOs. They were correct, in a way, but not in the way that they thought: Ramnagar is a creation of an organization, the Sangathan, and it had not been real ten years earlier. Ramnagar was *made* real through the ongoing creation of legal evidence and legal interpretation by Geeta, Dr. Vinayan, visiting anthropologists, and endless rallies. Ramnagar was produced and, in the absence of formal titles, could be maintained only through the continuous work to produce proof, legal interpretations, and political maneuvers.

The interpretations and the political struggles that produce Ramnagar drew the villagers into older struggles that have reconfigured caste and class in Duddhi, Left-Ambedkarite and Gandhian political infrastructures, and analyses that had been dialogically engaged for sixty years. In Duddhi, the indeterminacy of the FRA's text in no way explained the range of political projects that had successfully enlisted it. Nor did the word traps embedded within the law by its many authors in Delhi or the narratives in which they framed the forest rights struggle. Instead, these competing political traditions were engaged in competing and contradictory practices of regularization of the FRA's meaning (Moore 1978), a struggle that was itself a recent instantiation of a longer history of their competing projects of regularization on the same symbolic ground: low-caste and forest landlessness.

In Ram Lakhan's narrative, the FRA is much more than its text: it represents the once-lost promise of Indian Independence, now finally recovered. The act was in fact drafted specifically to enable such multiple enlistments. It was written to weaken the authority of the court system and the forest bureaucracy over India's forest land and, as a result, bureaucratic efforts to fix the meaning of the law face challenges by forest dwellers, activists, and politicians. It is not the law itself, then, but the relationship between the law and a local state with multiple loci of authority that has been entangled with infrastructures of older movements—from the Marxist Left to Gandhian Bhoodan movements—and has brought about the specific redefinitions of the law that are transforming Duddhi's landscape.

Ram Lakhan's narrative points to a vision of the Constitution that curiously echoes the vision outlined by the Supreme Court in its doctrine of a nonarbitrary "basic structure" of the Constitution, as discussed in chapter 1. The Constitution, for both Ram Lakhan and the Court, exists outside any given citation of the law or action of the executive state. For Ram Lakhan, however, the Constitution is a lost charter that guarantees economic and social rights as well as sovereignty to Dalits and Adivasis. In usurping the prime ministership from Ambedkar and hiding the Constitution, the Indian state, as led by Nehru and his successors, simultaneously effected the economic and political dispossession of Dalits and Adivasis. Many (e.g., Jaffrelot 2003; Guru 2011; Roy 2014) have argued that Ambedkar was torn between his roles as leader of a more radical project of Dalit liberation and a project of liberal institution-building, emblemized in his role in drafting the Constitution. For Ram Lakhan, this contradiction between Ambedkar's two roles is denied: because Ambedkar drafted the Constitution and was an important leader in the movement to liberate Dalit people, the Constitution itself liberates Dalit people.

The FRA presents the possibility of a reorganization of property and labor relations in Duddhi and across the nearly one quarter of India's land area that is owned by the Forest Department. The act reorganizes land relations not according to existing land relations, however, but according to caste and forest land tenure categories. It grants land to Scheduled Tribes who "occupied forest land" before December 13, 2005, and to "other traditional forest dwellers" who can prove seventy-five years of residence. The most accessible path to land rights through the law, therefore, is for those people who are members of tribes recognized by the state government who can also prove illegal residence on forest land before December 2005, typically including, in Duddhi, members of the Gond, Agaria, and Ghasiya communities who had ties to village political authorities. The reorganization of property relations in Duddhi, therefore, is contingent on struggles over the exact meaning of the law and of the legal categories of caste.

The FRA is framed in its preamble as reversing the "historic injustice" of the dispossession of India's forest dwellers, resolving their years of exploitation and eviction and solving the problem of the forest. The law has been used by NGOs and political movements across India's forest belt as a powerful tool to rework the relationship between caste and property. The law, however, in entering Duddhi via the Sangathan and the Banwasi Seva Ashram, has been subject to the same indeterminacy that ensnarled previous attempts to resolve forest-dweller landlessness in the area. The sediments of those previous attempts—in the form of an existing unequal distribution of property among castes and in relationships created between forest-dweller constituencies, organizations, and state actors—have, in turn, bounded the FRA's indeterminacy, granting land rights to already landed Scheduled Tribes and leaving Ramnagar's residents in a legal limbo.

Because the law's categories are indeterminate and membership in them is ambiguous, the Ramnagaris are caught up in two forms of extralegal politics. First is a knitting together of pasts and futures to produce acting collectives, solidarities across lines of caste and gender that might bring land rights to villages like Ramnagar. The villagers were brought together under the banner of Dalit Adivasi rights, an alignment of indigenous and Dalit pasts through a promise of political rights and land in the future. This knitting also allowed for new negotiations around gendered forms of sociality and labor, as Baldeva made clear that night by the fire.

These promised futures were subject to a second form of extralegal politics, however, as the village's destruction would make all too clear: a politics of proof, through which journalists like Raju and Alok, Delhi-based lawyers and academics, and visiting anthropologists are caught up in establishing the truth of caste and land tenure claims. These politics of proof and legal interpretation are not available to all to participate in equally. The precariousness of Ramnagar, its vulnerability to attack, reveals that the relationship between economic and political dispossession, and between economic and political power, has continued beyond the original sin of India's independence in Ram Lakhan's narrative.

Ramnagar's villagers occupied their land, but it would become clear that they lacked the political power on their own to stay on that land or to gain land rights. Land rights, in turn, would provide them with the ability to make further claims on the state that would make the land habitable and useful agriculturally: this included water, most importantly, but also roads, schools, and clinics. Their landlessness was not only an economic problem, then, but also a political problem. On their own, they were not able to furnish acceptable forms of proof that would enable them to make claims on the state. The work of Govindnagar's Yadavs to prevent Ramnagar's villagers from gaining land rights was therefore simultaneously work to prolong their political disempowerment. The dialogical relationship between the Sangathan and the Banwasi Seva Ashram was not only discursive but also would extend to the pragmatic politics of claiming each other's land and blocking each other's access to state resources. The arrival of the law had opened up a new channel for claims upon the state, but it did not guarantee the success of those claims, as the destruction of Ramnagar would show. The next chapter moves to the period following the attack, to the Ramnagaris' efforts to reconfigure their relationship to the state that had allowed it, and to patronage as the social and political form these efforts took.

ABANDONED SOLIDARITIES AND NEW LEGAL FUTURES

Dr. Vinayan, Geeta, and the Sangathan had promised the landless villagers who settled Ramnagar more than land: through land, the activists had told the villagers that they would obtain freedom from exploitative political, social, and economic relationships. With land was to come an end to relationships of patronage with landed members of higher castes, as landless Dalits and Adivasis gained for the first time the ability to withhold their labor from particular employers. With land was to come the possibility of new claims upon the state, for wells, schools, roads, and government welfare schemes. With land was to come reclaimed sovereignty.

Unlike in the plains of Uttar Pradesh, Tamil Nadu, or Maharashtra, where Dalit land occupations had been attempted before, not all land in forest areas is cultivated: the majority of Duddhi's land is uncultivated and is owned not by large private landlords but by the Forest Department. Attempts to rework caste and labor relations through the occupation of land, therefore, do not only require the dispossession of landed groups: the autonomy gained through land ownership is available to Dalits and Adivasis in forest areas through the occupation of previously unoccupied land. Because the land was state-owned, challenges to the occupation came from state actors citing conservation law, the Joint Forest Management (JFM) policy, and their own readings of the Forest Rights Act (FRA). Protection against eviction therefore required access to legal knowledge and state resources, access that is unevenly distributed and sets the stage for new patronage relationships. As it had in Govindnagar, as discussed in chapter 3, a solution to the problem of property in the forest would bring about a new relationship to the state—but it appeared that it could only come about through the support of state actors.

The tactics of the Sangathan that were produced through the alignment between the imaginaries of leftists and Dalit radicals thus ran into unintended effects as they were worked out in political practice. A bid to escape exploitative caste-based labor relations became entangled in new labor relations and new caste-based identifications. The failure of the future that they had been promised—of land rights and liberation—would challenge the new patronage relationships of the movement and the caste- and class-based identifications of the Ramnagaris.

This chapter is organized around a series of stories, organized chronologically, beginning with my first visit to Ramnagar in late 2010, nearly a year before the village was destroyed in September 2011. I recount the emergence of tensions and conflicts between a group of men in Ramnagar and Geeta and the work done by Geeta to maintain her role and authority within the village. Following the attack on the village, Geeta and the villagers briefly excluded me from the village, as they tested the loyalty of an anthropologist who had been, until then, trying to maintain friendly relations with both the villagers of Ramnagar and Govindnagar. The final two stories look at a new legal strategy presented by Geeta to the villagers, a move to claim collective land rights, and its unintended consequences both for Geeta's authority and for solidaristic relations within Ramnagar.

These stories track the falling apart of collective futures and efforts to repair them, to piece together a common project to achieve land rights across categories of gender and caste. New forms of suspicion take hold and new forms of solidarity are offered to index both a set of rules grounded in the FRA that will ensure a secure future for the Ramnagaris in Ramnagar and the outlines of a collective that might enact that future. A new caste identification took shape against this future of land rights, that of Dalit-Adivasis—but this identification would splinter as that future came to seem less likely, and recriminations and withdrawn solidarities took the shape of narrower caste identifications and the language of *jativadi* or casteism. Yet for all the work to produce a collective capable of action, the avenues toward land rights that the Ramnagaris explored all operated through a second political logic, a logic that in many ways they were trying to escape: that of patronage. Knowledge of the law, knowledge of the English language, and the forms of social knowledge that might allow a legal interpretation to gain approval from state authorities—the tools necessary to give legal force and meaning to the Ramnagaris' collective action—were held by activists, lawyers, journalists, and politicians from outside the village. Efforts to unmake relations of patronage would be mediated, in other words, by new forms of patronage. It is to the unmaking of potential collective futures and their remaking through the logics of patronage that this chapter turns.

Take This Issue, Sister

During my first visit to Ramnagar in November 2010, almost a year before it was destroyed, I met Geeta in Robertsganj, the dusty district headquarters in the north of Sonbhadra. Geeta stayed in a small and dusty flat on an unpaved road in a poor neighborhood. There was no time to keep the flat clean, Geeta apologized. The walls, stained with water damage, were decorated with images of Geeta's parents, Dr. Vinayan, and the Rani of Jhansi, a queen from the small state of Jhansi who fought in the 1857 rebellion against the British and has become a feminist and nationalist icon. Geeta's flat and her life in Robertsganj were far removed from middle-class Delhi, where she was raised and in which her relatives and peers from school and university remained. She had moved to Robertsganj in 2002 but had been living in forest villages and in small towns near them like Robertsganj since the early 1990s, when she became politically involved as a college student.

Shubha, who coordinated the Sangathan with Geeta, joined us in the flat in the morning to travel to Duddhi. The three of us hired a jeep to carry us south, over the Kaimur hills to the town of Duddhi, the largest town in Duddhi block, where block-level government offices were located. We parked outside a closed shop, and Geeta and I sat under an awning that stretched into the street. Residents of the area's occupied villages organized by the Sangathan began to trickle in—first a few, then a dozen at a time, and finally hundreds. Most of the people arriving were women, talking excitedly. The mood was festive. Winter was arriving, but as the sun rose higher in the sky the temperature still climbed into the high thirties Celsius.

Soon after we arrived, a large group of women arrived on the road, marching toward us and chanting: "*Mahila shakti zindabad!*" (Long live women's strength!), "*Inqilab zindabad!*" (Long live the revolution!), and the Bahujan Samaj Party's (BSP's) slogan, "*Jo zameen sarkari hai, woh zameen hamari hai!*" (The government's land is ours!). We started marching, the women in front, and a group of three abreast—a flag-bearer, a lone man, and a woman wearing all red and carrying a taught bow and arrow—walking in the lead. The group grew to be thousands strong, and the chants resonated in the small trading town, which was home to only twelve thousand people. They put the Sangathan's twist on the

BSP slogan, *"Jo jangal sarkari hai, woh jangal hamari hai!"* (The jungle which is the government's, that jungle is ours!) and added *"Van vibhag jangal chhode!"* (Leave the jungle, Forest Department!). Other chants referenced the ongoing legal battles with the Forest and Police Departments, which had filed cases against the villagers not only for occupying forest land but also for gathering sticks and other forest produce: *"Farji muqadama wapas lo, wapas lo!"* (Withdraw the false cases!) and *"Police prasashan murdabad!"* (Death to the Police Department!).

A few onlookers in the market joined and, except for one moment when we marched past a shop blaring loud pop music that overpowered the chants, the chants continued to grow louder. *"Adivasi ekta zindabad!"* (Long live Adivasi unity!), *"Dalit ekta zindabad!"* (Long live Dalit unity!). The categories "Dalit" and "Adivasi" were being used almost interchangeably in the chants, as they were in Ramnagar.

Geeta approached me in the crowd, a pleased grin on her face. "We don't have to do anything anymore," she said. "They organize the protests themselves! We used to have to encourage them and organize the rallies, but now they do the work and we just come along." Her role in the organization was diminishing, she said, as the women especially took on greater responsibilities. I asked Geeta what effects she thought these protests had, as the demands echoing out were much larger than the day-to-day project of land rights through the FRA. She explained that the protests demonstrated the strength of the group, both to itself and to its adversaries. Protests kept morale up, reminding everyone that the many small occupied villages in the region added up to a considerable constituency.

We moved off the street and onto a parade ground, on which we made a large circle, and as we turned, we could look across the ground to see the rest of the group, allowing us to apprehend its size for the first time. Back on the street after the parade grounds, we made our way to the block administrative headquarters for a rally. As the speeches and songs and slogans began, the women sat in front, raising their fists and cheering, while the apparently less interested men arranged themselves in the rear of the grounds.

Ram Lakhan took the stage, dressed in a white kurta pajama with a pen tucked into his front pocket. He began to sing in a high, thin voice about the struggle of landless Adivasis and Dalits and about using the law to escape slavery.

Ego mudda le la bhai
Ban jaye yatra
Kahin dekha nahin nam nisaan
Kahin dekha khatra

Ego mudda le la didi ji
Ban jaye yatra
Varg cher bhoomi ka banabar dharabis hui
Dekhla par kahi lata bada lage khi hui
Kahin ghere gondha kanake kahin ghere patra

Ego mudda le la didi ji
Ban jaye yatra
Kahin national park kahin sanctuary ho
Kanun le ke jailata bhagi humse deri ho
Kahin dar bhage huse
Kahin bane jabra
Ego mudda le la bhaiji
Ban jaye yatra

Take this one issue, brother
It will become your journey
We have no name or identity to be seen
Sometimes we see danger

Take this one issue, sister
It will become your journey
They transfer Section Four land to Section Twenty
They take land by digging pits and putting stones
Take this one issue, brother

It will become your journey
Sometimes it is in a national park, sometimes in a sanctuary
When we take the law and show them, sometimes they run far from us
Sometimes they intimidate us
Sometimes we become helpless
Sometimes we become confident
Sometimes they talk about the law, but they act ignorant
Take this one issue, sister
It will become your journey.

For a song sung at a rally, Ram Lakhan's lyrics were oddly uncertain about the future of their movement: the issue of land rights had indeed become their journey, but he was not sure where that journey would lead them. When the people of the Sangathan showed the law to the Forest Department, the Police

Department, the heads of the village councils, the bureaucracy, the "them," sometimes they would run far, he said, and sometimes they would respond with intimidation. Sometimes the villagers would be confident; sometimes they would feel helpless. The Forest Department was capable of many legal tricks, reclassifying land to make claims ineligible or shifting boundaries by moving physical markers.

For all the law's promise, it was not quite enough on its own to secure land rights for Ram Lakhan and his comrades. I would return to town with villagers from Ramnagar many times, but following the defeats that they would face in the coming months I would never see the villagers quite so confident there again. Usually when they reached Duddhi, its public spaces dominated by members of the higher-caste trading communities, the Dalits and Adivasis from Ramnagar would shrink, and they would temper their voices. Their collective presence that day had, then, indicated their power, at least to themselves.

After the rally, Geeta, Shubha, Ram Lakhan, and I piled back into the jeep that had brought us to Duddhi to travel on to Ramnagar. We drove fifteen kilometers east of the town, passing rows of small shops along the highway and fields of green wheat beyond. We pulled off the main road in the town of Govindnagar and began to drive through the village and across a small river toward Ramnagar. As we came up on the far bank of the river, however, the road ended and was replaced by small paths that were hard for me to discern. The paths led up and between hills that had occasional patches of farmland but that, on the whole, were brown and arid, far from the river and without irrigation. A Ramnagar man named Gaurav Agaria, who was driving the car, complained to Geeta that the tangle of dirt paths was confusing him, which prompted Ram Lakhan to hop out of the jeep and run ahead of us. As he ran, he pointed out to Gaurav the surest and easiest path for the vehicle.

As we approached the summit of the hills, we could see clusters of one-room mud huts with roofs made from red clay tiles and tree branches, small agricultural plots abutting them. In the center was a clearing, the *maidan*, with an open-air covered structure to provide shade. Ram Lakhan started calling out, "Ho! Everyone come to the maidan! Geeta is coming! Get everything ready!" People began scrambling. A large wooden charpoy, or cot, appeared, followed by someone carrying biscuits, salty snacks, and water. As we left the jeep, a man took Geeta's bag from her, a woman offered her a seat on the charpoy, and a young boy brought her water and biscuits.

Geeta reclined on the charpoy and asked for a cup of tea. The villagers took their seats on the ground around her. She asked about some children who were sitting nearby, playing a game with stones. Were they going to school? How old were they now? But the conversation gradually became serious, and

Geeta began to berate the villagers: The real enemy they now face is not external, not the capitalists, the Forest Department, or the landlords. It is them. They lack the strength to struggle.

Geeta's ire was directed principally at Ram Lakhan, who had sung at the rally. She addressed the entire group assembled, telling them that "You need to stand together" and "You must not lie," but it was clear that the collectively addressed "you" stood in for Ram Lakhan. The nearest school was two kilometers away, in Govindnagar, but Geeta felt strongly that the children should be attending it, and she blamed Ram Lakhan for the fact that they were not. "I knew I should not have let a man be the leader in Ramnagar," Geeta continued. "This is a women's movement, and women should lead it."

The next morning Geeta and Shubha returned to Robertsganj, and I remained in Ramnagar. Sitting around the fire outside Ram Lakhan's hut the next morning with his wife Baldeva and a few others, Ram Lakhan began to complain. "She shouldn't be talking to me like that," he said. "We didn't do anything to her." Without Geeta and Shubha, conversations were dominated by the men in the village, who mocked the women: "Without your big sisters here, you have nothing to say, huh?"

Tensions were emerging between Ram Lakhan and a number of men in the village and Geeta, and between Ratna and a number of other women and the village's existing male leadership. The village was in place, but the land rights that Dr. Vinayan and Geeta had promised through the law had not appeared. Without land rights and the possibilities of claims on the state for infrastructure—water, roads, schools, and clinics—life in Ramnagar was difficult. And for the men, the personalized labor relations with dominant-caste patrons that the villagers had left Govindnagar to escape seemed to have followed them. Instead of performing labor for a dominant-caste landlord patron, they now seemed to be performing it for a dominant-caste political patron.

Worker Solidarity and Labors of Patronage

In February 2011, Geeta invited me to an all-India trade union rally at Delhi's Jantar Mantar, an eighteenth-century observatory close to Parliament that had become the default, state-sanctioned site of protests in the capital. Multiple protests were often in progress on any given day on the street outside the observatory, and on this day, in addition to the union rally, there was also a small protest against government corruption and another against the 2009 Delhi High Court decision to decriminalize homosexual sex. The trade union protest was the largest of the rallies that day, however, with thousands of people from the

Communist Party–affiliated All-India Trade Union Congress and the Centre of Indian Trade Unions, the Congress Party–affiliated Indian National Trade Union Center, and the independent Left New Trade Union Initiative, among others.

The protest was organized against hikes in the prices of government-subsidized oil and the abolition of contract labor in factories. I was surprised, however, to see a large contingent of protestors from Ramnagar: 112 people had made the two-day journey and were now sleeping on the road outside Jantar Mantar for several days to protest the government's decision to raise prices on subsidized cooking gas and to push the government to abolish contract labor. Ram Lakhan carried a sign in English, a language he did not speak, demanding an eight-hour workday. Others carried English-language signs that demanded a living wage, a social security law, freedom of association, decent housing, and the release of Binayak Sen, a doctor who had been arrested on dubious charges of working with banned Maoist groups. Ramnagar's villagers were joined by many other landless forest dwellers involved in struggles for land rights. Another 50 villagers had come from other parts of Sonbhadra, 350 had come from the forested district of Lakhinpur Kheri in northern Uttar Pradesh, 250 from the state of Jharkhand, and 150 from Mirzapur, the district that borders Sonbhadra on the north.

Levien (2007) discusses a 2007 rally at Jantar Mantar by another umbrella organization that sought to bring together disparate groups of farmers to stop the use of eminent domain in agricultural land. That rally brought together groups representing landless forest-dwelling Dalits and Adivasis and the Bharatiya Kisan Union (Indian Farmers Union or BKU), representing dominant-caste landlords. The organizers of many rallies like to bring the BKU's constituents to their protests, as the group typically plays loud drums and chants and dances enough to multiply their visibility and leverage. But when the low-caste forest dwellers saw the BKU's dominant-caste constituents arriving, they left, telling the rally's leadership that they could not stay, that they would not protest in solidarity with the groups to whom they sold their labor. That day, the category of "farmer," which brought together landlords and landless laborers, failed to transcend the antagonistic relationships of exchange and patronage of the village. As this moment demonstrates, the political solidarity enacted in rallies— the collective that projects a shared set of demands for the future—is tenuous and can be brought down by, among other things, the absence of solidaristic relationships outside of the rallies.

The demands of the various protests held that day at Jantar Mantar were not all ultimately met. Contract labor has not, to date, been abolished, although Binayak Sen was released after widespread protests over his arrest. The thousands present at Jantar Mantar failed to persuade anyone in the national media to provide coverage of the rally. They did not seem to be threatening violence, and the show of strength in the rally was not enough to disguise the fact that the unions' ability to index possible futures was declining as their membership did.

Ram Lakhan told me at the rally that he was happy to be in Delhi; he was happy to have a chance to give a speech and happy to participate in the protest. Ram Lakhan, Baldeva, and others told me how much they enjoyed seeing other parts of the country, even if they found the people and the language in Delhi confusing. As Geeta had told me, the travels of Ram Lakhan and the other Ramnagaris also translated into a form of social and political capital back in Duddhi. I had seen members of dominant castes express surprise and even an amount of fear on learning that Dalits and Adivasis had been to the state capital Lucknow or Delhi. No one quite knew what they had learned there or what access to higher-level state resources they had acquired. Just as migration for employment gave the villagers access to alternatives to personalized labor relations with dominant-caste patrons, travel for political purposes gave them access to previously unknown alternatives to existing political relationships.

The journey took the Ramnagaris two days in each direction and took them away from their fields and jobs for six days. The slogans and demands of the protest were entirely distinct from those I had heard three months earlier in Duddhi. Gone were the demands for forest land and the angry denunciations of the Forest Department. They had been replaced by demands to improve the legal protections for industrial workers and to prevent increases in the prices of government-subsidized commodities. In principle, these commodities were available to Ramnagar's villagers at the subsidized rate available to all people below the poverty line, but only a few of the villagers had the necessary relationships with the leadership of the village council in Govindnagar that nominally represented them that would allow them to obtain the cards proving their poverty.

To the extent that Ramnagar's villagers do perform nonagricultural labor, an improvement in the legal protection of industrial workers would help them, Ram Lakhan explained to me. But he also explained that he and the others had come "because big sister called us." The villagers came, in other words, both to demonstrate their solidarity with industrial workers across the country, to come to understand themselves and their political work in Duddhi in terms of a larger workers' struggle, and also to fulfill a request of their patron, Geeta. In protesting in solidarity with industrial workers, the villagers were enacting a political identity that they would never enact in Duddhi: workers. "Worker" as a category becomes politically relevant in order to commensurate forest dwellers with factory workers. The categories Dalit and Adivasi, in contrast, had been deployed in Ramnagar to claim a notion of solidarity tied to the political project of claiming land rights in Ramnagar. The project that Ambedkar (1936) sees as necessarily following the annihilation of caste, the mobilization of India's working class as workers, could be enacted in a rally in New Delhi but not in Duddhi or in Ramnagar.

Fighting with the Law and Losing

As Dalit Adivasis seeking land together or as workers seeking a new economic settlement, the new forms of solidarity that the Ramnagaris enacted were, like the work that they did for Geeta, their political patron, tied to potential futures. Through solidarity and patronage, they sought land rights and the social and political transformations that they hoped would follow. However, those land rights seemed to be slipping out of reach.

As the Sangathan activists had presented it to the Ramnagaris, the FRA would secure their occupation of the forest. In March 2009, their homes built and fields planted, the villagers applied for rights through the act. Recognition for the village and their rights would be granted by a Forest Rights Committee that the FRA has village councils establish to evaluate claims. Ramnagar was not a recognized village, however, so its claims were submitted to a committee established in Govindnagar. This committee was largely composed of the Yadavs and dominant castes whose land the Ramnagaris once worked; many of these committee members were the same men who would attack Ramnagar two years later in 2011. The committee rejected Ramnagar's claims on the grounds that they had arrived on the land after the 2005 cutoff.

The committee ostensibly represented the entire community, landless and landed, who would together manage the forests. It had come under the control of landed dominant castes, however, and the committee now allowed these committee members to consolidate their caste and class positions. This was a form of collective action in its own right: through a state institution, members of a landed caste were extending their power. The Ramnagaris appealed the denial of their claims to the head of the local administration, District Magistrate Pandhari Yadav, only to face another denial. As Pandhari Yadav explained to me in December 2010, ten months before Ramnagar was destroyed, "The law states that the claimants should prove that they were on the land before 13 December 2005, and these villagers have no proof that they were on the land before that date."

The district magistrate did not order Ramnagar to be destroyed, but he was not alone in interpreting the FRA in a way that would deny rights to Ramnagar. In November 2011 I met Vikas Dubey, who ran a nongovernmental organization funded by the Japan International Cooperation Agency (JICA) that had

established and disbursed funds to a Joint Forest Management (JFM) committee in Govindnagar. I had been told by the Ramnagaris that it had been the
JICA-funded JFM committee, itself largely composed of dominant-caste Yadav
men, that had attacked their village in September, and Dubey did not dispute
their account.

Dubey offered to take me to meet with the Govindnagar JFM committee, so
that I could understand how and on what grounds they had attacked Ramnagar. His organization was established to implement the Government of
India's Joint Forest Management Guidelines of 1990, and unlike the village
Forest Rights Committee, he and the JFM committee lacked formal authority
to interpret the Forest Rights Act. JFM is a set of practices and policies first
implemented by local- and state-level forest officials in the 1980s and then
adopted by the Government of India, with support and funding from the Ford
Foundation and World Bank, to bring about forest conservation with the help
of forest residents by finding alternative sources of income and employment for
forest-dependent people. Among other reforms, the program paid forest residents in exchange for their planting and not cutting down trees, and Vasant
Saberwal, who was then the head of the Ford Foundation's Natural Resources
program in Delhi, explained to me in a 2011 interview that his program and the
World Bank had stopped funding the program in the late 1990s. They had
found, he told me, that forest residents seemed to resume cutting down trees as
soon as the funding ceased.

The policy languished from the late 1990s on—Saberwal told me that the
Government of India lacked the funds to support JFM on its own, and international funders were no longer interested in paying for the program, believing it
to be ineffective. Vineeth Sarin, at the time JICA's Lead Development Specialist
in India, explained to me in a 2011 interview that JICA was more willing to
cooperate with the Indian government than the World Bank or Ford Foundation were. JICA puts fewer restrictions on the ways its funds are used, he said,
in part because it faces less activist and media scrutiny than do the World Bank
or the Ford Foundation. For that reason, he said, and because it processes loan
requests relatively quickly, JICA had at that point become the largest bilateral
lending agency in India. In 2002, JICA began to fund state-level JFM programs.
In 2008, at the request of the Uttar Pradesh Forest Department, JICA extended
a forty-year loan of 13,345 million Yen (Rs. 8.6 billion or US$170 million) to
restart the JFM program, which led to the establishment of organizations like
Vikas Dubey's in Duddhi.

Dubey explained to me that his organization had selected for JFM funding
villages that bordered the forest, but in which everyone had a land title. They
agreed to give the villages grants and loans for a nursery, for handicraft

programs, for hand pumps, and for a new road—on the condition that they would clear the forest area surrounding their village of what Dubey called "encroachments," illegal settlement on forest land. Govindnagar, in other words, was only eligible for JFM funding if its residents could somehow get rid of Ramnagar. When I asked why the committee had to attack Ramnagar, Dubey echoed District Magistrate Pandhari Yadav's interpretation of the FRA, telling me that the Ramnagaris had misunderstood the new law: "they think they can use it to go and settle on new land, when the law says you can only claim land that you occupied before December 2005."

District Magistrate Pandhari Yadav and Vikas Dubey were right that the villagers did not have proof that they had been on the land before 2005. The FRA's text, however, does not provide a straightforward answer to the question of who is eligible for rights. The act requires claimants to have "occupied forest land" before December 13, 2005, but the land that they claim need only have been under occupation on the date of commencement of the act, December 31, 2007. Taken together, these requirements can be interpreted in two ways. Either the claimants must have lived on any piece of forest land before December 2005 and only must have occupied the specific piece of land they were claiming before December 2007, as the Sangathan activists had told the Ramnagaris. Or, as the Forest Rights Committee, the district magistrate, and the JFM committee claimed, they must have lived on the specific piece of land they were claiming prior to the 2005 cutoff.

Under the second interpretation, the FRA would provide rights only to those people who had managed successfully to claim land prior to its passage. The act would, then, formalize the informal and unequal distribution of land that preceded its passage. The law did not strictly define the rules that it would establish—which conditional futures of land rights or evictions would follow from it. Instead, its text established the grounds of contestation over which struggles over forest land could be waged. In defending their claim to District Magistrate Yadav and others, the Ramnagaris turned to another passage in the law. They cited the phrase "historic injustice," or *etihasik anyay*, that the Campaign for Survival and Dignity (CSD) conveners Pradip Prabhu and Madhu Sarin had inserted into the law, which conservationists had opposed. I was told repeatedly, by Ram Lakhan, Ratna, and others, that they were clearly the victims of the historical injustice. It was their land, and they were reclaiming it.

The FRA was being brought to life through two opposed interpretations. Each interpretation, each set of rules through which the law would shape life, was tied to a different vision of a future and the social and economic relations that would constitute it. In the Ramnagaris' case, this was a future in which they would have their own land and escape oppressive caste relations. In the case of the attackers, this was a future in which caste-based economic relations were preserved and the public forest surrounding their village would be protected or in which the elite conception of the public and its rights would be defended. These interpretations of the law were being mobilized not exclusively by bureaucrats and judges, state actors trained to interpret legal texts according to fixed procedures and within certain boundaries, but instead through collective action by landless forest dwellers and the landed farmers for whom they had once worked.

Ultimately, frustration at their failure to achieve land rights for the villagers prompted a number of men, led by Ram Lakhan, to seek an alternative to Geeta's methods and her patronage in July 2010. What Akhil Gupta (1995) has identified as a discourse of corruption, an idiom through which state actors' actions are analyzed as the self-interested actions of individuals, pervaded political talk among the Ramnagaris. If the state operated through corruption, Ram Lakhan asked me, why should they be punished by refusing to participate?

The group approached state actors directly, offering the Sonbhadra district magistrate and district forest officer Rs. 25,000 (roughly US$500 in the exchange rates of the time) each in exchange for recognition of their rights. By approaching the state actors directly, Ram Lakhan made clear to me, he was not rejecting Geeta's patronage but seeking an alternative to it. He was, in other words, seeking to make Geeta's patronage itself commensurable with that of other patrons, depersonalizing the relationship.

The attempted bribes failed. Perhaps Ram Lakhan and the men had not known the correct procedures to successfully bribe the officers, perhaps they lacked the requisite social status for their bribes to be accepted, perhaps they had not offered enough money. Pandhari Yadav, the district magistrate, would later be accused by the Union Rural Development Minister Jairam Ramesh of stealing Rs. 400 crore (roughly US$80 million in the exchange rates of the time) from the funds allocated to the district under the National Rural Employment Guarantee Act (*Times of India* 2012). Cash, as Björkman puts it, can be "a sign and instantiation of the networks of knowledge, authority, and resources" (2014, 631) that powerful politicians have access to, but in this instance, cash coming from the hands of those who evidently lacked access to such networks failed to instantiate and failed to act. Despite constantly pointing out instances of corruption, none of these villagers knew how corruption actually takes place. The acts that they deemed corrupt were not themselves visible, and such acts, as Bourdieu (1990) has shown, succeed through a second concealment, a concealment of the calculation behind the gesture. Whatever reason lay behind the district magistrate's refusal, the future that the Ramnagaris had hoped for, of land rights and liberation, seemed to be disappearing from view.

In the days that followed the failed corruption attempt, word of what had happened spread, and Geeta learned of it. She was furious with the villagers for their moral failure. "It gives our organization a bad name," she told me a few days later. "People will think that we're corrupt, too."

Geeta drew a distinction between her work to implement the FRA through an expansion of its meaning through demonstrations, persuasion, and coercion and the act of corruption that Ramnagar's villagers attempted. Despite sharing an end, the distribution of titles to the villagers, and despite her claim to me to see the law in exclusively instrumental terms, she was asserting clear moral and practical differences between the two modes of political practice. The Sangathan attempted to implement what she saw as the spirit of a more or less just law by bending its meaning, whereas bribery violated both the spirit and text of the law.

Controlling Channels

Ten months after the district magistrate rejected the Ramnagaris' appeal and two months after the failed attempt to bribe him, the village was destroyed. The future the Ramnagaris had imagined appeared to have been foreclosed, and with that future slipping away, the present changed as well. The mood in the village was despondent. Accusations abounded regarding what had gone wrong, who had failed to gain the support of which activists, politicians, or police officers who might have protected the village.

In November 2011, I made my second trip to Govindnagar since the attack. I called Ram Lakhan from Delhi to ask if it was all right if I came and when would be convenient for him. "Next week," he said. "Can you come Wednesday?" I booked my train ticket to Mirzapur, caught a bus to Robertsganj, and from there, one to Duddhi. As the bus pulled into Duddhi, I called Ram Lakhan, to tell him that I would be arriving in Govindnagar in an hour. "Oh, oh," he said. "Where will you stay?"

No one from Ramnagar had asked me this before; someone from the village had always arranged accommodation for me. I stammered, and Ram Lakhan, realizing that I did not have anywhere to stay, said that he would arrange something and that I should find him when I got to the village. He did not offer to send anyone to meet me at the highway in Govindnagar, though, as the villagers had always done in the past. Instead, I caught one of the jeeps that work as shared taxis, plying the roads around Duddhi. I disembarked in Govindnagar and started making my way to the Dalit and Adivasi neighborhood of Govindnagar where the Ramnagaris were now staying on my own, unsure why their usual hospitality was not being offered to me.

I walked past Gaurav Agaria's hut on my way, said hello, and asked how he was doing. "Everything is fine," he replied, "but I'm not involved with those people anymore, with Geeta and everyone." He did not invite me in for water or biscuits, and I walked on. When I reached the central clearing in the middle of the Agaria neighborhood, I saw Ram Lakhan, who offered a weak greeting. He pulled up a charpoy, and Lalti and five or six others joined us to sit and talk. We made small talk, but everyone was hesitant. Something was clearly on their minds.

Finally, Ram Lakhan asked me, "Anand brother, are you on our side or not?"

"What do you mean?" I asked. "Of course I'm on your side. Why are you asking this?"

"No, because we have heard some things. Geeta told us that you have been spending a lot of time at the Banwasi Seva Ashram and you are actually on their side."

"Yes," Lalti interjected, "Why do you go there so much? We have heard that you might be with the JICA people."

I fumbled around for an explanation. As a researcher, I could travel to places and talk with people they could not. I could tell them what their attackers were planning, what they were thinking, but I was on their side.

"Look," I said to them, "I am on your side. Completely. I swear. But because I am a researcher, and because I'm from America, those people trust me and they let me see what they do. I can take that knowledge and use it for your cause."

"But why do you have to go there so much?" Ram Lakhan pushed.

"Because I'm trying to understand what they do! So that I can use it for you!"

Lalti was unconvinced. "We need to call big sister," she said, referring to Geeta. "To see what she thinks." She pulled out her phone and dialed Geeta, back in Delhi. They spoke for a minute, and she handed the phone to me.

"Hi, Anand?" Geeta asked in English. "It seems they have some idea in their heads. For some reason they are suspicious. They say you have been going to the Banwasi Seva Ashram too much. I can't convince them that they have nothing to be worried of. It's up to you. You need to make them trust you. Frankly, we have some concerns too. You just went there this time without telling us. It's a very dangerous, feudal area. You shouldn't be going there alone. We don't know how much time you spend with the Banwasi Seva Ashram or what you're doing with them. Can you give the phone back to Lalti?"

I continued to protest for a few minutes, but I could see that there was no use. The hospitality I had enjoyed before—even the friendships I had developed with Lalti and Ram Lakhan—had been put on hold. Lalti said that I could stay that evening but, in the morning, I would have to return to Delhi to see Geeta.

I caught a 4:30 a.m. bus the next morning from Govindnagar and made my way back to Delhi. A few days later, I visited Geeta in her Delhi apartment. She expressed regret over what had happened on my visit and suggested that

I do two things to regain the trust of the villagers. First, I should stop my field-work with the Banwasi Seva Ashram, the staff of JICA, and the dominant-case villagers of Govindnagar. "These are very feudal people, you see," Geeta explained. "And our people cannot trust them, and they cannot trust you if they feel that you are with them." The second thing I should do, Geeta told me, was to write an essay for the Sangathan's newsletter explaining what JICA had done, how they were equivalent in their lending structure and goals to the much-mistrusted World Bank, and how they were using the pretense of conservation to support what she called "feudal elements" in forests.

I wrote the essay, and Geeta called me the day after to say that she liked what I had written. She suggested that I return to Govindnagar the next week, but she again cautioned me against returning to the Banwasi Seva Ashram. The attack had destroyed any remnants of goodwill or trust that might have existed toward the ashram, and the roles I was playing—both that of an engaged anthropologist who was working with and for the movement for land rights and that of a dis-passionate anthropologist who was attempting to understand a larger social context in Ramnagar and Govindnagar—were now in deep and unsustainable contradiction. Another researcher from the United States, Geeta had told me earlier, had worked with the Sangathan for a year and had disappeared. They suspected that he had been working with the Central Intelligence Agency. Activists with the Sangathan and Ramnagaris all had stories of Intelligence Bureau officers and police officers who had knowledge of the content of private meetings that they could not have had without someone leaking it to them. When Ramnagar was destroyed by people from Govindnagar, therefore, my attempt to maintain access to both groups could be considered suspicious. Publicly repudiating the position of the Banwasi Seva Ashram and the JICA JFM committee proved my alliance with Ramnagar and the Sangathan and ended any relationship I had with the Govindnagar Yadavs and the Banwasi Seva Ashram.

I was not the only person whose loyalties and solidarities were questioned in the months following the attack on Ramnagar. In November, Geeta chose Lalti to replace Ram Lakhan as the leader of the Ramnagaris. Ram Lakhan was a member of the Agaria Scheduled Tribe, while Lalti was a Ghasiya. Of the 120 families who had settled Ramnagar, eighty are Agarias, and these eighty had lived apart from the rest of the village, in an older settlement on the eastern side of a deep ravine that separates them from the newer areas of the village, where Chamars, Gonds, Ghasiyas, Bhuiyas, and others live. With Lalti assuming leadership, therefore, the leader of the Ramnagaris was, for the first time, not a man, a member of its majority community, or a resident of its largest settlement. This shift in the gender and the *jati*, or subcaste, of leadership would begin to produce a new series of shifts in the political and economic dynamics of the Ramnagaris.

Patronage and Unity

In December 2011, I stayed in Lalti's house in Govindnagar for a few nights. She had grown up in this house and returned to it when there was no agricultural work to be done in Ramnagar or, as in this case, when her home in Ramnagar was destroyed and she was not sure whether or not she would be able to move back. It was an earthen hut like her hut in Ramnagar, but it was older, sturdier, and larger, with three rooms for its seven occupants. Lalti's Govindnagar hut received four hours of electricity each night and had an uncovered well next to it. Water was close at hand here, unlike in Ramnagar, but it was greenish and had garbage and leaves floating on top. Despite the advantages of this home, Lalti and her husband Shankar had tried to move to Ramnagar because behind the hut they had only half a hectare of land, which was not enough land to feed their family.

Food and money were short, but Lalti's husband Shankar had still killed a chicken for me and Lalti had made me a large curry that evening. We sat by a fire outside the hut. Shankar offered me some *mahua*, a strong liquor made from the flowers of the mahua tree that is drunk across the central Indian forest belt, to wash the spicy curry down. We quickly grew tipsy, and I asked Lalti and Shankar what they were going to do now, with Ramnagar destroyed.

"I'm not scared of those people. We can go back, we can do anything at all," she said, "but only if we keep our unity. Nowadays, we are falling apart. Some people are still with Ram Lakhan, and some are with me. How can we win if we are divided? Tell me, brother!"

Ram Lakhan, Lalti explained to me, still commanded the respect and authority of many people in the village, but mostly of members of his Agaria community. Ram Lakhan continued to make many of the decisions concerning the village, but Lalti was now responsible for representing the village to outsiders: to Geeta, to local politicians and bureaucrats, and when villagers traveled to the state capital Lucknow or Delhi for large rallies. Lalti had the recognition of some members of the village, mostly among women and the members of the one-third of Ramnagar's villagers who were not Agarias, but political authority and political representation had essentially been split.

The attack on Ramnagar, the apparent failure of one path toward land rights, would go on to produce new splits among the villagers in relation to the terms and composition of their solidarity and their relationship with the law. A movement to claim land that had begun in order to reorganize caste- and gender-based labor relationships ended up, in turn, producing a series of new labor relationships that would shape the subsequent group identifications and demands of the movement. It had also challenged the gendered distribution of political authority in the village, making a woman, Lalti, the village's leader.

One aspect of the future held out by the Sangathan activists—land rights leading to changed labor relations—materialized, but only in part. Ramnagar's villagers held land and farmed it themselves. They had stopped selling their labor to the Yadavs in Govindnagar. But every family in the village was dependent on migration outside the village, to a nearby cement factory, to Delhi, or even to Kerala in South India. Ram Lakhan could tell me the average pay for a day of unskilled labor in every state in the country. They depended on labor migration of different durations, from a day to a year, because their holdings were still small and unirrigated, and with the possibility of future attacks from Yadavs and the Forest Department, it was uncertain whether they would be able to harvest the crops they did grow.

The legal future promised by the activists did not seem to be arriving. In attempting to bribe the divisional forest officer and the district magistrate, Ram Lakhan and the male leadership of Ramnagar had attempted to short-circuit Geeta's patronage by reaching out directly to a state actor, multiplying their paths to the more just future they were working toward. If one goal of Ambedkarite politics in Uttar Pradesh can be seen as the abstraction of labor, ending both patronage and the stigma of caste and making Dalit labor commensurable with the labor of others, then the attempt by Ram Lakhan and others from Ramnagar to bribe local officials for land rights can be seen as a failed attempt to enlist other patrons and to make patronage itself commensurable. By multiplying the number of potential patrons available to the Ramnagaris, patrons would become comparable to other patrons, both in terms of the demands they would be able to make on their clients and in terms of the political changes they would be able to provide.

But the attempt to bribe the local officials failed, and as word traveled around Duddhi that Geeta was no longer protecting Ramnagar, the plan to destroy the village was formulated. Vikas Dubey, the JICA-funded organizer of the JFM committee that had participated in the attack, told me that the attackers knew that Geeta had distanced herself from Ramnagar and had attacked because the village was without political protection. Still resenting the loss of their old laborers and grazing land, Yadavs in Govindnagar used the JFM committee to destroy Ramnagar. An older repertoire of violence used to punish Dalits and Adivasis who challenged their place in the caste order thus aligned with JICA's conservationist project. This alignment, however, simultaneously punished Ramnagar's Dalits and Adivasis for challenging two forms of patronage and their attendant personalized labor relations in seeking abstracted forms of exchange: the agrarian patronage and labor with respect to the Yadavs and the political patronage and labor with respect to Geeta. Without Geeta's patronage, Ramnagar's villagers were vulnerable to attack by their old patrons, the land-owning Yadavs from

Govindnagar. The latter were punishing the villagers for occupying forest land and escaping their patronage, but they were inadvertently also punishing the Ramnagaris for attempting to find patrons other than Geeta.

Patronage thus appears in Ramnagar as a transactional means to an end, as a gifting relationship that entails the provision of scarce goods available only through the patron—whether food by landlords or state resources by activists—in exchange for labor in fields and in homes for landlords and in rallies and in homes for political patrons. Patronage is, however, at the same time, a relationship of sincere affection, as between women like Lalti and Geeta. To the extent that some Ramnagaris have tried to escape from such relationships, they cannot be seen as entailing a "mutuality of being" between patron and client, characterized by "a moral logic of selflessness" on the part of the patron, as Piliavsky (2014, 23) argues, drawing on Sahlins (2013). The resentment that prompted the villagers to escape two patronage relationships points instead to a perception, held particularly by Ramnagar's men, of exploitation.

The resentment by Ram Lakhan and the other men at Geeta's patronage was not shared by many of the village's women, who repeatedly expressed to me their affection for Geeta. The men's resentment of Geeta and desire to escape from her patronage was inseparable from their resentment of the way in which Geeta had successfully changed gendered relationships of authority, if not labor, among the villagers. This challenge to men's authority was expressed most clearly when Geeta and Shubha left Ramnagar and the men would taunt the women for their lack of authority in their patrons' absence. Geeta's patronage, in other words, promises different things to different residents of Ramnagar: both land and new social relations with higher castes to all residents and a reworking of the gendered division of political authority to women.

Subramanian (2009) argues that patronage "can encode meanings and relations more complicated than the exercise of top-down authority circumscribing the agency of the client. As it did in the eighteenth and nineteenth centuries, patronage can function more dialectically as a mechanism through which loyalty is conditional on the granting of specific rights and privileges" (177). She thus argues for the possibility of patronage "from below," through which subalterns can "actively negotiat[e] terms of engagement within an emergent political configuration" (177). Loyalty in Ramnagar clearly was "conditional on the granting of specific rights and privileges," as Ram Lakhan and the male political class of the village attempted to demonstrate to Geeta when they tried to circumvent her patronage. Their attempt to negotiate the terms of engagement with their patrons, however, failed because the district magistrate rejected their bid to create a new patronage relationship. The political project of Ramnagar—claiming land rights through the favorable reinterpretation of a law—relied on access to legal and state resources that were not evenly distributed in Duddhi. Despite Geeta's efforts at sharing her skills, none of the villagers could produce a persuasive argument in court in favor of a given reading of the FRA. Moreover, Geeta could never share with the villagers the social capital that she was able to deploy in interactions with officials, indicating familiarity with higher-level officials in the state capital Lucknow and in Delhi, and indicating knowledge of their corruption. Her skills were rare enough in Ramnagar, it turned out, that an attempt to make her patronage commensurable in order to enact patronage "from below" was difficult.

Geeta ultimately attempted to strengthen women's leadership in what she saw as a women's organization by removing the rebellious and, in her view, corrupt Ram Lakhan from political power. She replaced Ram Lakhan, a member of the majority Agaria jati, with Lalti, who was a Ghasiya. In choosing as a new representative a member of a minority jati, however, Geeta produced two new, unexpected dynamics. First, Ram Lakhan maintained legitimacy as a political leader within a large segment of Ramnagar's population, separating local hegemony from the channel of representation through which Geeta operated and alienating a large portion of the population from Geeta and her project. Second, jati began to emerge as a newly salient category, politically and socially. Jativadi became an increasingly frequent accusation within Ramnagar, as villagers began to accuse other villagers of favoring members of their own caste. And the Agaria jati began to draw apart from Geeta and the rest of the village, seeking to build their own channels of political representation.

But jativadi runs counter to the projects of political abstraction through solidarity that had brought Ramnagar together. These projects aimed to unite the many landless people of Govindnagar in struggle not as members of individual caste communities but as workers, as Dalits, or as Adivasis, to subsume individual and jati identities within larger political categories of solidarity. These were all attempts to make caste categories do something, to change existing property and labor relations, and as they seemed to fail, new caste categories began to be worked into political projects: the categories of jati. What did carry over to these new political projects, however, as the next two stories show, was the legal means that Geeta was producing, which could be isolated from the Sangathan's political narratives and identities.

Collectivization

The next week, I traveled with Ram Lakhan to Baijpur, an occupied forest village in Sonbhadra that lies north of the Kaimur Range. The water table is higher north of the Kaimurs, and as the region receives more rainfall than Duddhi does, the area is strikingly lush following the rains. Baijpur is the result of the first land occupation that Geeta organized in Sonbhadra. A group of forty women occupied and started to farm this land in 2004. They faced multiple attacks from the Police and Forest Departments and were arrested, but they kept returning to the village multiple times. Like the Ramnagaris, by 2011, the villagers still did not have land rights, but the attacks had slowed, and the villagers were gradually achieving de facto control over the land.

When we arrived in Baijpur, a large colorful tent had been set up in the central open grounds of the village. Under this tent were two large speakers on stands, out of which was emanating a loud Bhojpuri pop song, to which seven or eight children were dancing, their arms waving dramatically. In a field some distance away from the open ground, a second tent had been erected. Under it, women from Baijpur and from the occupied villages across Sonbhadra were cooking dal, rice, rotis, and potatoes in huge pots over large fires.

The infrastructure was in place for a rally, but the audience for the speeches and songs would be composed of the occupying villagers themselves. Geeta and the Sangathan had brought villagers from across the region together to discuss a new legal strategy that, she promised, would finally bring them formal land rights: rather than claiming individual land rights, they would claim collective rights.

The meeting began in the late morning. Ram Lakhan and Shankar, another Ramnagari, held a notebook between them and stood in front of the microphone to sing a song hailing the victories of the movement in Duddhi. Following the song, Geeta took the stage to introduce Comrade D. Thankappan, a man in his sixties dressed in a clean untucked button-up shirt, trousers, and sandals. Thankappan, Geeta said, was an important leader from the Mumbai mill workers' labor movement, and he had been central to the 1982 textile strike, a year-long strike of 250,000 workers whose failure was a turning point in the Indian labor movement. In 2002, he had been among the founders of the New Trade Union Initiative, which worked to bring new constituents into the labor movement, including forest dwellers.

Geeta had invited Thankappan to Baijpur because he had experience organizing the collectivization of factories in Mumbai, and Geeta hoped that this experience would allow Thankappan to help the landless of Duddhi in instituting collective farming. Because the villagers in Baijpur, Ramnagar, and the other forest villages of Duddhi had small plots and were not accumulating profits that would allow them to hire labor, they often helped one another with plowing and harvesting. The plots were not collectively owned but were instead parceled out to individual families. In Ramnagar, these plots had been twenty bighas (five hectares) per family before the attack and were now reduced to an average of eight bighas (two hectares) each. Now, Geeta and the organization were attempting to claim collective property rights for the villagers of Duddhi, and they had brought in Thankappan to help them.

The move to collectivization, however, was not intended to bring about a complete collectivization of property. It was, rather, a new legal strategy that dovetailed neatly with both a longstanding leftist agricultural project and, in name at least, the ownership and organizational practices of the union-owned factories in Mumbai that Thankappan had been involved in organizing. As I discuss in chapter 2, the CSD had successfully created the possibility of claiming rights through the FRA both as individuals, which the Ramnagaris had attempted but failed to do, and as communities. In section II 3(1)(i) of the act, communities are allowed to claim the "right to protect, regenerate or conserve or manage any community forest resource which they have been traditionally protecting and conserving for community use." The law provides the same restrictions on applicants regardless of which form of property they are claiming: residence before December 2005 for members of Scheduled Tribes or seventy-five years of residence for people who are not members of Scheduled Tribes.

The law, however, does not provide a procedure for evaluating community land claims by mixed groups that include both Scheduled Tribe and non–Scheduled Tribe members. Geeta argued that the law took for granted that villages would consist entirely either of Scheduled Tribes or non–Scheduled Tribes. As a result, a mixed community like Ramnagar would be able to file for land rights under the FRA, and because there were members of Scheduled Tribes among its members, they would only need to prove residence since 2005, and not for seventy-five years.

Geeta was attempting, in other words, to create a new possible legal future through a novel reading of the FRA. By reading the law as enabling collective rights for mixed communities of Scheduled Tribes and non–Scheduled Tribes, she was attempting to stitch back together Ramnagar's collective, which was threatening to come apart on lines of gender and jati. The two forms of claims enabled by the FRA provided Geeta with two chances, but this second form required her to prove that the agriculture and forest management in each village was, in fact, collective. Shubha explained to me that the villagers had always practiced collective agriculture by default and that the goal of this consultation was both to formalize and improve their collective agriculture and to plan for the collective claim process. To enable a new form of legal claim to the land, the practice of extending help to one another during the planting and harvesting periods—a generalized reciprocity (Sahlins 1972) of agricultural labor—was being reframed as collective farming.

Collective and common forms of property have two distinct genealogies in India, one on the Marxist Left and another derived from an influential school of environmentalists who have attempted to reconcile the livelihood needs of forest dwellers with conservation goals. Both genealogies informed Geeta's new legal tactic, but neither, as we will see, could account for the ends to which the tactic would be used.

The leftist lineage of collective property in India stretches back to the 1940s Telangana movement, a peasant uprising in what was then the princely state of Hyderabad and is now Andhra Pradesh, discussed in chapter 3. Geeta explained to me that the Sangathan derives its inspiration from "the revolutionary struggles of Bhagat Singh," the 1920s Punjabi anticolonial socialist, "and Telangana." In the Telangana movement, the Communist Party organized peasants in three thousand villages to redistribute property, which was subsequently owned and managed by communes for five years, until Hyderabad's violent incorporation into the Indian union in 1951 (see Roosa 2001).

A second lineage derives from an influential body of work on conservation and property, led most notably by Elinor Ostrom (1990), who has argued that properly managed common closed property regimes can exist that simultaneously provide for people's livelihoods, are egalitarian (or at a minimum democratic), and allow for the conservation of environmental resources. Ostrom argues against Hardin's (1968) influential argument about the "tragedy of the commons," which states that commonly owned resources will be vulnerable to excessive use and abuse because each user's individual rational interest will lead them to maximize their short-term gain from the resource, whereas if the resource were owned by individuals, they would seem to maximize their long-term gain. For Ostrom, instead, with the institutions and rules governing use in place, collective groups could manage and use common resources without depleting them.

Starting in the 1970s, a series of policy efforts in Asia and Latin America attempted to formalize common property arrangements. In the late 1970s, Mark Poffenberger of the Ford Foundation's Indian office began to collaborate with two projects designed to involve forest dwellers in conservation projects and to share revenues with them. One project was with foresters in West Bengal, and a second was in Haryana, led by Madhu Sarin, who would go on to be a co-organizer of the CSD and an author of the FRA. Poffenberger and the Ford Foundation organized a series of meetings with sympathetic forest officials and activists from across India (and soon from across South and Southeast Asia) to promote participatory forest management.

These efforts culminated in the incorporation of the JFM program into the 1988 National Forest Policy and the above-mentioned 1990 JFM Guidelines. Neither granted forest dwellers rights to forest land, but they established institutions, JFM committees, to share revenues with the Forest Department and participate in conservation. Sarin, who had been involved in some of the early attempts at participatory forest management that the JFM policy was based on, told me in a 2012 interview that she saw the failure to grant land rights as a betrayal of the original project. JFM committees, she said, were now no more than agents of the Forest Department, and they were complicit in the eviction of unauthorized forest dwellers, as they had been in Ramnagar.

The project of common resource management in forests, however, had a second legal life after the JFM policy, in the community forest rights provision of the FRA. In interviews with activists involved with the CSD, I found that many saw the community rights provision as recognizing an indigenous tradition of environmental protection and common property. For Geeta and the Sangathan, however, this putatively indigenous tradition was being aligned with a leftist tradition of common ownership to create a new legal tactic that would escape the legal obstacles posed by the local administration's reading of the FRA. A collective claim to land and forest management through the FRA implies the existence of a collective social unit that will own and manage the land. But the legal future promised by Geeta and promoted by Thankappan through collective claims had the unexpected result of enabling a fracture in Ramnagar. Over the winter of 2011, I began to hear more frequent accusations by villagers who were not Agarias of the Agarias practicing jativadi—that is, favoring members of their community over the others. As the political project foundered, so too did the forms of identification that had been associated with it.

Jativadi

One day in January 2012, while I was staying in Govindnagar with Lalti and Shankar, both members of the Ghasiya caste, we walked over to the Agaria hamlet for a chat with Ram Lakhan and the others to discuss the possibility of the villagers filing legal cases against the Forest Department officers who had recently filed cases against five villagers for occupying forest land illegally and cutting down trees. "If they file cases against us, we'll file cases against them!" Shankar had brought the paperwork for the case along with him, and he and Lalti were collecting the statements of villagers who either were not literate or lacked comfort with the legal forms.

Water and some snacks had been served, but as the sun set and it grew dark, we all began to grow hungry. Baldeva went inside their hut and began to cook. At around 8:00 p.m., she started coming out with plates piled with steaming heaps of rice, dal, and potatoes, but only served them to Ram Lakhan and the two other Agarias present. Shankar and the visitors from the other hamlet said nothing while they were eating, but when we started walking back from the hamlet after 11:00 p.m., they began to complain: "We would never do anything like that. If they came to our homes, we would either feed them or wait until they left!" "How can they leave us hungry like that while they are eating?" "This is just jativadi."

I began to hear complaints and accusations of jativadi more and more frequently among the displaced Ramnagaris. Shankar, Lalti, and other non-Agarias claimed that the Agarias had abandoned the forms of reciprocity that held the movement for Ramnagar together. Not only that, but in privileging their jati over the categories of solidaristic identification assumed by the Sangathan's struggle—Dalit, Adivasi, worker—they were undermining the struggle itself. As Lalti had asked me, "How can we win if we are divided?"

A new form of caste identification had emerged, both through the BSP's electoral politics and through the Sangathan-organized land occupation, that drew together Agarias, Chamars, and Ghasiyas first into the equated categories of Dalit and Adivasi and then, as needed, into workers. These forms of solidarity could be drawn on in collective action around land rights and workers' rights but also produced everyday forms of reciprocity that indexed long-term solidarities: sharing food and helping in one another's fields. The withdrawal of these everyday forms of reciprocity, in turn, was taken to index the return of an older form of caste-community-based, or jati-based, solidarity.

If the accusation of jativadi itself only ran from non-Agarias to Agarias, the emergent talk of jatis ran in both directions. In the Agaria settlement, when Shankar and Lalti were out of hearing distance, I would hear Ram Lakhan and his friends complain about them. "These Ghasiyas, they're always bothering us, telling us what to do. Always disturbing us." The political project that had built Ramnagar was breaking down and a form of caste identification and solidarity was breaking down along with it, at least between the Agarias and the others.

Among the villagers who were not Agarias and who were still politically aligned with Geeta, the categories of Dalit and Adivasi still held. If anything, the categories came to be used more interchangeably than before, as the new potential legal future that was promised by a collective claim no longer required all claimants to be members of Scheduled Tribes.

The divisions among the Ramnagaris had deepened by 2012, and alliances in the area had been reshuffled in ways I had not anticipated a year earlier. Communication between the Agarias and others had diminished, and Ram Lakhan and the Agaria leadership were making new alliances. On the eastern side of the village, past the Agaria settlement, a grove of trees had been cut down and several new huts had been built by the very Yadavs who had been involved in the attack. I asked Baldeva Agaria about the huts, and she said that there had been nothing anyone in Ramnagar could do to stop it. The Yadavs, through the JICA-funded JFM committee, enclosed the land, ostensibly to conserve it, but then they started building huts on it. "But how will the Forest Department allow that?" I asked. She said that she was not sure, but that her husband Ram Lakhan, who still had considerable authority among the Agarias, had been visiting the recently arrived Yadavs over the previous few days, offering them a deal. "If we STs [Scheduled Tribes] file for community rights, then it does not matter who files for rights with us," she explained.

Geeta had proposed a new legal tactic that took advantage of the ambiguity in the FRA's procedures for community claims to allow both Scheduled Tribes and non–Scheduled Tribes to claim land only based on proof that they had lived there before 2005, and not for seventy-five years as was required for non–Scheduled Tribes for individual claims. But this ambiguity, it appeared, was in fact enabling joint claims and a new alliance between the Agarias and the Yadavs.

Ram Lakhan and the Agarias had entered a solidaristic relationship with the members of other Scheduled Castes and Tribes who made up Ramnagar and a patronage relationship with Geeta to escape the patronage relationships that existed with the Yadavs. Now, in response to Geeta's replacement of him with Lalti as Ramnagar's leader, Ram Lakhan was returning to the old patrons as replacements for the new one. If, however, the Ramnagaris had land, the patronage relationship with the Yadavs would change. They might work on Yadav property again, but they would do so only with the option of also refusing to work and instead working on their own land or migrating out of Duddhi to work. And they might perform various political favors for the Yadavs, but they would do so with the always-present possibility of refusing the favors and returning to Ramnagar and Geeta's patronage.

Questions remain, however. Why and how did a political project that aimed to end the personalized patronage relationships that Ramnagar's villagers found themselves in continue to produce new patronage relationships? Why did the villagers need to turn to Geeta in the first place to escape the Yadavs? Why did Ram Lakhan go to Pandhari Yadav, the district magistrate, to get around Geeta? Why was he approaching the Yadavs again, to escape Geeta? Why, moreover, did the everyday and domestic forms of labor associated with economic and caste-based patronage relationships carry over to the villagers' relationship with Geeta?

Patronage here appears to be recalcitrant, persisting and reappearing even as the participants of the relationship or their political project changed. It persists both as individuated and personalized labor relations and as a set of domestic labor practices. It appears to persist as a habitus, an expectation on Geeta's part that is easily fulfilled by the Dalit and Adivasi villagers of Ramnagar that, despite forgoing a middle-class life in a larger city in order to be an activist, she would not have to sweep her own floor, cook her own food, wash her own clothes, or carry her own bags. It simultaneously persists as a mode of access to state resources: the Dalit and Adivasi villagers do not have unmediated access to state actors or state institutions. They expect certain state actors to be biased against them in favor of higher-caste groups, such as Forest Department officials or Samajwadi Party representatives, and after their failed individual claims, they do not expect to achieve justice through the formal mechanisms of state institutions either. State actors, whether acting through the formal procedures of the law or as potentially bribed individuals, would not recognize their land claims.

Caste categories, as a number of recent studies have argued (e.g., Rao 2009; Deshpande 2013; Subramanian 2015), are not the fixed social categories that many social scientists imagine them to be. They have, instead, emerged through political projects, bringing people together to demand new rights or to consolidate existing privileges. In Ramnagar, however, caste categories have not only appeared; they have also disappeared. Political projects are tied to the production of futures, and to the extent that the futures promised do not arrive, the caste categories associated with the mobilization toward that future becomes imperiled. Collective action, as Geeta told me at the rally in Duddhi, not only demonstrates the collective's strength to state actors and publics outside of the collective but also demonstrates the collective's existence and its strength to its own members. In Ramnagar, the weakening of the possible future tied to the collective action seems to have weakened the collective identification itself.

The problem for the Ramnagaris, however, was that the collective action through which they attempted to gain land rights required the presence of a patron. What Geeta called "skills"—her legal knowledge and social and cultural capital in state spaces from Robertsganj to Delhi—was not something that she could teach the Ramnagaris, despite her efforts. The explicit denotational meaning given to their collective protests therefore had to be provided by someone who had legal knowledge and social capital that are unknown among landless Dalits and Adivasis. The legalization of politics, then, provides the conditions of possibility for a reproduction of patronage.

The new skills, legal tactics, and political possibilities opened by the land occupation movement, however, had lives beyond the purposes Geeta intended them to have. Ram Lakhan and the Agarias did not give up on the goal of gaining land rights when they distanced themselves from Geeta, the rest of the village, and the solidaristic categories that had once brought them together. They continued to attempt to gain land rights through the very legal means, community claims, that Geeta had proposed to the entire village.

Nonetheless, Geeta's political patronage was evaluated differently by Ram Lakhan and the Agaria men who made up the older political class of the village and Lalti and the mostly non-Agaria women who made up the newer political class. For Ram Lakhan, the relationship was transactional: the villagers were to protest when and where Geeta told them to and to defer to her when she was present, in exchange for her procuring land rights for them. For Lalti, the relationship was a solidaristic one that presented different possibilities: Geeta's patronage was transformative, changing her relationship with state actors, with higher castes, and with men in and outside the village. The arrival of land rights or their failure to arrive had not shaken her affection for the woman who she called her "big sister." Patronage as a social form, in other words, cannot be reduced to a transactional or a solidaristic essence: as with laws for Moore (1978), a formal continuity or identity can in fact mask dissent and rupture.

A New Opening

Matthew Hull (2012) argues that we should consider state institutions as collective agents themselves. Bureaucratic organizations, he writes, are "a social form designed for collective action, a social technology for aligning the efforts of a large number of people so that they act as one" (129). Hull recognizes that this is a tentative achievement, however, and this alignment of individual state agents into a single, coordinated collective agent does not always occur in India's forest belt. On the one hand, Gupta's (1995) discourse of corruption frequently reduces the actions of state institutions to the self-interested actions of individuals. On the other hand, state institutions often do not coordinate with one another and even act at cross-purposes, as happened when the JFM committee and the BSP aligned behind different constituencies and different interpretations of the law in Ramnagar.

The disaggregation of the state along these lines is common, but action by state actors can be understood as collective action in a second sense: to the extent that individuals act on behalf of the state, they do so by indexing a range of others, whether present or absent, on whom they can call. The threats issued by police officers become conditional futures or rules enforced not only through the gun or stick they may carry but also through their ability to call on other police officers, not to mention the court and prison systems, for support. In many cases, these state actors appear to be aligned, but in the area around Ramnagar, this apparent alignment was absent and these conditional futures could be challenged, their rules weakened.

The attack on Ramnagar in 2011 was initiated by one set of actors with access to state resources, and it was stopped by a second. The series of efforts by the Ramnagaris to claim rights can be seen as a series of efforts to align their cause with the collective action of state actors, such as the Forest Rights Committee and the district magistrate, to protect against the Forest Department. My conversations with Ram Lakhan, Baldeva, and others often took the shape of analyses of such state actors, the logics according to which they operated and the openings that they provided. In the spring, an apparent loss of access to one state actor would ultimately provide such an opening.

In March 2012, the BSP, which had ruled the state since 2007, was voted out of power. The BSP had campaigned on a range of policies favorable to Dalits, including the redistribution of land to the landless (Lerche 1999). The party had aligned itself with the Ramnagaris on several occasions, including the previous September when a representative of the party had stopped the attack on their village. The discourse of corruption identified by Gupta was not the only idiom through which Ramnagaris analyzed state actors. Caste was also central. As other work on North Indian politics has noted (Lerche 1999; Michelutti 2004), the state was not sequestered from the social relations of caste; its actors both emerged out of caste relations and acted to shape them, as for example the police forces describes by Jeffrey (2001) are understood to be acting on behalf of the landowning castes that make up their ranks. State actors are able to act by indexing the possible collective action of nonstate actors, and nonstate actors are able to act by indexing the collective action of state actors. And so, without the pro-Dalit BSP in power, it appeared, the Ramnagaris had lost their access to and ability to invoke state actors and thus much of the force of their own collective action, their ability to establish conditional futures.

The new representative to the state assembly was an independent candidate named Parvati Gond, a new politician who was herself Adivasi. Geeta and the Ramnagaris began to discuss the possibility of courting her support. As an independent, she did not have the clear constituencies that parties provide. At Geeta's urging, Lalti, Ram Lakhan, Baldeva, and the others decided to attempt to win her support by inviting Gond to hold a rally in Ramnagar. Gond's own political future, as a first-time representative, was in doubt, and so the Ramnagaris hoped to align their future with hers, to join what Cody (2020) calls her "wave," in order to protect both.

In April, Parvati Gond came to a rally for the Ramnagaris in Govindnagar. In a clearing, the Ramnagaris erected a large tent, set up loudspeakers, and cooked a meal for hundreds. Vendors, anticipating the crowd that would come, gathered around the compound's entry, selling boiled eggs and tea. An audience of hundreds arrived, most of them Adivasis and Dalits from villages established by the Sangathan. The village council leadership was absent, although a few dominant-caste men lurked around the edges of the rally.

Geeta took the microphone first, to introduce Gond. Gond was on the side of the "public," Geeta said, using the English word in her Hindi speech to refer to the area's landless. She understood the historic injustice that had been committed against the landless and was going to work to reverse the decisions to deny them rights. Gond, a woman in her late thirties dressed in a purple silk sari, had worked as a doctor before running for office, and she took the stage with some hesitation, without the easy stage manner of most politicians. She would reconstitute the Forest Rights Committee, Gond said, this time including residents of Ramnagar, and she would ask the committee to reconsider its decision. She would make their movement strong and take control of the implementation of the Forest Rights Act herself. Moved by her rhetoric, the crowd began to cheer. Gond was growing more comfortable, and she closed on a militant note, raising her voice as she promised to align herself and the state resources she controlled with the Ramnagaris' future even beyond the bounds of legality: "Now we will fight with the law. If we do not win with the law, then we will do what we have to do!"

Word of the new representative's declaration of support was carried in at least two local newspapers the next day, intimating not a change in the text of the FRA but a new range of state collective actors aligned with the Ramnagaris. The Forest Rights Committee was not reconstituted, despite Gond's assurances, but, with the planting season approaching, the Ramnagaris took Gond's declaration of support to be sufficient protection to begin to move back to Ramnagar. Slowly, a few at a time, they began to rebuild their huts and to prepare the fields to plant lentils, wheat, and potatoes. The text of the FRA had not changed, but through Gond's support, the Ramnagaris had rearranged the conditional futures that they and their attackers faced and had changed the rules of life in the area to allow their return. Gond did not authorize a resettlement of Ramnagar, and she failed to reconstitute the Forest Rights Committee, as she had assured the Ramnagaris she would. The Forest Department and police officers who, it was hoped, would protect—or at least refrain from attacking—a rebuilt Ramnagar were never informed of their new roles.

Without deeds to the land or authorization by the Forest Rights Committee, the Ramnagaris had found a tentative solution to the problem of the forest by rearranging their relationship to the state. By the time the rains arrived, Ramnagar had nearly reached its original strength of two hundred–odd people. To maintain Gond's support, villagers continued to attend her rallies, leaving their fields to travel for hours to attend rallies that had nothing to do with Ramnagar. The goal, Ram Lakhan explained to me, was to be the most visible part of

Gond's constituency. The threat, the conditional future, implied by their presence was the loss of that constituency if she did not continue to support the Ramnagaris' struggle. In turn, Gond's public support for the Ramnagaris, which did not include an explicit authorization of the village's resettlement, was enough to produce a new set of conditional futures and consequent set of rules through which dominant-caste men would not attack for the time being. State actors, including the police and the Forest Department, played a crucial role in the events that led to Ramnagar being resettled, and yet a conditional future that included their collective action was produced without the Ramnagaris coordinating with them at all. The divisions along lines of jati and gender were by no means resolved, but Gond's support and the possibility of resettling the village allowed for a temporary détente.

The meaning of the FRA was continuing to be redefined and contested in Duddhi, as political projects enacted through it challenged existing hierarchies and economic relations. Similar contests over the law's meaning were being played out across India's forest belt, with compounded effects that came to be perceived at state and national scales. The law, it turned out, seemed to draw together scales of politics, in which reworking and rereadings at one scale had effects at others. Preservationists challenged the law's constitutionality in high courts and in the Supreme Court, and forest rights activists worked to maintain the law's constitutionality through lower courts that did not have the formal authority to rule on constitutional matters. The FRA, drafted in Delhi because of mobilization in the forests, had been brought to forests by a range of political networks such as the Sangathan and the Banwasi Seva Ashram. Now, as the law produced new mobilizations against dispossession and new occupations of land nationally, it came to challenge economic relations at a much larger scale. In the next chapter, I travel from Sonbhadra to Delhi to track the ongoing collective mobilizations to contest the meaning of the Forest Rights Act at the national scale.

NATIONAL POLITICS AND THE SCALES
OF THE FOREST RIGHTS ACT

One afternoon early in my fieldwork in June 2009, I accompanied Geeta, Shubha, and Baldeva on a visit to the district magistrate of Sonbhadra, Pandhari Yadav, in his office in the district headquarters, Robertsganj. The three women had arranged the meeting to challenge the arrest of Aadesh, a man who lived in Ramnagar and whom the police had charged with poaching animals in a forest close to Ramnagar. The police in Sonbhadra report to the district magistrate, and the three women were hoping that Yadav would be able to have the charges against Aadesh dropped.

It was a Sunday and Yadav was not in his office, but at one side of the walled compound on the outskirts of Robertsganj where he lived was a structure where he met visitors. The four of us entered the building through a heavy, fortified door and were seated in an antechamber by a receptionist, who pushed a buzzer to announce our arrival to Yadav, whom he respectfully addressed with the Arabic-derived term for master: "DM *sahib*." Five minutes later, we were ushered in to the meeting room along with a small group of others who had come to meet the district magistrate.

Cody (2009) has pointed to continuities between a bureaucrat's public meeting room in South India and the *darbar* hall, the room in which precolonial kings would meet visitors and hear supplicants, both in the stance taken by the bureaucrat to visitors and in the hall's spatial arrangement. Such continuities between the royal patron and the bureaucrat-patron were evident here in North India. A large wooden desk was placed on an elevated platform at one end of the room. Facing the platform were ten rows of plastic chairs. On the wall behind the desk a series of images had been hung: a reproduction of a painting of Gandhi, another of the anticolonial socialist Bhagat Singh with an inscription at its bottom indicating that it had been donated by the All India Youth Congress, and the images of a number of Hindu gods. On the desk were two telephones, a stack of papers, and a marble sign that had been engraved "P. K. Yadav, IAS," short for "Indian Administrative Service." Yadav entered the room and began to hold court, asking each visitor in turn what we had come to see him about, but only offering his attention in drops, a nod at a time, with interruptions to take phone calls or sign the papers his assistant pushed in front of him.

When it was our turn, Geeta spoke. She and Yadav had met before, and she dispensed with the pose of supplicant that the other visitors had adopted, choosing instead to address him respectfully but as an equal. She introduced the case: Aadesh had been charged the previous week, she said, and not only was he not guilty of poaching, but the police in fact no longer had jurisdiction over poaching cases in the area. Geeta argued that the Forest Rights Act (FRA) gave this authority to the newly created Forest Rights Committees, which were to be composed entirely of forest dwellers. Yadav disagreed. He had read the act in its entirety, he said, and Geeta was misinterpreting the role that it laid out for the Forest Rights Committees. They could manage what it termed minor forest produce, but jurisdiction over poaching cases still lay with the police and the courts.

Their discussion grew heated, and the conflict resolved only when Geeta pulled out her cellular phone to show the district magistrate that she had on her phone the numbers of six members of the committee that had written the first draft of the FRA. "Which one shall I call," she asked Yadav, "to tell us what they meant?" Geeta's demonstration of her superior access to the law's authors enabled a temporary victory. Without needing to follow through on her suggestion and make any phone calls or even show or read aloud the names on her phone, Geeta's indication of her access to people who had been involved in the law's drafting led Yadav to concede her point.

The victory was limited. Yadav agreed to look into the case, but the charges against Aadesh were not ultimately dropped. In a court, Geeta's argument would not have been effective. The intentions of the authors of a bill cannot be cited to change the interpretation of the law. Yet in the district magistrate's office that day, Geeta's indexing of direct social ties to a number of the law's authors granted her an interpretive authority that trumped both Yadav's formal authority and the authority he had gained from reading the law's text. Her invocation of unnamed drafters with political and legal authorities, which were unnamed and yet, as Gupta and Ferguson (2002) put it, were "above" and "encompassing" of Yadav's authorities, held sway.

This book so far has proceeded through a gradual narrowing of scale: to answer the question of how Ramnagar was built and destroyed, it began with the Emergency and the production of forests as a national political problematic in its aftermath, tracked the emergence of a national movement for forest rights and the drafting of the FRA, and finally followed the FRA to Ramnagar and Govindnagar. And yet despite this narrowing of focus, it is clear that the struggle over Ramnagar and thousands of other forest villages has never been distinct from larger scales of politics. The ability to call on villagers from across the district, journalists in other towns, courts in larger cities, and larger national movements—reframing the terms and scale of their politics at each moment—was key to the successes of the Sangathan. The ability to invoke, even without naming or calling on the phone, Delhi-based activists who were involved in the drafting of the law allowed for Geeta's minor victory over the district magistrate that day in 2009.

The FRA emerged, as I detailed in chapter 1, following an incorporation of forests within India's political economy. Such an expansion of scale, bringing in new spaces and populations, has long been argued to be central to the logic of capitalist accumulation (Luxemburg 1913; Smith 1990; Harvey 1999). Brenner (2001) has suggested that we approach contentious politics as similarly operating through an ongoing rescaling, a rearrangement of the spatial, temporal, and social parameters through which politics are made. Indeed, as chapter 1 details, the movement for the FRA emerged through such a rescaling, as forests were brought into a national political infrastructure.

Yet, in its circulation, the new law allowed for a shift in the topology of these scales. It traveled between Delhi, Lucknow, and Ramnagar, and its interpretation in one site that was ostensibly the scalar subordinate—"below" and "encompassed by" in Gupta and Ferguson's terms—could be drawn on and used to challenge interpretations in other, ostensibly superior sites. Legal meaning may be shaped through collective action and interpretive discourses that circulate independently of laws, but this ongoing reshaping of legal meaning takes place through the invocation both of what Moore (1978) has described as the regularities in the symbolic form of legal texts and of ongoing efforts to present shifts in legal meaning as continuities. In other words, the circulation of legal text along with an ideological presupposition that the meaning of that text is or should be consistent across scales and sites enables new claims and relationships across those sites. Such a presupposition is given doctrinal form by the Common Law principle of *stare decisis*, the doctrine that courts must follow not only statutory law but also precedents set by earlier courts in deciding cases.

This chapter turns to the new scalar politics enabled by the FRA. It begins with a consideration of the multiscalar legal politics in which the forest rights movement participated, taking advantage of the mobility of the new law across legal scales to play courts and other sites of interpretation off one another. I then turn to the political-economic implications of the law, as it came to be contested not only in forests and courtrooms but also in the national media by corporate lobbyists and economists. As millions claimed land rights, one of the largest rearrangements of property relations in independent Indian history was underway. The FRA, passed as a measure to gain hegemony within a population that had frequently been dispossessed by accumulation, began to be seen by representatives of large companies as threatening accumulation itself. A new set of contests began to take shape between these representatives, state actors, and forest rights activists over the text and meaning of the FRA.

Judicial Scales

In August 2011, I was in the office of Uma, the Delhi-based lawyer who, as I discussed in chapter 2, circulated the Supreme Court orders that the Ministry of Environment and Forests (MoEF) cited in its 2002 eviction drive in forests across the country. Uma and I were discussing the increasing hostility of the court and forest bureaucracy to forest dwellers and the uses and abuses of public interest litigation, including the 1996 *Godavarman v. Union of India* case discussed in chapter 2, through which the Court had claimed broad authority over forest matters.

I brought up a public interest litigation that a group of conservationists and retired forest officers had filed in the Court, which seemed to me to be another instance of forest bureaucrats working together with the court against land rights for forest dwellers. I had not heard any updates on the case in several years and wanted to know the latest developments.

In 2008, four groups, led by the Bombay Natural History Society, India's oldest environmental conservationist group, and a number of retired forest officers, filed identical petitions in a number of regional high courts for a public interest litigation that challenged the FRA on constitutional grounds. The petition made eighteen arguments against the act, including the following:

1. Parliament does not have the authority to pass a law like the FRA that concerns land and land rights, which under the Constitution fall under the authority of state legislatures.
2. The FRA would not in fact correct the "historical injustice" that its preamble claims it would. By giving forest dwellers rights to forest land, the law would force them "to live at subsistence level" with "no access to public

health facilities, education, power, sanitation, public distribution system, etc. without any other source of income or livelihood other than selling or transferring the land that may be allotted to them under the said Act." (Bombay Natural History Society & Ors. v. Union of India & Ors.)

3. The FRA, in giving rights to public forest land to private individuals, violates the right of the broader public to the "ecological importance and benefits derived from forests." (Bombay Natural History Society & Ors. v. Union of India & Ors.)

The petition argued that the law was not only a case of Parliament overstepping its constitutional authority in passing a law that granted land rights, but it in fact furthered the very historical injustice that it claimed to be undoing. Debi Goenka, a conservationist associated with the Bombay Natural History Society and one of the authors of the petition, explained to me in a 2008 interview that the law gave forest dwellers low-quality land that they would not be able to farm productively and did not allow them to sell it. They would be tied to a piece of land, he said, that would not be able to support them, and they would not be able to move to cities in search of more remunerative employment. Not only forest dwellers would be hurt by the FRA, however. The petition also invoked as a victim of the law the "public," discussed in chapter 1, whose right of access to and enjoyment of the environmental benefits of forest land was threatened by the granting of use and tenure rights to forest dwellers.

When the petitions were filed in 2008, they seemed to threaten the future of the FRA, presenting the possibility that it would be struck down before it went into effect. In our 2011 meeting, however, Uma did not seem concerned about the petitions.

"Oh, they all went straight to the Supreme Court Forest Bench," she explained. "They were identical, so the Supreme Court asked to hear them all together." But what had happened to them? "Nothing! We have had ways of preventing the Court from hearing them."

I pressed her: "What sort of ways?"

"Oh, I can't tell you that," she replied, smiling.

Uma explained that whatever other means were available to it, she hoped the forest rights movement would be able to use the authority of lower courts against the challenge to the act in the Supreme Court. By 2011, 1.23 million land titles had already been distributed under the FRA (Shrivastava 2011). Each year, dozens of cases had made their way to local and high courts. The courts had seen debates of the act's meaning, but in their rulings, they had always assumed that the law was constitutional. "In India," Uma explained to me, "high courts are constitutional courts, and their rulings therefore apply nationally." The Supreme Court is the country's apex court and it can reverse high court verdicts, but as more and more titles were distributed, overturning the FRA would both pose a political problem and would require the Court to reverse the precedents of the constitutional judgments already implicitly established by the high courts. Withdrawing land rights from more than one million families whose rights had already been recognized would surely present a greater threat of political unrest than had existed before the act, written in part to quell such unrest, was passed. And as more rulings in the high courts assumed the constitutionality of the act, the Supreme Court would face greater obstacles in challenging its constitutionality.

Uma's hopes seemed to be borne out in the years following our meeting. In August 2012, the Bombay Natural History Society, the most prominent party to the petition, quietly withdrew its support without explanation. The case languished in the years that followed, with the occasional hearing conducted but no judgments issued. The Supreme Court might occupy the highest and most enveloping position in the spatial imaginary of the Indian judiciary, but its capacity to overturn the decisions of lower bodies was being constrained by procedural and political considerations.

The growing political infrastructure that tied forest dwellers to New Delhi enabled this reversal of the relations between scales of the judiciary. The more cases forest rights groups brought to the high and lower courts to adjudicate on the meaning of the FRA while assuming its constitutionality, and the faster such groups helped forest dwellers claim rights, the greater the political threat forest dwellers would pose and the greater the legal obstacle would be if the Supreme Court overturned the FRA. As discussed in chapter 1, the Supreme Court had claimed vast authority over India's forests, derived from its writ of continuing mandamus in the 1996 *Godvarman* case. In 2002, the MoEF had cited this authority in initiating the eviction drive that inspired the movement for the FRA. By 2012 the Court and the MoEF seemed to have had their authority checked, as Uma and the Campaign for Survival and Dignity members who had first pushed for the new law had intended.

The court system, however, was in no way irrelevant to the ongoing contests across the country to establish the meaning of the FRA—*who* would get *what* land through the law and what they would be able to do with the land after they received titles. Geeta and dozens of villagers in Ramnagar had been taken to court by the Forest Department, charged with trespassing on forest land, illegally cutting down trees, and, in Geeta's case, threatening public order and security. Geeta and the villagers responded with their own set of court challenges.

Lawyers regularly dropped by Geeta's Robertsganj flat, strategizing which courts to take to which forest officers on what ground. They would take a case to the Allahabad High Court, the high court nearest to Sonbhadra, where they suspected that at least one judge would be friendly to the forest rights cause. "If they file cases against us, we will file cases back against them," Shankar had told me, and they charged the Forest Department with assaulting them and with illegally destroying their homes. The FRA, Geeta and the lawyers argued, forbade the Forest Department from evicting anyone until all claims had been settled, and they did not consider the Ramnagaris' claims to have been settled.

But courts in Sonbhadra were only one site among many in which the law's meaning was being worked out, and courts were only one of many sets of state resources that the villagers drew on. Courts could be expected to fix the meaning of the law in certain ways, introducing a limited regularity to legal meaning, but they were among multiple institutions to be entered and used according to need. Courts were considered against other state resources, with authorities and jurisdictions at other scales.

The FRA—its text, the circulating interpretations of that text, the institutions and movements citing and regularizing those interpretations, the existing political narratives that become legally grounded in the text through these citations, and the political and property relationships being rearranged through these political projects—brought together subjects of politics in new arrangements across sites and scales. Its broad circulation by forest rights activists and other groups meant that any debate over its meaning in Delhi was susceptible to arguments about the millions of people who were using the law outside of Delhi. Just as contests over the law's meaning in Ramnagar challenged local political and economic relations between landless Dalits and Adivasis and land-owning members of dominant castes, in contests over its meaning in Delhi, the aggregated populations claiming land through the FRA came to be seen as challenges to nationally scaled political and economic relations.

Enclosure and Accumulation

In the first decade of the new millennium, India began to be hailed widely as an economic success story: from 2003 to 2010, the country's gross domestic product (GDP) grew at a rate of 7 or 8 percent each year except 2008. In 2001, Chair of Goldman Sachs Asset Management Jim O'Neill classified India along with Brazil, Russia, and China as a member of the BRIC group of countries— that is, relatively poor countries whose economies he forecasted would grow faster than the G7 group of major industrial economies and which therefore, he argued, should play a larger role in global economic governance (O'Neill et al. 2001). India was positioned as a second China, an Asian country whose economy was set to grow rapidly enough for it to become a major power.

Capturing the mood of the moment, economist S. S. A. Aiyar wrote in a white paper for the Cato Institute in 2011 that

> the Indian elephant has indeed morphed into a tiger. It averaged 8.5 percent growth in the last decade and survived the Great Recession of 2007–09 with only minor bumps before returning to 8.5 percent growth in 2010–11. Its per capita income has shot up from $300 in 1991 to almost $1,700 today, and its GDP this year will exceed $2 trillion in nominal terms and maybe $4.5 trillion in PPP (purchasing power parity) terms, which would make it the third-largest economy in the world after the United States and China. It is hailed today as a potential superpower and has been proposed by the United States for a permanent seat on the United Nations Security Council. Political analysts see it as perhaps the only credible Asian check on Chinese hegemony in the 21st century. Many analysts (including Goldman Sachs, who coined the term BRICs to mean Brazil, Russia, India, and China) predict that India will soon overtake China as the fastest-growing economy in the world. (2)

Yet there was evidence that what Harvey (2003, 67) calls "accumulation by dispossession"—or what Smith (2011, 4) calls "enclosure"—played a key role in the rapid growth of India's GDP in these years, that the vast profits that underpinned this GDP growth were built less on commodity production and trade than on the enclosure of already existing value through dispossession, extraction, and rent-seeking. Ahmed and Varshney (2012) have argued along such lines that the country's "crony capitalism" resulted in capital accumulation being directed toward businesses with close connections to the government. *The Economist* observed in 2014 that India's "politically connected" firms outperformed the stock market dramatically between 2009 and 2011, and that some 17 percent of India's GDP growth in 2008 was made by billionaires in "rent-seeking sectors" such as mining and property (*The Economist* 2014).

"Politically connected firms" and "crony capitalism" name relationships between capital, corporations, and the state. They name groups engaged in collective action. The collectives that this book has tracked so far, whether in Ramnagar or in Delhi, have included forest dwellers and have acted in their name, whether those forest dwellers were the Ramnagaris or their dominant-caste attackers. Ramnagaris and the Sangathan can be seen as part of a larger range of mobilizations that observers have noted in India in recent decades, mobilizations that challenge enclosure and dispossession (e.g., Sanyal 2013; Chatterjee 2008; Levien 2018). These various antienclosure mobilizations would, however, themselves produce a collective reaction, as groups that acted on behalf of fractions of Indian capital began to identify threats to their profits and India's economy. These national-level struggles would in turn bring attention to the FRA and the transformations it was bringing to India's forests, and they would once again reshape the law's meaning.

The observation that political connections were enabling the large corporate profits of the first decade of the twenty-first century was echoed in a charge that was leveled by a movement against corruption that would mobilize large numbers of people across India's cities. In March 2010, the Comptroller and Auditor General of India, which supervises state accounting, released a report accusing the United Progressive Alliance (UPA) government of auctioning 2G wireless spectrum to a few private companies that had close ties to the government for US$28 billion less than its market value. In May 2010, transcripts of tapes recorded by the Directorate General of Income Tax Collection of conversations between a corporate lobbyist and various politicians in the ruling party were published in the magazines *Open* and *Outlook*. The transcripts seemed to reveal a conspiracy between the corporation and senior politicians to bend laws and manipulate public opinion for their shared profit.

Some journalists and academics argued that the leak revealed the inner workings of the Indian state: its full corruption was now visible, as was the complicity of major Indian capitalists and journalists with that corruption. In the government's defense, its finance minister Montek Singh Ahluwahlia argued in a January 2011 interview that subsidies to corporations were necessary to allow them to build important infrastructure such as the cellular network. He argued that the goal of the 2G spectrum auction had not been to raise revenue for the state but, in fact, to keep prices low for companies to facilitate the spread of a "transformative technology" (*Business Standard India* 2011).

Such arguments did little to stop the storm of criticism the government was facing. In November 2010, Webb (2012) recounts, what had been a small, largely ignored protest at New Delhi's Jantar Mantar grew into a demonstration of twenty-two thousand. Coordinated by an organization called India Against Corruption and led by Anna Hazare, an activist and social reformer from Maharashtra, the movement quickly spread across India's large and small cities. Magazines and news channels provided enthusiastic coverage of the nascent movement, representing its participants back to themselves, to nonparticipants, and to state actors. The movement's leadership made demands on the state that were echoed and emphasized by reporters: to create an entirely independent Jan Lokpal, or people's protector, with the power to investigate and punish corruption at all levels of the state.

Akhil Gupta's (1995) "discourse of corruption," explaining inexplicable state actions in terms of corruption, here formed the grounds for a large national movement. Like the Campaign for Survival and Dignity during its push to shape and pass the FRA, the anticorruption movement drew on idioms of protest that presented their movement within the time-space of the Indian independence struggle. Anna Hazare, dressed in white, sat in front of a photo of Gandhi and went on a hunger strike to force Parliament to pass a bill to create an agency that would investigate and punish state corruption.

Sanjoy Chakravorty (2013) estimates that rural land prices increased between five and twenty times over the first decade of this century, driven by cheap credit, rising incomes, and a search for assets in which untaxed wealth could be invested. Along with these rising prices came an increasing use of eminent domain to gain increasingly expensive rural land. Another set of mobilizations, less centrally coordinated than either the forest rights or anticorruption movements, took shape against the use of eminent domain to claim agricultural land in India. Starting in the 1990s, organizations of the nonparty Left began to protest the use of the 1894 Land Acquisition Act to acquire mostly agricultural land for public infrastructure and private real estate developments. The *Narmada Bachao Andolan* (Movement to Save the Narmada), a movement against the massive Sardar Sarovar Dam in Western India, gained visibility over the 1990s and 2000s, and its leadership soon built a larger coalition of organizations, the National Alliance of People's Movements, oriented around antidispossession movements.

In 2005, the UPA passed the Special Economic Zone (SEZ) Act. SEZs are enclaves created by state governments to attract investment by relaxing import and export duties, taxes, and labor standards. Levien (2012) estimates that the six hundred SEZs approved by 2012 would occupy half a million acres of land across the country. The antidispossession movement, what Levien calls India's "land wars" (934), grew, both through political parties and through umbrella organizations such as the National Alliance of People's Movements, to struggle against SEZs as well.

Attempts by the Communist Party of India (Marxist) to use the SEZ Act in West Bengal to build a car factory and a petrochemical plant spurred local protests that were quickly drawn into both Maoist politics and a campaign by the rival Trinamool Congress Party that was central to the Communist Party's loss in the 2011 state elections (*Hindustan Times* 2021). Attempts by the Bahujan Samaj Party government to use the Land Acquisition Act to dispossess villagers in Uttar Pradesh to build a new expressway produced a mobilization that led to the kidnapping of two police officers, a gun battle between farmers and police, and the Congress politician Rahul Gandhi joining a protest against the project (*Economic Times* 2011). The rate of new approvals of SEZs declined quickly, and by 2013, the government passed a new act to govern land acquisition, the Right to Fair Compensation and Transparency in Land Acquisition, Rehabilitation and Resettlement Act, which replaced the 1894 Act. The new act requires that 80 percent of families affected by land acquisition provide consent for the transfer of land to the government, and it provides for greater compensation for those whose property or livelihood is affected by land acquisition.

India Against Corruption, the mobilizations against agrarian dispossession, and the movement for forest rights all mobilized against what they diagnosed to be a close link between the Indian state, capital, and enclosure. Each challenged this form of enclosure through the translation between scales of the state and scales of collective action. One turned an incident of bribery into an analysis of the Union government's political economy and demanded the creation of a new national watchdog. The second took discrete events of dispossession and used them to demand changes to the national legal framework through which agricultural land was claimed by the state and capital. The third translated events of forest-based dispossession into a new national law, the FRA, which it then used to initiate hundreds of thousands of claims across the nearly one-quarter of India's land area that is forest land. Together, the three antienclosure movements would set off dramatic changes to India's political economy.

Accumulation and Popular Struggle

In the years following the passage of the FRA, India's economic growth appeared to slow. In 2007–2008, at 10.7 percent, Indian corporate profits reached the highest rate they had achieved since the early 1990s. Economic growth seemed to outlast the downturn faced in the US and European economies with the 2008 financial crisis. In 2010, however, Indian GDP growth fell to 5 percent, and it would remain low for the next several years. Corporate profits dropped to 7.8 percent (Mody, Nath, and Walton 2010).

A number of economists and representatives of large companies began to articulate an analysis of the slowdown in GDP growth and the decline in corporate profits, arguing that efforts to slow or prevent dispossession in rural and forest areas were slowing accumulation on a national scale. Raghuram Rajan, who was at the time governor of the Reserve Bank of India, argued that the country's economic problems resulted from the laws and institutions governing property:

> New factories and mines require land. But land is often held by small farmers or inhabited by tribal groups, who have neither clear and clean title nor the information and capability to deal on equal terms with a developer or corporate acquirer. Not surprisingly, farmers and

tribal groups often felt exploited as savvy buyers purchased their land for a pittance and resold it for a fortune. And the compensation that poor farmers did receive did not go very far; having sold their primary means of earning income, they then faced a steep rise in the local cost of living, owing to development. In short, strong growth tests economic institutions' capacity to cope, and India's were found lacking. Its land titling was fragmented, the laws governing land acquisition were archaic, and the process of rezoning land for industrial use was non-transparent. (Rajan 2013)

Dispossession had caused political problems that had slowed accumulation, Rajan argued, but the solution to these political and economic problems could be found in a fix to the country's archaic property laws and bureaucracy.

Shankar Sharma, the chief global trading strategist of the securities firm First Global, told the *Economic Times* in 2011 that the anticorruption movement would have a similar effect on accumulation: "If this drive against corruption has the effect (and it will) of reducing decision-making and project implementation, it will reduce GDP growth, and erode corporate profitability. Remember, fairly-won public contracts rarely have any profitability. It's almost always sweetheart deals that carry supernormal profits. Mark my words . . . if lynch mobs are going to run the country, we are heading for a very dark period" (quoted in Menon 2011).

Others, inside and outside the government, took the view that the FRA, a law intended to prevent the political reaction to dispossession that Rajan was describing, was an obstacle to continuing accumulation, and they began to try to change the way in which it was implemented. Debates over the new law and its effects on state policies and practices emerged within the UPA government soon after the FRA came into effect in early 2008. Depending on their constituencies, allies, and ideologies, politicians within the government found themselves with very different orientations toward the law.

In October 2008, Kishore Chandra Deo, general secretary of the Congress and a member of a Scheduled Tribe himself, wrote a letter to the prime minister complaining that forest land was being diverted for public and private uses without considering the rights—settled or unsettled—of forest dwellers. Deo led the Joint Parliamentary Committee that had reviewed the draft Forest Rights bill, as discussed in chapter 3, and had sided in his recommendations with the demands of the Campaign for Survival and Dignity and Left parties. In an interview to the *Times of India*, Deo complained, "It is unfortunate that both the courts and the government are flagrantly flouting the provisions of the [forest rights] law" (quoted in Ghildiyal 2008).

In July 2009, under the leadership of its new minister Jairam Ramesh, the MoEF issued a circular that seemed to meet Deo's demand. The ministry would not, it said, issue environmental clearance to a project without a letter from the state government certifying that the claims process under the FRA had been completed in the affected area and that the local Gram Sabha, or village council, had agreed to the project. To make land available for investment in mines, factories, or any other purpose in the 23 percent of India's land area that is forest land was now made subject to both the FRA and the approval of local political bodies. The meaning of this circular, the uses to which it would be put, and its continuing authority, however, would be subject to contestation over the next several years, as the meaning of the FRA continued to be contested at multiple scales.

Two large projects in the eastern state of Odisha brought forests into the emerging national political problematics of corruption and dispossession. POSCO, a South Korean steel manufacturer, signed a memorandum of understanding with the state of Odisha in 2005 to build a steel plant and port. POSCO planned to spend Rs. 52,000 crores, or roughly US$10 billion, on the project, making it the largest foreign investment the country had seen. The state of Odisha assured the MoEF that no one had rights to the 4,004 hectares of forest in which the project was to be built. In August 2009, Minister of Environment and Forests Jairam Ramesh wrote to the Odisha government that the July 2009 MoEF circular on the FRA required not only that the state government assure that the act had been enacted before clearance was granted but also that local Gram Sabhas had to provide approval. None of these councils had given permission to the project and, following agitations by several local groups, the MoEF sent a committee to review the case. The committee's report said that the state government had not, in fact, consulted with local councils and recommended that POSCO be denied clearance.[1]

Ramesh's ministry blocked a second large project in Odisha on the grounds that it violated the FRA. The British company Vedanta Resources planned to invest US$8.1 billion to build a bauxite mine in the Niyamgiri hills in the eastern portion of the state. Local Adivasis in the Dongaria and Kutia communities reportedly consider the hills to be sacred, and as of 2010, none of them had been given titles through the FRA. As he had done in the case of a movement against the acquisition of land for an infrastructure corridor in Uttar Pradesh, the Congress politician Rahul Gandhi took up the cause of the threatened villages, saying in a 2008 rally, "Personally I am against mining at Niyamgiri hills as it would destroy the environment of the area, and affect water sources, livelihood sources and culture" (*The Hindu* 2008). The local village councils refused to approve the project, and in August 2010, Ramesh's ministry denied Vedanta environmental clearance. The same month, K. C. Deo wrote to the Ministry of Mines demanding that it withdraw clearance to two bauxite projects in his home state of Andhra Pradesh on the grounds that they also violated the FRA (Patnaik 2010).

The sentiment that politics had come in the way of accumulation was repeated across newspapers and among the country's political and economic elites. At the same time that a group of Ramnagar's villagers were attempting unsuccessfully to bribe local officials in exchange for land rights, newspapers and think tank reporters accused the anticorruption movement of slowing down the gears of government. Those gears needed to be greased in order to operate smoothly, and bureaucrats were becoming afraid to accept bribes. Rajan was not alone. A wide consensus existed that low wages, cheap land, and bribable bureaucrats were necessary for economic growth. The narrative circulated by think tanks and op-ed writers held that the anticorruption movement had made bureaucratic discretion itself dangerous for bureaucrats, and they had stopped pushing files along. With the added obstacles of the FRA and antidisplacement movements, bureaucrats and ministers had stopped giving clearance to large important projects in rural and forest areas. The number of new SEZs fell. Antidisplacement movements had made land not only expensive but politically unavailable.

Clearances

The proper functioning of a bureaucracy and its place in issuing clearances—permission for a project to proceed—came into question in the national English-language media in this period. Public and private companies that want to use forest land for projects are required to receive clearance from the state Forest Department and the national MoEF, both of which evaluate the environmental impacts of the proposed projects. Jairam Ramesh, as minister of environment and forests, had presented himself as committed to environmentalism and as an ally of landless forest dwellers. He created a National Green Tribunal to hear civil cases related to the environment, passed a two-year moratorium on the sale of genetically modified eggplants, and spoke about the need to balance economic growth, environmental conservation, and the livelihood needs of India's poor.

In 2009, Ramesh announced that private companies and the public corporation Coal India would be given clearances to mine areas with coal reserves—including those that had already been assigned to individual companies—only if they had thin tree density and low ecological value. With money already invested in coal reserves that could no longer be legally mined, companies began to lobby the government to replace Ramesh as environment minister. In early 2011, the Confederation of Indian Industry and the minister of power lobbied the government directly, and a number of politicians with connections to the mining industry began to give interviews to the media criticizing Ramesh.

Electricity consumption in India increases in the summer, as fans, refrigerators, and air-conditioners draw more from the existing supply and as hydroelectric power supplies diminish before the monsoon arrives. Positing a threat of looming power shortages, the coal secretary Sriprakash Jaiswal told reporters that the thermal power supplies that were needed to compensate for the shortage of hydroelectric power were threatened by the MoEF's failure to clear coal mining projects (Singh and Watts 2011). Prodipto Ghosh, the former secretary of the MoEF and lobbyist for the Federation of Indian Chambers of Commerce and Industry, wrote editorials comparing the environmental clearance system under Ramesh to the "license raj," the system of regulations that existed before the 1991 liberalization of India's economy: "License raj refers to quantitative restrictions on output or purchase, and conjures the imagery of unaccountable discretion, inconsistency, unpredictability and uncertainty about the timeframe of government decisions. Environmental regulation, if it has the effect of stalling investment, and if operated in an ad hoc, subjective manner, without clear timelines, clearly would have these features" (Ghosh 2011). The threat of declining electricity supplies as the result of an excessively stringent forest rights and environmental clearance process was repeated in the English-language media by the Association of Power Producers, an industry lobbying group, the power minister, and the Planning Commission, the body that produced India's five-year plans, until the government relented and replaced Ramesh as minister of environment and forests (Sethi 2013).

Ramesh's replacement, Jayanti Natarajan, was brought to the MoEF in July 2011, reportedly for the purpose of smoothing the process of environmental clearance. Unlike Ramesh, Natarajan did not cultivate a public image as a defender of forest dwellers or the environment; she in fact gave few interviews with the media. The rate of clearances remained low, however. Complaints about the low clearance rate made by companies and industry lobbying groups centered, as they had during Ramesh's tenure, on the obstacles presented by the FRA and environmental laws, which were alleged to be too stringent. The two ministers, one journalist alleged, had inaugurated a reign of "green terror" (Kumar 2012).

Natarajan entered into contests with other ministers over the environmental clearance system and the FRA. The journalist Nitin Sethi (2013) found that the Forest Advisory Committee, which was charged with ensuring that projects had been approved by local village councils before giving them clearance, was in fact giving clearances based only on assurances from state governments. Following these reports, Natarajan held a meeting with the Forest Advisory Committee, which she told Sethi was to ensure that they did not give clearances without village council approvals. On this basis, Natarajan refused to give clearance to the massive Mahan coal block proposed in Singrauli, Madhya Pradesh, which borders Sonbhadra. In September 2012, Finance Minister P. Chidambaram proposed to speed the implementation of "mega projects" by creating a National Investment Board, which would provide approval to projects that were investing more than Rs. 1,000 crore (roughly US$200 million) without going through other clearance processes, including environmental clearance. The board would, in effect, sidestep the FRA and all environmental legislation for very large investments. Natarajan wrote a public letter to the prime minister opposing the proposal, arguing that it would "be used for the benefit ONLY of large investors, but not ordinary people, local citizens and stakeholders dedicated to preserving environmental integrity" (quoted in Singh 2012, emphasis in original).

K. C. Deo, who had been appointed minister of tribal affairs in July 2011, also wrote a letter to the prime minister criticizing the proposal: "No environment clearance should be given to any project until there is total compliance with the Forest Rights Act (FRA) and also unless the provisions of Panchayat Extension to Scheduled Areas (PESA) are fully met" (quoted in NDTV 2012). The next month, in October 2012, the Law Ministry proposed to "delink environmental and forest clearances" from highway projects, allowing the Ministry of Road Transport and Highways to acquire land to build new highways and widen existing highways without either environmental clearances or the recognition of rights under the FRA.

In January 2013, the Prime Minister's Office wrote to the MoEF and the Ministry of Tribal Affairs, asking them to waive the requirement that projects in forest areas receive consent from local village councils, as the FRA requires. In February 2013, the MoEF conceded, issuing a notification that exempted "linear projects"—highways, canals, and power transmission lines—from requiring village council approval.

Some reports alleged that the low rate of clearances under Natarajan was a result of the large bribes she supposedly demanded. A January 2014 report in the *Indian Express* claimed that Natarajan had in her home 350 files that had not been given clearance, 180 of them unsigned. The following day, the *Economic Times* ran an editorial criticizing Natarajan:

> Jayanthi Natarajan, it would appear, has done immense damage to the economy and to her own party's electoral prospects. She had, it has been reported, been sitting on hundreds of files for no plausible reason, delaying their clearance for months on end, some of them for years.

This amounted to criminal negligence, aborting new projects at a time of waning economic sentiment and slowing investment. It is amazing that she was given such a long rope and not relieved of her ministerial responsibility earlier. The long rope, instead of tripping her up, has choked off the economy's oxygen supply. The fall in real capital formation as a share of GDP by about six percentage points is at the root of the slowdown in economic growth over the last several quarters. (*Economic Times* 2014)

By not signing the files and preventing their circulation, the editorial claimed, Natarajan was in fact asphyxiating the economy. In December 2013, following continued lobbying, Natarajan was replaced as minister of environment and forests with Veerappa Moilly. Under Moilly, the rate of project clearances finally returned to the level at which it had been before Ramesh had been appointed minister. The reign of green terror had ended. Forest land was once again easily available to investors, and forest dwellers' authority to prevent dispossession through the FRA had been weakened.

Bureaucratic discretion and arbitrariness appeared in a political critique leveled against Ramesh and Natarajan as ministers of environment and forests. They were acting on behalf of environmental interests that ran counter to the national interest, it was alleged, or on behalf of companies allied with the Congress Party, granting these companies clearances for their factories and coal mines while denying clearances to those allied with the party's rivals. Although they were part of a large bureaucracy, Ramesh and Natarajan were its only elected members, and their role was to reconcile bureaucratic rationality with political ends. The nature of this arbitrariness was different from the arbitrariness of a district magistrate; Ramesh and Natarajan were visible public and political figures in their own right, and each could be directly assigned responsibility for the decline in environmental clearances.

The hapless victim of bureaucratic indifference and discretion has loomed large in anthropological work on bureaucracy (e.g., Herzfeld 1992; Gupta 2012; Mathur 2016), but the victims of Ramesh's and Natarajan's discretion were able to achieve redress. All reports indicate that Ramesh and Natarajan were replaced as a result of lobbying done by companies that lost or stood to lose money as a result of the lower clearance rate under their ministerships. Ramnagar's villagers struggled to reverse District Magistrate Pandhari Yadav's decision to deny them forest rights, but India's coal companies were able to replace two environment ministers.

The means through which coal companies acted on the MoEF, however, were not the means through which Ramnagar's villagers attempted to act on the local bureaucracy in Duddhi. Both threatened the bureaucracy with collective action. Through their protests and their presence at political rallies, the Ramnagaris indexed potential futures, presenting the possibility of their voting for or against particular politicians and embarrassing the local bureaucracy through sit-ins. The protests against Ramesh and Natarajan, however, successfully conjured absent, or not-yet-present, collectives: through interviews and op-eds, company representatives were able to index both potential public anger and a future slowing economy if coal supplies dwindled and electricity production declined. The scale of forest politics had once again been recast. From the individual or family of forest dwellers who had been deprived of rights, such politics were now presented as threatening the national economy and the national public. A solution to the problem of the forest was now a problem for the nation.

The discretion of bureaucrats and politicians that the anticorruption movement pointed to as the culprit for corruption became, for mining industry lobbyists, the culprit for their inability to realize profits from their investments and for the decline in the country's economic growth. A Weberian ([1921] 2019) understanding of bureaucracies as institutions that would ideally absolve individuals of responsibility and discretion, limiting their actions to a set of prescribed rules, animated both criticisms, even if the ends associated with these criticisms were opposed. Jayanti Natarajan, by not allowing files to move, violated the shared expectation of anticorruption activists and industry lobbyists that her role as environment minister was to keep files moving, by either rejecting or clearing them.

The Weberian ideal of the indifferent bureaucracy is, Herzfeld (1992) argues, a fiction to which both bureaucratic and nonstate actors can appeal. Ministers can appeal simultaneously to a second vision of the national interest, however, one framed by political and electoral considerations. The 2014 *Economic Times* editorial criticizing Natarajan points to a mechanism through which the demands of capital make their way to state actors: they arrive mediated, tied to specific threats and potential futures.

At risk, if production and accumulation slow, are state finances, popular opinion, and the ability of political parties to raise funds for the next election.[2] The new rights of forest dwellers to determine whether or not they would be dispossessed were thus recast through the collective action of corporate representatives as a threat to productivity on a national scale and a threat to the future political fortunes of the ruling parties.

Accumulating Demands

This chapter began with an encounter between Geeta, Shubha, and Baldeva and Sonbhadra's district magistrate, Pandhari Yadav. In a debate over the meaning of the FRA, Yadav's interpretive authority—grounded in his position within the bureaucracy and his reading of the law's printed text—was momentarily trumped by Geeta's demonstration that she had access to some of the law's authors through her cellphone which, unlike a printed legal volume, was a two-way channel that could potentially allow the authors to clarify their meaning and intention in drafting the bill.

The demands made by the Ramnagaris and forest-dweller organizations across India for substantive citizenship—for enforceable property rights and a solution to the problem of the forest—took the shape of a national movement and a national law. The first, composed of a shifting coalition of collectives and their representatives, produced the second, a text that circulated nationally alongside its many paratexts and interpretive discourses. Among the interpretive discourses were those that assumed a regularity in the meaning of the law, an assumption that I have argued produces new relationships between people involved in different stages of a law's interpretive life, even across geographic and temporal distances. In courts, this assumption takes doctrinal form in the common law principle of *stare decisis*, or the binding force of precedent: interpretations and rulings made about a law in one place and time ostensibly hold in other places and times.

These assumptions of regularity produce the social geometry of legal politics: If legal meaning is consistent and high courts can set constitutional precedents, then the outcome of a Supreme Court case can be shaped from outside of the Supreme Court itself. The assumption of legal regularity allows the actions of other people in other places to be called on to act again in new ones. But the emergence of a movement oriented toward legal politics at a national scale allowed these assumptions to disrupt the scales of politics in India: if legal meaning is consistent and the networks produced by a movement produce channels to circulate legal meanings that run parallel to state channels that circulate legal meanings, then an activist with the phone numbers of the law's authors can contest the interpretation provided by a bureaucrat.

The accumulation of successful claims to forest rights, of partial solutions to the problem of the forest, came to produce a new scalar politics in its own right. The increasing difficulty companies faced in acquiring forest land for mines, factories, and other uses brought a new set of collective actors, corporate lobbyists, into the ongoing struggle to define the FRA. India's economy and the national public that depended on reliable electricity and economic growth for its livelihood were at stake, they argued, as they intervened in the bureaucratic channels through which the law circulated, helping to replace two cabinet ministers in two years, reshaping the law and restricting the terms of the substantive citizenship forest dwellers were able to claim.

CONCLUSION

In late 2019, a movement emerged across India's cities in protest of two measures that had been proposed by the ruling Hindu-nationalist Bharatiya Janata Party (BJP): a new law, the Citizenship Amendment Act, which would create a naturalization process for adherents of all religions with the notable exception of Islam, and a proposed National Register of Citizens, which would create a register of all citizens. Protests erupted, responding to fears, grounded in the long-stated mission of the BJP to build a Hindu nation, that the two measures would be used to strip Indian Muslims of their citizenship. This movement to claim citizenship—or to guard against its removal on the basis of religion—took on the name of the Muslim-majority Delhi neighborhood that saw the first and the longest-lasting protests against the proposed measures: Shaheen Bagh.

The protests in Shaheen Bagh and elsewhere ended abruptly in March 2020, following the imposition of lockdowns at the start of the COVID-19 pandemic. The proposed Citizenship Amendment Act and National Register of Citizens were subsequently put on hold by the government. In May 2022, residents of Shaheen Bagh returned to the streets of their neighborhood to protest in response to the arrival of bulldozers that had been sent by the BJP-run South Delhi Municipal Corporation, ostensibly to destroy "illegal encroachments" in the area (*The Wire* 2022). The threat to destroy homes in Shaheen Bagh followed a wave of demolitions in Muslim-majority neighborhoods in BJP-ruled states across India—demolitions that ostensibly simply enforced property law by clearing private structures on public land without regard for religion, but whose religious motivation was clear both to their targets and to the larger public (Housing and Land Rights Network 2022). Indeed, the bulldozer itself came to stand in for a muscular Hindu nationalism, representing the threat of state-led dispossession of Muslims as far away as an Indian Independence Day parade in Edison, New Jersey (Dev 2022).

The residents of Shaheen Bagh, with help from sympathetic politicians, succeeded in stopping the bulldozers in 2022. Following their large protests, the bulldozers turned around. A message had been sent, however: property rights for Muslims, whether formal or informal, were as tenuous as their citizenship, and those Muslim people who protested the government or its new religious criteria for citizenship would be punished. As Lenin Raghuvandhi from the People's Vigilance Committee on Human Rights told an Associated Press reporter in June 2022, "It was a threat that if you raise your voice against the government or the BJP, your house will be demolished."

An attempt to make citizenship contingent, removable, or deniable on the basis of religion was put on hold, but was followed by an effort to make property rights contingent. If formal citizenship could not yet be removed, the substantive citizenship expressed in enforceable property rights perhaps could—not through the courts but by a bulldozer. And yet, at least in Shaheen Bagh, the same infrastructures of collective action that had enabled its residents to force the government to delay its measures to make citizenship contingent allowed them to prevent their own displacement.

The legality of the municipal corporation's attempt to dispossess residents of Shaheen Bagh in 2022 was not determined by deeds, titles, precedents, and statutes on their own—these needed to be brought into social life through the collective action of men in bulldozers and the protests of the people of the neighborhood. As it is in the forests, legal meaning in Shaheen Bagh is a product of collective action. The collective action of the Campaign for Survival and Dignity, the Ramnagaris, their attackers from Govindnagar, and many others worked both to fix and unfix the new Forest Rights Act as it was produced as a text and as that text made its way to the forest. By indexing potential futures—whether the promise of a new electoral coalition or the threat of a repeated attack on Ramnagar—collective action reworked the rules through which the law came into life. It reworked the rules through which land was allotted and used, initially allowing the Ramnagaris to establish their village, later for dominant-caste groups to destroy Ramnagar, and finally for the Ramnagaris to rebuild. In reorganizing property relations, labor relations were remade. In unfixing the organization of social life to produce new collectives that could act, caste and gender were reshaped. In shifting practices of cultivation, habitation, and management, the ecological world of a corner of Duddhi subdistrict was transformed. All these shifts took place through the citation of the same law.

The Forest Rights Act has been brought into social and political life, not only in being read but also in being cited, debated, fought over, and waved around and thrust at people as an object. As I have argued, the outcomes of these contests are determined neither by the law and its text nor by the contingencies of the moment of contestation; the story of the Forest Rights Act has been a story of ongoing efforts at rulemaking, at fixing the future and fixing the relationship between people and the forests they live in. The law emerged from a history of contentious collective action, and its text contains the traces of that contention *in potentia* as potential chronotopes through which the law might be brought into life. Its meaning continues to be fixed and unfixed through the reworking of collectives and their futures from Ramnagar to India's Supreme Court.

The creation of the law and the citation of that law, however, aimed to solve what I have called the problem of the forest, the problem of property for low-caste and indigenous forest dwellers whose presence had been defined by an inability to claim property rights. The problem is one of the relationship between Dalit and Adivasi forest dwellers and the state that would enforce property rights or would deny them, as happened when Kalla and his family were dispossessed and when Ramnagar was destroyed. The forest rights movement hoped to use a law to transform forest dwellers' relationship to land, by transforming long histories of settlement into possibilities of property claims, conservation authority, and political sovereignty. The new law would serve as a charter for the establishment of Ramnagar, but it in fact offered little protection when the village was destroyed: on its own, the law did not solve the problem of the forest. The Ramnagaris would be able to claim land not by receiving deeds from the Forest Rights Committee, but by rearranging their relationship to the state through collective action—as the residents of Shaheen Bagh would do as well.

Years after the passage of the Forest Rights Act the problem of the forest remains unresolved. Millions of families have claimed pattas through the law, but the rights that these pattas grant remain contested across scales, from villages to the national capital. In 2019, the National Democratic Alliance government led by Prime Minister Narendra Modi proposed a new Indian Forest Act that would allow the forest bureaucracy to revoke rights that were already granted under the Forest Rights Act. In the same year, the Supreme Court ordered all forest dwellers who had not successfully claimed rights under the Forest Rights Act to be evicted, although it would ultimately stay the order after national protests. In 2022, the national government announced that private companies would be allowed to harvest timber without consulting the communities who had gained rights and authority under the Forest Rights Act, including authority over conservation.

Property claims made by low-caste and indigenous forest dwellers continue to be rejected and revoked after they were granted. As of 2022, Ramnagar's villagers have not received pattas under the Forest Rights Act to their village. Nonetheless, the village has remained in place: the homes and fields that were destroyed in 2011 have been rebuilt and expanded. The state government built a handpump in Ramnagar in 2014, providing a relatively safe source of drinking water to the villagers. The rebuilt homes sheltered Ramnagaris who returned to Duddhi during the national 2020 COVID-19 lockdown, when tens of millions of migrant workers were forced to leave cities and worksites across India.

Ramnagar remains in place, Geeta told me in 2022, because of the strength of the Sangathan and the relationships that it has built with local politicians like Parvati Gond. It remains in place, she said, because it has now been in place for more than fifteen years: it is a fact on the ground, and to destroy it would cause political difficulties for any politician, bureaucrat, judge, or dominant-caste landowners who might try. The Forest Rights Act served as a charter for the Ramnagaris, a promise of land and sovereignty for Dalit Adivasis, but it did not on its own solve the problem of the forest. The problem of the forest has instead been held off for the time being, through collective action, through the new futures it promises, and through the new relationship to the state that it has brought to Ramnagar's residents.

This is an unfixed conclusion, then, to a story about an effort to fix the future. Ram Lakhan, at least, offered hope that with their new knowledge of the law, this unfixed future might eventually contain not only rights to their small patch of land and forest, but also liberation and sovereignty for all forest dwellers. I end with his words:

> Our Adivasi people will not stay quiet. Today they won't talk. Tomorrow they won't talk. But the day after tomorrow, they will talk. . . . The struggle is old, but we did not have the knowledge until now. As our people have slowly learned to read and write and they have traveled around the country and abroad, we have learned about the law, we have learned that the law is true, and we have begun to struggle.

Notes

PREFACE

1. The term "Dalit" refers to members of the castes lowest within South Asia's caste hierarchy. A discussion of the term and its history can be found in the introduction.

2. The term "Adivasi" can be translated as "indigenous," and refers to members of communities that have been held to be outside of South Asia's caste order. A discussion of the term and its history can be found in the introduction.

INTRODUCTION

1. See Kapila 2008 and Guha 2015 for discussions of the history and politics of the caste-tribe distinction.

2. But see Dube 2023 for a discussion of settler colonialism following Partition in certain forest regions of central India.

3. See Sivaramakrishnan 1995 and Gadgil and Guha 2013 for a discussion of the debates between Brandis and Baden-Powell.

4. To point to the role of courts and bureaucracies in restricting legal meanings is not to deny the varied social and ideological stakes of interpretation within either. As Baxi (2014) shows, the adjudication of rape trials in India cannot be understood outside a larger context of structural caste and gender violence in the country. Bureaucratic proceduralism itself has ideological stakes and exclusionary consequences, as Sharma (2013) shows—and efforts to reduce bureaucratic discretion through the formalization of "transparency" through documentation themselves can render laws and schemes "unimplementable," as Mathur (2016) shows.

5. These popular mobilizations to shape and interpret a law can be seen as part of a larger set of practices around legal and constitutional politics in India, as Dasgupta (2024) describes in the creation of India's Constitution and De (2018) presents in his account of the Constitution being drawn on in popular struggles and claims.

6. Prashant Sharma's 2014 account of the making of India's Right to Information Act details an overlapping set of networks across popular movements and the bureaucracy.

1. HOW THE FORESTS BECAME INDIAN

1. Scholars including Hussain (2007) and Raman (2018) have understood the emergency and the exception in colonial India as responses to the specter of insurgency. For Hussain, the exceptional became routine in colonial India because sovereignty itself was held to be at stake in obedience to law, not simply particular laws. Discussing the East India Company's conquest of Wayanad in the early nineteenth century, Raman describes the subsumption of law to imperatives of governmentality such that "law was splintered—neither in suspension nor firmly in place" (123). Indeed, such a legal splintering describes the problem of the forest in Duddhi accurately, but although Duddhi's political and legal status was produced through its incorporation into a larger Indian legal framework of counterinsurgency, no insurgent political movement of any significance would take shape in the region until many decades later, following the Emergency.

2. These efforts to prevent tribal indebtedness, in particular to nontribals and outsiders, can be placed in a larger context of colonial anxieties about debt and peasant unfreedom described by Bose (1986) and the economic protectionism that Mantena (2010) describes accompanying the post-1857 imperial shift to indirect rule.

3. See Austin 1999 for a detailed discussion of the debates over property and land reform in the Constituent Assembly.

4. See Wahi 2015 and Khosla 2020, respectively, for discussions of the debates over property and Parliament's ability to amend the Constitution.

5. See Noorani 2001 and Polzin 2021 for discussions of Conrad's impact on the Supreme Court and basic structure doctrine.

6. See Chatterjee 2024 for an analysis of the Emergency in relation to the global energy crisis and an increasing—and increasingly centralized—use of coal in India.

2. HISTORICAL INJUSTICES AND THE MOVEMENT TO CREATE THE FOREST RIGHTS ACT

1. For Gramsci ([1926] 2005), common sense consisted of the diffuse and broadly shared conceptions that a social group holds of the world. It contains within itself the seeds of "good sense," a critical conception of reality.

3. THE LAW AS RUMOR

1. For an account of debates over the extent and systematic nature of jajmani as well as an attempt to rehabilitate the concept's explanatory power, see Piliavsky 2014.

2. See Hota 2023 for a rich ethnographic account of the potential anti-Dalit exclusions of indigenist Adivasi politics.

3. See Lerche 1999 and Mendelsohn and Vicziany 1998.

5. NATIONAL POLITICS AND THE SCALES OF THE FOREST RIGHTS ACT

1. In May 2011, despite protests among forest dwellers in the affected area and the fact that local village councils had not given approval to the project, Ramesh gave clearance to the POSCO project.

2. Indeed, political parties in India often require more funds to win elections than are allowed by Election Commission rules (Jaffrelot 2003).

Bibliography

Agha, Asif. 2007. "Recombinant Selves in Mass Mediated Spacetime." *Language and Communication* 27 (3): 320–35.

Agrawal, Arun. 2005. *Environmentality: Technologies of Government and the Making of Subjects.* Durham, NC: Duke University Press.

Ahmed, Sadiq, and Ashutosh Varshney. 2012. "Battles Half Won: Political Economy of India's Growth and Economic Policy Since Independence." In *The Oxford Handbook of the Indian Economy.* Edited by Chetan Ghate, 1–61. Oxford: Oxford University Press.

Aiyar, Mani Shankar. 2003. "Can the Congress Find a Future?" *Seminar* 526.

Aiyar, Swaminathan S. Anklesaria. 2011. "The Elephant That Became a Tiger: 20 Years of Economic Reforms in India." *Cato Institute Center for Global Liberty and Prosperity Development Policy Analysis* 13, July 20.

Ambedkar, Bhimrao Ramji. 1936. *Annihilation of Caste: Speech Prepared for the Annual Conference of the Jat-Pat-Todak Mandal of Lahore, but Not Delivered.* Bombay: B. R. Kadrekar.

Ambedkar, Bhimrao Ramji. 2004. *The Essential Writings of B. R. Ambedkar.* New Delhi: Oxford University Press.

Anand, Nikhil. 2017. *Hydraulic City: Water and the Infrastructures of Citizenship in Mumbai.* Durham, NC: Duke University Press.

Austin, Granville. 1999. *The Indian Constitution: Cornerstone of a Nation.* New York: Oxford University Press.

Baden-Powell, Baden Henry. 1892. *The Land-Systems of British India.* Oxford: Clarendon.

Baden-Powell, Baden Henry. 1893. *Forest Law: A Course of Lectures on the Principles of Civil and Criminal Law and on the Law of the Forest.* London: Bradbury, Agnew.

Bahuguna, V. K. 2002. "Eviction of Illegal Encroachment of Forest Lands in Various States/UT's Time Bound Action Plan." Delhi: Government of India, Ministry of Environment and Forests.

Bakhtin, Mikhail Michajlovič. 1982. *The Dialogic Imagination: Four Essays.* Translated by Michael Holquist. Austin: University of Texas Press.

Banerjee, Prathama. 2006. *Politics of Time: "Primitives" and History-Writing in a Colonial Society.* New York: Oxford University Press.

Banerjee, Sumanta. 1984. *India's Simmering Revolution: The Naxalite Uprising.* New York: Zed.

Bate, Bernard. 2009. *Tamil Oratory and the Dravidian Aesthetic: Democratic Practice in South India.* New York: Columbia University Press.

Baviskar, Amita. 2004. *In the Belly of the River: Tribal Conflicts over Development in the Narmada Valley.* New Delhi: Oxford University Press.

Baxi, Pratiksha. 2014. *Public Secrets of Law: Rape Trials in India.* New Delhi: Oxford University Press.

Baxi, Upendra. 1982. *The Crisis of the Indian Legal System.* New Delhi: Vikas.

Baxi, Upendra. 1986. *Towards a Sociology of Indian Law.* New Delhi: Satvahan.

Baxi, Upendra. 1999. "Constitutionalism as a Site of State Formative Practices." *Cardozo Law Review* 21: 1183.

Bear, Laura. 2015. "Capitalist Divination: Popularist Speculators and Technologies of Imagination on the Hooghly River." *Comparative Studies of South Asia, Africa and the Middle East* 35 (3): 408–23.

Benjamin, Walter. (1921) 2009. *One-Way Street and Other Writings*. New York: Penguin.

Bhattacharjea, Ajit. 1978. *Jayaprakash Narayan: A Political Biography*. Delhi: Vikas.

Bhushan, Prashant. 1978. *The Case That Shook India*. New Delhi: Vikas.

Bhuwania, Anuj. 2017. *Courting the People: Public Interest Litigation in Post-Emergency India*. New York: Cambridge University Press.

Björkman, Lisa. 2014. "'You Can't Buy a Vote': Meanings of Money in a Mumbai Election." *American Ethnologist* 41 (4): 617–34.

Boggs, Carl. 1977. "Marxism, Prefigurative Communism and the Problem of Workers' Control." *Radical America* 6 (Winter): 99–122.

Bose, Ajoy. 2009. *Behenji: A Political Biography of Mayawati*. London: Penguin UK.

Bose, Sugata. 1986. *Agrarian Bengal: Economy, Social Structure and Politics, 1919–1947*. Cambridge: Cambridge University Press.

Bourdieu, Pierre. 1990. *The Logic of Practice*. Translated by Richard Nice. Palo Alto, CA: Stanford University Press.

Brahma, S. 1963. *Working Plan for the Erstwhile Forests and Wastelands of the North Mirzapur Forest Division, Uttar Pradesh, 1961–62 to 1970–71*. Nainital, India: Working Plans Circle, U.P.

Brass, Paul R. 1980a. "The Politicization of the Peasantry in a North Indian State: I." *Journal of Peasant Studies* 7 (4): 395–426.

Brass, Paul R. 1980b. "The Politicization of the Peasantry in a North Indian State: II." *Journal of Peasant Studies* 8 (1): 3–36.

Brenner, Neil. 2001. "The Limits to Scale? Methodological Reflections on Scalar Structuration." *Progress in Human Geography* 25 (4): 591–614.

Brooks, Peter, and Paul Gewirtz. 1998. *Law's Stories: Narrative and Rhetoric in the Law*. New Haven, CT: Yale University Press.

Business Standard India. 2011. "Q&A: Montek Singh Ahluwalia, Deputy Chairman, Planning Commission." January 17.

Cabinet Secretariat, Government of India. 2006. "Extracts from the Minutes of the Meeting of the Cabinet Held at 1830 Hours, on Thursday, 7th December, 2006, in Panchvati, 7, Race Course Road, New Delhi."

Callon, Michel. 1984. "Some Elements of a Sociology of Translation: Domestication of the Scallops and the Fishermen of St Brieuc Bay." *Sociological Review* 32 (1): 196–233.

Campaign for Survival and Dignity. 2003. *Endangered Symbiosis: Evictions and India's Forest Communities*. New Delhi: Delhi Forum.

Campaign for Survival and Dignity. 2005. "Press Release of the Campaign on the Jail Bharo." Press release, December 16.

Carr-Harris, Jill. 2005. "Struggle-Dialogue: Tools for Land Movements in India." New Delhi: Ekta Parishad.

Chakravorty, Sanjoy. 2013. *The Price of Land: Acquisition, Conflict, Consequence*. New Delhi: Oxford University Press.

Chandra, Bipan. 2003. *In the Name of Democracy: JP Movement and the Emergency*. New Delhi: Penguin.

Chatterjee, Liz. 2024. "Late Acceleration: The Indian Emergency and the Early 1970s Energy Crisis." *American Historical Review* 129 (2): 429–66.

Chatterjee, Partha. 2004. *The Politics of the Governed: Reflections on Popular Politics in Most of the World*. New York: Columbia University Press.

Chatterjee, Partha. 2008. "Democracy and Economic Transformation in India." *Economic and Political Weekly* 43 (16): 53–62.

Chaudhry, Faisal. 2016. "A Rule of Proprietary Right for British India: From Revenue Settlement to Tenant Right in the Age of Classical Legal Thought." *Modern Asian Studies* 50 (1): 345–84.

Chowdhury, Nusrat Sabina. 2019. *Paradoxes of the Popular: Crowd Politics in Bangladesh.* Stanford, CA: Stanford University Press.

Cody, Francis. 2009. "Inscribing Subjects to Citizenship: Petitions, Literacy Activism, and the Performativity of Signature in Rural Tamil India." *Cultural Anthropology* 24 (3): 347–80.

Cody, Francis. 2013. *The Light of Knowledge: Literacy Activism and the Politics of Writing in South India.* Ithaca, NY: Cornell University Press.

Cody, Francis. 2020. "Wave Theory." *American Ethnologist* 47 (4): 402–16.

Coneybeare, H. C. A. 1879. *Note on Pargana Dudhi of the Mirzapur District, with Special Reference to Its Land Assessment.* Allahabad, India: North-Western Provinces and Oudh Government Press.

Conrad, Dietrich. 1970. "Limitation of Amendment Procedures and the Constituent Power." *Indian Year Book of International Affairs 1966–67,* 375–430.

Cover, Robert M. 1983. "Nomos and Narrative." *Harvard Law Review* 97 (1): 4–69.

Cronon, William. 1983. *Changes in the Land: Indians, Colonists, and the Ecology of New England.* Revised edition. New York: Hill and Wang.

Constituent Assembly. 1976. "Excluded and Partially Excluded Areas (Other than Assam) Sub-Committee, 1947—Final Report." In *Committees and Commissions in India.* Vol. 1, *1947–54.* Edited by Virendra Kumar. Delhi: Concept.

Dasgupta, Sandipto. 2024. *Legalizing the Revolution: India and the Constitution of the Postcolony.* Cambridge: Cambridge University Press.

De, Rohit. 2018. *A People's Constitution: The Everyday Life of Law in the Indian Republic.* Princeton, NJ: Princeton University Press.

Derrida, Jacques. 1988. "Signature Event Context." In *Limited Inc.* Edited by Gerald Graff, translated by Samuel Weber and Jeffrey Mehlman, 1–23. Evanston, IL: Northwestern University Press.

Deshpande, Satish. 2013. "Caste and Castelessness." *Economic and Political Weekly* 48 (15): 32–39.

Dev, Atul. 2022. "A Bulldozer among the Floats at Indian Parade Divides New Jersey Town." *Reuters,* September 22.

Dhavan, Rajeev. 1993. *Law as Struggle: Notes on Public Interest Law in India.* Madison: Institute for Legal Studies, University of Wisconsin–Madison Law School.

Divan, Shyam, and Armin Rosencranz. 2001. *Environmental Law and Policy in India: Cases, Materials, and Statutes.* New Delhi: Oxford University Press.

Drake-Brockman, D. L. 1911. *Mirzapur, a Gazetteer, Being Volume XXVII of the District Gazetteers of the United Provinces of Agra and Oudh.* Allahabad, India: Government Press.

Drèze, Jean. 2005. "Tribal Evictions from Forest Land." New Delhi: National Advisory Committee.

Dube, Pankhuree R. 2023. "Theorizing the Adivasi's Absence in Partition Histories: Indigenes, Refugees, and the Settler State in Dandakaranya Forest." *Settler Colonial Studies* 14 (1): 94–113.

Duncan, Ian. 1999. "Dalits and Politics in Rural North India: The Bahujan Samaj Party in Uttar Pradesh." *Journal of Peasant Studies* 27 (1): 35–60.

Eckert, Julia, Brian Donahoe, Christian Strümpell, and Özlem Biner. 2012. "Introduction." In *Law against the State: Ethnographic Forays into Law's Transformations.*

Edited by Julia Eckert, Brian Donahoe, Christian Strümpell, and Özlem Biner. Cambridge: Cambridge University Press.

The Economic Times. 2011. "Land Acquisition Stir: Rahul Gandhi Meets Greater Noida Farmers." September 29.

The Economic Times. 2014. "Ex-Environment Minister Jayanthi Natarajan Has Damaged India and Her Party." January 14.

The Economist. 2010. "Politics with Bloodshed." April 7.

The Economist. 2014. "A Bad Boom." March 15.

Edelman, Marc. 1999. *Peasants against Globalization: Rural Social Movements in Costa Rica.* Stanford, CA: Stanford University Press.

Elwin, Verrier. 1942. *The Agaria.* New Delhi: Oxford University Press.

Elyachar, Julia. 2010. "Phatic Labor, Infrastructure, and the Question of Empowerment in Cairo." *American Ethnologist* 37 (3): 452–64.

Engels, Friedrich, and Tristram Hunt. 2010. *The Origin of the Family, Private Property, and the State.* London: Penguin Classics.

Epp, Charles R. 1998. *The Rights Revolution: Lawyers, Activists, and Supreme Courts in Comparative Perspective.* Chicago: University of Chicago Press.

Evans-Pritchard, E. E. 1940. *The Nuer: A Description of the Modes of Livelihood and Political Institutions of a Nilotic People.* Oxford: Oxford University Press.

Frankel, Francine R. 2006. *India's Political Economy, 1947–2004: The Gradual Revolution.* New Delhi: Oxford University Press.

French, Rebecca R. 1996. "Of Narrative in Law and Anthropology." *Law and Society Review* 30: 417.

Gadgil, Madhav, and Ramachandra Guha. 2013. *This Fissured Land: An Ecological History of India.* 2nd ed. New Delhi: Oxford University Press.

Galanter, Marc. 1984. *Competing Equalities: Law and the Backward Classes in India.* New Delhi: Oxford University Press.

Ganapathy, Nirmala. 2005. "Environment Ministry Strikes at Root of Tribal Land Rights Bill." *Indian Express*, April 14.

Gandhi, Sonia. 2005. "Letter to the Prime Minister." Prime Minister's Office, Government of India.

Gauri, Varun. 2014. "Fundamental Rights and Public Interest Litigation in India: Overreaching or Underachieving?" In *The Shifting Scales of Justice: The Supreme Court in Neo-Liberal India.* Edited by Mayur Suresh and Siddharth Narrain, 79–108. New Delhi: Orient Blackswan.

Geological Survey of India. 1873. *Records of the Geological Survey of India.* Government of India Press.

Ghildiyal, Subodh. 2008. "'Settle Forest Rights First, Industry Can Wait.'" *Times of India*, October 6.

Ghosh, Prodipto. 2011. "A Murkier Shade of Green." *Indian Express*, February 12. https://indianexpress.com/article/opinion/columns/a-murkier-shade-of-green/.

Ghurye, Govind Sadashiv. 1980. *The Scheduled Tribes of India.* New Brunswick: Transaction.

Gluckman, Max. 1940. "Analysis of a Social Situation in Modern Zululand." *Bantu Studies* 14 (1): 1–30.

Goldman, Michael. 2020. "Dispossession by Financialization: The End(s) of Rurality in the Making of a Speculative Land Market." *Journal of Peasant Studies* 47 (6): 1251–77.

Gopalakrishnan, R. 2005. "Brief for the Meeting." Prime Minister's Office, Government of India.

Gopalakrishnan, Shankar. 2010a. "Forest Areas, Political Economy and the 'Left-Progressive Line' on Operation Green Hunt." *Radical Notes*, May.

Gopalakrishnan, Shankar. 2010b. "Rights Legislations and the Indian State: Under-standing the Meaning of the Forest Rights Act." http://www.academia.edu/360289 /Rights_Legislations_and_the_Indian_State_Understanding_the_Meaning_of _the_Forest_Rights_Act.

Gramsci, Antonio. (1926) 2005. *The Southern Question*. Translated by Pasquale Verdic-chio. Toronto: Guernica Editions.

Greenough, Paul. 2001. "Naturae Ferae: Wild Animals in South Asia and the Standard Environmental Narrative." In *Agrarian Studies Synthetic Work at the Cutting Edge*. Edited by James C. Scott and Nina Bhatt. New Haven, CT: Yale University Press.

Group of Ministers, Government of India. 2006. "Draft Minutes of the 2nd Meeting of the Group of Ministers (GoM) to Consider the Issues Relating to the Scheduled Tribes (Recognition of Forest Rights) Bill, 2005 Held on 13.11.2006 at 1100 Hrs."

Grove, Richard. 1996. *Green Imperialism: Colonial Expansion, Tropical Island Edens and the Origins of Environmentalism, 1600–1860*. Cambridge: Cambridge University Press.

Guha, Ramachandra. 1990. "An Early Environmental Debate: The Making of the 1878 Forest Act." *Indian Economic and Social History Review* 27 (1): 65–84.

Guha, Ramachandra. 2007. "Adivasis, Naxalites and Indian Democracy." *Economic and Political Weekly* 42 (32): 3305–12.

Guha, Ranajit. 1982. *A Rule of Property for Bengal: An Essay on the Idea of Permanent Settlement*. New Delhi: Orient Blackswan.

Guha, Ranajit. 1999. *Elementary Aspects of Peasant Insurgency in Colonial India*. Dur-ham, NC: Duke University Press.

Guha, Sumit. 2006. *Environment and Ethnicity in India, 1200–1991*. Cambridge: Cam-bridge University Press.

Guha, Sumit. 2015. "States, Tribes, Castes: A Historical Re-Exploration in Comparative Perspective." *Economic and Political Weekly* 50 (46/47): 50–57.

Gupta, Akhil. 1995. "Blurred Boundaries: The Discourse of Corruption, the Culture of Politics, and the Imagined State." *American Ethnologist* 22 (2): 375–402.

Gupta, Akhil. 2012. *Red Tape: Bureaucracy, Structural Violence, and Poverty in India*. Durham, NC: Duke University Press.

Gupta, Akhil, and James Ferguson. 2002. "Spatializing States: Toward an Ethnography of Neoliberal Governmentality." *American Ethnologist* 29 (4): 981–1002.

Gupta, Dipankar. 2000. *Interrogating Caste: Understanding Hierarchy and Difference in Indian Society*. New Delhi: Penguin.

Guru, Gopal. 2011. "Introduction: Theorizing Humiliation." In *Humiliation: Claims and Context*. Edited by Gopal Guru, 1–22. London: Oxford University Press.

Guyer, Jane. 2007. "Prophecy and the Near Future: Thoughts on Macroeconomic, Evan-gelical, and Punctuated Time." *American Ethnologist* 34 (3): 409–21.

Habermas, Jürgen. 1981. *The Theory of Communicative Action: Reason and the Ratio-nalization of Society*. Boston: Beacon.

Habermas, Jürgen. 2011. "'The Political': The Rational Meaning of a Questionable Inheritance of Political Theology." In *The Power of Religion in the Public Sphere*. Edited by Eduardo Mendieta and Jonathan VanAntwerpen, 15–33. New York: Columbia University Press.

Haraway, Donna J. 2003. *The Companion Species Manifesto: Dogs, People, and Signifi-cant Otherness*. Chicago: Prickly Paradigm.

Hardin, Garrett. 1968. "The Tragedy of the Commons." *Science* 162 (3859): 1243–48.

Harvey, David. 1999. *The Limits to Capital*. New York: Verso.

Harvey, David. 2003. *The New Imperialism*. Oxford: Oxford University Press.

Herring, Ronald J. 1983. *Land to the Tiller: The Political Economy of Agrarian Reform in South Asia*. New Haven, CT: Yale University Press.

Herzfeld, Michael. 1992. *The Social Production of Indifference*. Chicago: University of Chicago Press.

Hetherington, Kregg. 2009. "Privatizing the Private in Rural Paraguay: Precarious Lots and the Materiality of Rights." *American Ethnologist* 36 (2): 224–41.

Hetherington, Kregg. 2011. *Guerrilla Auditors: The Politics of Transparency in Neoliberal Paraguay*. Durham, NC: Duke University Press.

The Hindu. 2005. "North-East Civil Groups Seek Region-Wise Discussion on Bill." July 27.

The Hindu. 2008. "Rahul Opposes Mining of Niyamgiri Hills." March 11.

The Hindu. 2010. "Naxalism Biggest Threat to Internal Security." May 24.

Hindustan Times. 2021. "West Bengal Election: How Mamata Banerjee Emerged as a Giant Killer in 2011." February 27.

Hoddy, Elizabeth. 1999. *The Banwasi Seva Ashram in Gandhi's Footsteps—A Model Gandhian Development Project*. New Delhi: Gandhi Peace Foundation.

Holston, James. 2009. *Insurgent Citizenship: Disjunctions of Democracy and Modernity in Brazil*. Princeton, NJ: Princeton University Press.

Hota, Pinky. 2023. *The Violence of Recognition: Adivasi Indigeneity and Anti-Dalitness in India*. Philadelphia: University of Pennsylvania Press.

Hussain, Nasser. 2007. "Hyperlegality." *New Criminal Law Review* 10: 514–31.

Housing and Land Rights Network. 2022. *Forced Evictions in India: 2021*. New Delhi: Housing and Land Rights Network.

Hull, Matthew S. 2012. *Government of Paper: The Materiality of Bureaucracy in Urban Pakistan*. Berkeley: University of California Press.

Indian National Congress. 1945. *What Congress Fights for: Being the Election Manifesto of the Indian National Congress, 1945–46*. Bombay: Indian National Congress, Central Election Board.

Ives, Peter. 2004. *Gramsci's Politics of Language: Engaging the Bakhtin Circle and the Frankfurt School*. Toronto: University of Toronto Press.

Iyer, Venkat. 2000. *States of Emergency: The Indian Experience*. New Delhi: Butterworths India.

Jaffrelot, Christophe. 2003. *India's Silent Revolution: The Rise of the Lower Castes*. London: C. Hurst.

Jahan, Ishrat. 2023. "India's Landmark Law to Empower Indigenous Forest-Dwellers to Sustainably Access and Use Forest Resources." *Pathfinders*, June 6. https://www.sdg16.plus/policies/indias-landmark-law-to-empower-indigenous-forest-dwellers-to-sustainably-access-and-use-forest-resources/.

Jakobsen, Jostein, Kenneth Bo Nielsen, Alf Gunvald Nilsen, and Anand Vaidya. 2019. "Mapping the World's Largest Democracy (1947–2017)." *Forum for Development Studies* 46 (1): 83–108.

Jaoul, Nicolas. 2006. "Learning the Use of Symbolic Means: Dalits, Ambedkar Statues and the State in Uttar Pradesh." *Contributions to Indian Sociology* 40 (2): 175–207.

Jeffrey, Craig. 2001. "'A Fist Is Stronger than Five Fingers': Caste and Dominance in Rural North India." *Transactions of the Institute of British Geographers* 26 (2): 217–36.

Jones, William. 1869. "Our Mission in Singrowli." In *The Christian Witness and Congregational Magazine*, 5: 53–57. London: Snow.

Joshi, M., and P. P. Singh. 2003. *Tropical Deforestation and Forest Degradation: A Case Study from India*. Twelfth World Forestry Congress, Quebec City, Canada.

Kapila, Kriti. 2008. "The Measure of a Tribe: The Cultural Politics of Constitutional Reclassification in North India." *Journal of the Royal Anthropological Institute* 14 (1): 117–34.

Kapila, Kriti. 2022. *Nullius: The Anthropology of Ownership, Sovereignty, and the Law in India*. Chicago: HAU.

Kaviraj, Sudipta. 1997. *Politics in India*. New Delhi: Oxford University Press.

Kesavananda Bharati Sripadagalvaru v. State of Kerala. 4 SCR 225 (1973).

Khanna, Shomona, and T. K. Naveen. 2005. *Contested Terrain: Forest Cases in the Supreme Court of India*. New Delhi: Society for Rural Urban and Tribal Initiative.

Khosla, Madhav. 2020. *India's Founding Moment: The Constitution of a Most Surprising Democracy*. Cambridge, MA: Harvard University Press.

Kodiveri, Arpitha. 2024. *Governing Forests*. Melbourne: Melbourne University Press.

Kohli, Atul. 2006a. "Politics of Economic Growth in India, 1980–2005: Part I: The 1980s." *Economic and Political Weekly* 41 (13): 1251–59.

Kohli, Atul. 2006b. "Politics of Economic Growth in India, 1980–2005: Part II: The 1990s and Beyond." *Economic and Political Weekly* 41 (14): 1361–70.

Kohn, Eduardo. 2013. *How Forests Think: Toward an Anthropology beyond the Human*. Berkeley: University of California Press.

Koselleck, Reinhart. 2004. *Futures Past: On the Semantics of Historical Time*. New York: Columbia University Press.

Kothari, Rajni. 1970. *Politics in India*. New Delhi: Orient Blackswan.

Kumar, Prachi. 2012. "Green Terror: Outdated Environmental Laws and Inflexible Ministers Strangle Indian Economy." *India Today*, October 15.

Kunnath, George J. 2012. *Rebels from the Mud Houses: Dalits and the Making of the Maoist Revolution in Bihar*. New Delhi: Social Science.

Lerche, Jens. 1999. "Politics of the Poor: Agricultural Labourers and Political Transformations in Uttar Pradesh." *Journal of Peasant Studies* 26 (2–3): 182–241.

Levien, Michael. 2007. "India's Double Movement: Polanyi and the National Alliance of People's Movements." *Berkeley Journal of Sociology* 51: 119–49.

Levien, Michael. 2011. "Special Economic Zones and Accumulation by Dispossession in India." *Journal of Agrarian Change* 11 (4): 454–83.

Levien, Michael. 2012. "The Land Question: Special Economic Zones and the Political Economy of Dispossession in India." *Journal of Peasant Studies* 39 (3–4): 933–69.

Levien, Michael. 2018. *Dispossession without Development: Land Grabs in Neoliberal India*. New York: Oxford University Press.

Li, Tania. 2007. *The Will to Improve: Governmentality, Development, and the Practice of Politics*. Durham, NC: Duke University Press.

Li, Tania. 2011. "Centering Labor in the Land Grab Debate." *Journal of Peasant Studies* 38 (2): 281–98.

Locke, John. (1690) 2003. *Two Treatises of Government and a Letter Concerning Toleration*. New Haven, CT: Yale University Press.

Malinowski, Bronislaw. 1923. "The Problem of Meaning in Primitive Languages." In *The Meaning of Meaning*. Edited by C. K. Ogden and I. A. Richards, 296–336. London: K. Paul, Trend, Trubner.

Mantena, Karuna. 2010. *Alibis of Empire: Henry Maine and the Ends of Liberal Imperialism*. Princeton, NJ: Princeton University Press.

Mathur, Nayanika. 2016. *Paper Tiger: Law, Bureaucracy and the Developmental State in Himalayan India*. Oxford: Oxford University Press.

Marx, Karl. (1887) 1990. *Capital*. Vol. 1 of *A Critique of Political Economy*. Translated by Ernest Mandel and Ben Fowkes. London: Penguin.

Marx, Karl. n.d. "Debates on the Law on Thefts of Wood." In *Supplement to the Rheinische Zeitung*. Translated by Clemens Dutt. http://www.marxists.org/archive/marx/works/1842/10/25.htm.

Mauss, Marcel. (1925) 1990. *The Gift: The Form and Reason for Exchange in Archaic Societies*. Translated by W. D. Halls. New York: Norton.

Mendelsohn, Oliver, and Marika Vicziany. 1998. *The Untouchables: Subordination, Poverty, and the State in Modern India*. Cambridge: Cambridge University Press.

Menon, Shailesh. 2011. "India's Growth Story Gone Down the Drain: Shankar Sharma, Chief Global Trading Strategist, First Global." *Economic Times*, September 30.

Mertz, Elizabeth. 2007. *The Language of Law School: Learning to "Think Like a Lawyer."* New York: Oxford University Press.

Messick, Brinkley. 1996. *The Calligraphic State: Textual Domination and History in a Muslim Society*. Berkeley: University of California Press.

Michelutti, Lucia. 2004. "'We (Yadavs) Are a Caste of Politicians': Caste and Modern Politics in a North Indian Town." *Contributions to Indian Sociology* 38 (1–2): 43–71.

Michelutti, Lucia. 2008. *The Vernacularisation of Democracy: Politics, Caste and Religion in India*. New Delhi: Routledge India.

Ministry of Tribal Affairs, Government of India. 2006. "Memo No.17014/4/2005-S&M/PC&V: Note for the 2nd Meeting of the Group of Ministers on the Scheduled Tribes (Recognition of Forest Rights) Bill, 2005."

Misra, Amaresh. 1993. "Land Struggle in Uttar Pradesh." *Economic and Political Weekly* 28 (39): 2059.

Mitchell, Lisa. 2023. *Hailing the State: Indian Democracy Between Elections*. Durham, NC: Duke University Press.

Mody, Ashoka, Anusha Nath, and Michael Walton. 2010. "Sources of Corporate Profits in India—Business Dynamism or Advantages of Entrenchment." IMF Working Paper. http://www.imf.org/external/pubs/ft/wp/2011/wp1108.pdf.

Mohanty, B. B. 2001. "Land Distribution among Scheduled Castes and Tribes." *Economic and Political Weekly* 36 (40): 3857–68.

Moore, Donald S. 2005. *Suffering for Territory: Race, Place, and Power in Zimbabwe*. Durham, NC: Duke University Press.

Moore, Sally Falk. 1978. *Law as Process: An Anthropological Approach*. New York: Routledge.

Mosse, David. 2003. *The Rule of Water: Statecraft, Ecology and Collective Action in South India*. New Delhi: Oxford University Press.

Muñoz, José. 2009. *Cruising Utopia: The Then and There of Queer Futurity*. New York: New York University Press.

Murphy, John. 1992. "Insulating Land Reform from Constitutional Impugnment: An Indian Case Study." *Comparative and International Law Journal of Southern Africa* 25 (2): 129–55.

Narayan, Badri. 2011. *The Making of the Dalit Public in North India: Uttar Pradesh, 1950–Present*. New Delhi: Oxford University Press.

Nash, June C. 2001. *Mayan Visions: The Quest for Autonomy in an Age of Globalization*. New York: Routledge.

National Forum of Forest People and Forest Workers. 2008. *Forest Rights Act: A Weapon of Struggle*. New Delhi: National Forum of Forest People and Forest Workers.

National Forum of Forest People and Forest Workers. 2009. "Public Hearing on FRA at LKO." July 6.

Nayak, Rajesh Kumar. 2001. "History of Dudhi Estate Mirzapur 1858–1950." PhD diss., VBS Purvanchal University.

NDTV. 2012. "Jayanthi Natarajan Writes to PM against Chidambaram's Proposal: Full Letter." October 10. http://www.ndtv.com/article/india/jayanthi-natarajan-writes-to-pm-against-chidambaram-s-proposal-full-letter-277651.

Neale, Walter C. 1970. *Land Reform in Uttar Pradesh, India*. New York: Agency for International Development.

Niezen, Ronald. 2003. *The Origins of Indigenism: Human Rights and the Politics of Identity*. Berkeley: University of California Press.

Noorani, A. G. 2001. "Behind the Basic Structure Doctrine." *Frontline*, April 28.

Office of the Registrar General and Census Commissioner. 2011. *Census of India*. New Delhi.

Omvedt, Gail. 2008. *Seeking Begumpura: The Social Vision of Anticaste Intellectuals*. New Delhi: Navayana.

O'Neill, Jim. 2001. "Building Better Global Economic BRICS." *Global Economics* 66. New York: Goldman Sachs.

Ostrom, Elinor. 1990. *Governing the Commons: The Evolution of Institutions for Collective Action*. Cambridge: Cambridge University Press.

Ostrom, Elinor. 1998. "A Behavioral Approach to the Rational Choice Theory of Collective Action." *American Political Science Review* 92 (1): 1–22.

Pai, Sudha. 2002. *Dalit Assertion and the Unfinished Democratic Revolution: The Bahujan Samaj Party in Uttar Pradesh*. New Delhi: Sage.

Pai, Sudha. 2007. *Political Process in Uttar Pradesh: Identity, Economic Reforms, and Governance*. New Delhi: Pearson Education India.

Patnaik, Santosh. 2010. "Bauxite Mining in Vizag Put on Hold." *The Hindu*, August 22.

Paxson, Heather. 2012. *The Life of Cheese: Crafting Food and Value in America*. Berkeley: University of California Press.

Peirce, Charles S. 1991. *Peirce on Signs: Writings on Semiotic*. Edited by James Hoopes. Chapel Hill: University of North Carolina Press.

Peluso, Nancy Lee, and Peter Vandergeest. 2011. "Political Ecologies of War and Forests: Counterinsurgencies and the Making of National Natures." *Annals of the Association of American Geographers* 101 (3): 587–608.

People's Union for Democratic Rights. 1982. *Undeclared Civil War, Defend the Rights of Tribals, Oppose Forest Bill*. New Delhi: People's Union for Democratic Rights.

Philip, Kavita. 2003. *Civilizing Natures: Race, Resources and Modernity in Colonial South India*. New Brunswick, NJ: Rutgers University Press.

Piliavsky, Anastasia. 2014. "Introduction." In *Patronage as the Politics of South Asia*. Edited by Anastasia Piliavsky, 1–38. London: Routledge.

Planning Commission. 1979. *Report of the Working Group on Energy Policy*. New Delhi: Government of India.

Poffenberger, Mark. 2000. *Communities and Forest Management in South Asia*. Gland, Switzerland: IUCN.

Polzin, Monika. 2021. "The Basic-Structure Doctrine and Its German and French Origins: A Tale of Migration, Integration, Invention and Forgetting." *Indian Law Review* 5 (1): 45–61.

Pottage, Alain, and Martha Mundy. 2004. *Law, Anthropology, and the Constitution of the Social: Making Persons and Things*. Cambridge: Cambridge University Press.

Prabhu, Pradip. 2004. "The Scheduled Tribes & Forest Dwellers (Recognition of Forest Rights) Act 2005 (Draft)."

Pradhan, Itishree, Binayak Kandapan, and Jalandhar Pradhan. 2022. "Uneven Burden of Multidimensional Poverty in India: A Caste Based Analysis." *PLoS ONE* 17 (7): 1–18.

Prasad, Archana. 2004. *Environmentalism and the Left: Contemporary Debates and Future Agendas in Tribal Areas*. New Delhi: LeftWord.

Prime Minister's Office, Government of India. 2006. "Minutes of the Meeting Held on 28.9.2006 in the PMO under the Chairmanship of MOS in the PMO to Resolve the Issues Concerning Report of the JPC on the STS (Recognition of Forest Rights) Bill."

Raheja, Gloria Goodwin. 1988. "India: Caste, Kingship, and Dominance Reconsidered." *Annual Review of Anthropology* 17 (January): 497–522.

Rajagopal, Arvind. 2011. "The Emergency as Prehistory of the New Indian Middle Class." *Modern Asian Studies* 45 (5): 1003–49.

Rajan, Raghuram. 2013. "Why India Slowed." *Project Syndicate.* April 30.

Rajshekhar, M. 2011. "The Act That Disagreed with Its Preamble: The Drafting of the Scheduled Tribes and Other Traditional Forest Dwellers (Recognition of Forest Rights) Act, 2006."

Ram, Kanshi. 1997. *The Editorials of Kanshi Ram.* Lucknow: Bahujan Samaj.

Raman, Bhavani. 2018. "Law in Times of Counter-Insurgency." In *Iterations of Law: Legal Histories from India.* Edited by Aparna Balachandran, Rashmi Pant, and Bhavani Raman, 120–46. New Delhi: Oxford University Press.

Rancière, Jacques. 2004. "Who Is the Subject of the Rights of Man?" *South Atlantic Quarterly* 103 (2): 297–310.

Randeria, Shalini. 2007. "The State of Globalization: Legal Plurality, Overlapping Sovereignties and Ambiguous Alliances between Civil Society and the Cunning State in India." *Theory, Culture and Society* 24 (1): 1–33.

Rangarajan, Mahesh. 1994. "Imperial Agendas and India's Forests: The Early History of Indian Forestry, 1800–1878." *Indian Economic and Social History Review* 31 (2): 147–67.

Rangarajan, Mahesh. 1996. *Fencing the Forest: Conservation and Ecological Change in India's Central Provinces, 1860–1914.* New Delhi: Oxford University Press.

Rangarajan, Mahesh. 2005. *India's Wildlife History.* New Delhi: Orient Blackswan.

Rangarajan, Mahesh. 2009. "Striving for a Balance: Nature, Power, Science and India's Indira Gandhi, 1917–1984." *Conservation and Society* 7 (4): 299–312.

Rao, Anupama. 2009. *The Caste Question: Dalits and the Politics of Modern India.* Berkeley: University of California Press.

Rawat, Ramnarayan S. 2011. *Reconsidering Untouchability: Chamars and Dalit History in North India.* Bloomington: Indiana University Press.

Ray, Raka, and Mary Fainsod Katzenstein. 2005. *Social Movements in India: Poverty, Power, and Politics.* Lanham, MD: Rowman & Littlefield.

Reeves, Peter. 1985. "The Congress and the Abolition of Zamindari in Uttar Pradesh." *South Asia: Journal of South Asian Studies* 8 (1–2): 154–67.

Report of the United Provinces Zamindari Abolition Committee Volume I. 1948. Allahabad, India: M. G. Shome.

Richland, Justin B. 2008. *Arguing with Tradition: The Language of Law in Hopi Tribal Court.* Chicago: University of Chicago Press.

Ricœur, Paul. 1984. *Time and Narrative.* Chicago: University of Chicago Press.

Riles, Annelise. 2004. "Real Time: Unwinding Technocratic and Anthropological Knowledge." *American Ethnologist* 31 (3): 392–405.

Riles, Annelise. 2006. *Documents: Artifacts of Modern Knowledge.* Ann Arbor: University of Michigan Press.

Robb, Peter. 1993. *Dalit Movements and the Meanings of Labour in India.* New Delhi: Oxford University Press.

Roosa, John. 2001. "Passive Revolution Meets Peasant Revolution: Indian Nationalism and the Telangana Revolt." *Journal of Peasant Studies* 28 (4): 57–94.

Roseberry, William. 1994. "Hegemony and the Language of Contention." In *Everyday Forms of State Formation: Revolution and the Negotiation of Rule in Modern Mexico.* Edited by Gilbert M. Joseph and Daniel Nugent, 355–66. Durham, NC: Duke University Press.

Roy, Arundhati. 2014. "The Doctor and the Saint." In *Annihilation of Caste: The Annotated Critical Edition.* New Delhi: Navayana.

Sahlins, Marshall. 1972. *Stone Age Economics.* Chicago: Alder Atherton.

Sahlins, Marshall. 2013. *What Kinship Is . . . and Is Not*. Chicago: University of Chicago Press.

Sahoo, Uttam Kumar, and Geetanjoy Sahu. 2019. "Trends and Directions in the Implementation of the Scheduled Tribes and Other Traditional Forest Dwellers (Recognition of Forest Rights) Act 2006 after Twelve Years." Mumbai: Tata Institute of Social Sciences.

Saksena, H. S., and Chandra Sen. 1999. *Putting People Last: Tribal Displacement and Rehabilitation*. New Delhi: Inter-India.

Sampat, Preeti. 2015. "The 'Goan Impasse': Land Rights and Resistance to SEZs in Goa, India." *Journal of Peasant Studies* 42 (3–4): 765–90.

Sankhdher, Lalit Mohan. 1974. *Caste Interaction in a Village Tribe: An Anthropological Case Study of the Tribes in Dhanaura Village in Mirzapur District of Uttar Pradesh*. New Delhi: K. B.

Sanyal, Kalyan. 2013. *Rethinking Capitalist Development: Primitive Accumulation, Governmentality and Post-Colonial Capitalism*. New Delhi: Routledge.

Sarin, Madhu. 1995. "Regenerating India's Forests: Reconciling Gender Equity with Joint Forest Management." *IDS Bulletin* 26 (1): 83–91.

Sarin, Madhu. 2005. "Scheduled Tribes Bill 2005: A Comment." *Economic and Political Weekly* 40 (21): 2131–34.

Savyasaachi. 1998. *Tribal Forest-Dwellers and Self-Rule: The Constituent Assembly Debates on the Fifth and Sixth Schedules*. New Delhi: Indian Social Institute.

Schmitt, Carl. (1928) 2008. *Constitutional Theory*. Translated by Jeffrey Seitzer. Durham, NC: Duke University Press.

Scott, James C. 2009. *The Art of Not Being Governed: An Anarchist History of Upland Southeast Asia*. New Haven, CT: Yale University Press.

Sethi, Nitin. 2013. "Tribal Interests, Norms Ignored for Mahan Coal Block." *The Hindu*, September 21. http://www.thehindu.com/news/national/tribal-interests-norms-ignored-for-mahan-coal-block/article5151075.ece.

Shah, Ganshyam. 2001. *Dalit Identity and Politics*. New Delhi: Sage.

Sharma, Aradhana. 2013. "State Transparency after the Neoliberal Turn: The Politics, Limits, and Paradoxes of India's Right to Information Law." *PoLAR: Political and Legal Anthropology Review* 36 (2): 308–25.

Sharma, B. D. 1989. "Report of the Commissioner for Scheduled Castes and Scheduled Tribes: Twenty-Ninth Report 1987–89."

Sharma, B. D. 2010. *Unbroken History of Broken Promises*. New Delhi: Freedom.

Sharma, Nidhi. 2020. "1.75 Million Forest Rights Claims Rejected by State Governments." *Economic Times*, September 24.

Sharma, Prashant. 2014. *Democracy and Transparency in the Indian State: The Making of the Right to Information Act*. New York: Routledge.

Sherman, Taylor C. 2016. "A Gandhian Answer to the Threat of Communism? Sarvodaya and Postcolonial Nationalism in India." *Indian Economic and Social History Review* 53 (2): 249–70.

Shourie, Arun. 1984. *Mrs. Gandhi's Second Reign*. New Delhi: Vikas.

Shrivastava, Kumar Sambhav. 2011. "Forest Dwellers March for Their Rights." *Down to Earth*, December 16.

Silverstein, Michael. 2003. "Indexical Order and the Dialectics of Sociolinguistic Life." *Language and Communication* 23 (3–4): 193–229.

Silverstein, Michael. 2010. "Society, Polity, and Language Community: An Enlightenment Trinity in Anthropological Perspective." *Journal of Language and Politics* 9 (3): 339–63.

Silverstein, Michael, and Greg Urban. 1996. *Natural Histories of Discourse*. Chicago: University of Chicago Press.

Simone, AbdouMaliq. 2010. "2009 Urban Geography Plenary Lecture—On Intersections, Anticipations, and Provisional Publics: Remaking District Life in Jakarta." *Urban Geography* 31 (3): 285–308.

Sirur, Simrin. 2019. "Story of UP's Sonbhadra Which Saw a Massacre in July: Distance, Poverty and a Resource Curse." *The Print*, August 19. https://theprint.in/india /story-of-ups-sonbhadra-which-saw-a-massacre-in-july-distance-poverty-a -resource-curse/278833/.

Singh, G. P. 1966. *Working Plan for the Protected and Vested Forests of the Dudhi Forest Division, Mirzapur, Southern Circle, Uttar Pradesh, 1964–65 to 1973–74.* Nainital: Working Plans Circle, U.P.

Singh, Ramvir. 2005. "The Draft Scheduled Tribes (Recognition of Forest Rights) Bill, 2005: A Critique." Unpublished memorandum, September 6.

Singh, R. S. 1973. *Working Plan for the Dudhi Forest Division, Pipri (Mirzapur), Southern Circle, Uttar Pradesh, 1973–74 to 1982–83.* Nainital: Working Plans Circle, U.P.

Singh, Sarita, and Himangshu Watts. 2011. "Corruption, Inefficiency Eat 25% of CIL Output: Sriprakash Jaiswal." *Economic Times*, October 19.

Singh, Satyajit Kumar. 1985. "From the Dam to the Ghettos: The Victims of the Rihand Dam." *Economic and Political Weekly* 20 (39): 1643–44.

Singh, Shalini. 2012. "Jayanthi Assails Investment Super Committee Proposal." *The Hindu*, October 10.

Sivaramakrishnan, K. 1995. "Colonialism and Forestry in India: Imagining the Past in Present Politics." *Comparative Studies in Society and History* 37 (1): 3–40.

Sivaramakrishnan, K. 1997. "A Limited Forest Conservancy in Southwest Bengal, 1864–1912." *Journal of Asian Studies* 56 (1): 75–112.

Sivaramakrishnan, K. 1999. *Modern Forests: Statemaking and Environmental Change in Colonial Eastern India.* Palo Alto, CA: Stanford University Press.

Skoda, Uwe. 2005. *The Aghria: A Peasant Caste on a Tribal Frontier.* New Delhi: Manohar.

Smelser, Neil. 1963. *Theory of Collective Behavior.* New York: Routledge.

Smith, Gavin A. 2011. "Selective Hegemony and Beyond-Populations with 'No Productive Function': A Framework for Enquiry." *Identities* 18 (1): 2–38.

Smith, Neil. 1990. *Uneven Development: Nature, Capital, and the Production of Space.* Athens: University of Georgia Press.

Solum, Lawrence B. 2010. "Indeterminacy." In *A Companion to Philosophy of Law and Legal Theory.* Edited by Dennis Patterson, 479–92. Chichester: Wiley-Blackwell.

Srinivas, Mysore Narasimhachar. 1995. *Social Change in Modern India.* New Delhi: Orient Blackswan.

Strathern, Marilyn. 1999. *Property, Substance and Effect: Anthropological Essays on Persons and Things.* London: Athlone.

Subramanian, Ajantha. 2009. *Shorelines: Space and Rights in South India.* Palo Alto, CA: Stanford University Press.

Subramanian, Ajantha. 2015. "Making Merit: The Indian Institutes of Technology and the Social Life of Caste." *Comparative Studies in Society and History* 57 (2): 291–322.

Sundar, Nandini. 2001. *Branching Out: Joint Forest Management in India.* New Delhi: Oxford University Press.

Sundar, Nandini. 2008. *Subalterns and Sovereigns: An Anthropological History of Bastar 1854–2006.* New Delhi: Oxford University Press.

Sundar, Nandini. 2011. "The Rule of Law and Citizenship in Central India: Post-Colonial Dilemmas." *Citizenship Studies* 15 (June): 419–32.

Swyngedouw, Erik. 1997. "Glocalization and the Politics of Scale." In *Spaces of Globalization: Reasserting the Power of the Local.* Edited by Kevin R. Cox, 137–66. New York: Guilford.

Tarlo, Emma. 2003. *Unsettling Memories: Narratives of the Emergency in Delhi.* Berkeley: University of California Press.

Tarrow, Sidney. 1998. *Power in Movement: Social Movements and Contentious Politics.* Cambridge: Cambridge University Press.

Teltumbde, Anand. 2011. *The Persistence of Caste: India's Hidden Apartheid and the Khairlanji Murders.* New York: Zed.

TERI. 2020. "Estimation of the Current Emission and Sequestration, as well as Future Potential of Sequestration/Emission Reduction to Achieve Land Degradation Neutrality in India." New Delhi: The Energy and Resources Institute.

Thompson, E. P. 2013. *Whigs and Hunters: The Origin of the Black Act.* London: Breviary Stuff.

The Times of India. 2012. "Ramesh Seeks CBI Probe into State NREGS Scam." April 1.

Trubek, David M. 1984. "Where the Action Is: Critical Legal Studies and Empiricism." *Stanford Law Review* 36 (1/2): 575–622.

Tsing, Anna Lowenhaupt. 2004. *Friction: An Ethnography of Global Connection.* Princeton, NJ: Princeton University Press.

United Progressive Alliance. 2004. "Common Minimum Programme."

Uttar Pradesh Zamindari Abolition and Land Reforms Act, 1950.

Verdery, Katherine. 2003. *The Vanishing Hectare: Property and Value in Postsocialist Transylvania.* Ithaca, NY: Cornell University Press.

Viswanath, Rupa. 2014. "Rethinking Caste and Class: 'Labour,' the 'Depressed Classes,' and the Politics of Distinctions, Madras 1918–1924." *International Review of Social History* 59 (1): 1–37.

Voloshinov, V. N. 1986. *Marxism and the Philosophy of Language.* Cambridge, MA: Harvard University Press.

Wahi, Namita. 2015. "The Fundamental Right to Property in the Indian Constitution." https://ssrn.com/abstract=2661212.

Wani, Milind, and Ashish Kothari. 2008. "Globalisation vs India's Forests." *Economic and Political Weekly* 43 (37): 19–22.

Webb, Martin. 2012. "Activating Citizens, Remaking Brokerage: Transparency Activism, Ethical Scenes, and the Urban Poor in Delhi." *PoLAR: Political and Legal Anthropology Review* 35 (2): 206–22.

Weber, Max. (1921) 2019. *Economy and Society.* Edited and translated by Keith Tribe. Cambridge, MA: Harvard University Press.

Weil, Benjamin. 2006. "Conservation, Exploitation, and Cultural Change in the Indian Forest Service, 1875–1927." *Environmental History* 11 (2): 319–43.

West, Paige. 2006. *Conservation Is Our Government Now: The Politics of Ecology in Papua New Guinea.* Durham, NC: Duke University Press.

West, Robin. 1993. *Narrative, Authority, and Law.* Ann Arbor: University of Michigan Press.

The Wire. 2022. "Protests in Shaheen Bagh as Bulldozers Arrive for 'Anti-Encroachment Drive.'" May 9. https://thewire.in/government/shaheen-bagh-bulldozer-encroachment.

Wolford, Wendy. 2003. "Producing Community: The MST and Land Reform Settlements in Brazil." *Journal of Agrarian Change* 3 (4): 500–520.

Xaxa, Virginius. 1999. "Tribes as Indigenous People of India." *Economic and Political Weekly* 34 (51): 3589–95.

Zelliot, Eleanor. 1996. *From Untouchable to Dalit: Essays on the Ambedkar Movement.* New Delhi: Manohar.

Index

Page numbers in *italics* refer to figures.

accumulation. *See* capital accumulation

Adivasi. *See* Dalit: Adivasis solidarity; Indigenous peoples; Scheduled Tribes: Adivasi

Agarias. *See* Scheduled Tribes: Agarias

Ahirs. *See* Yadav caste

Ahmad, Fakhruddin Ali, 26. *See also* State of Emergency

Allahabad High Court, 44, 144

Ambedkar, Bhimrao Ramji, 92–97, 102, 105–6, 117; land politics of, 95–97. *See also* Indian constitution

Andhra Pradesh, 69, 101, 130, 152

antidispossession. *See* People's movements: and antidispossession

Article 21. *See* Indian constitution: right to life

ashram. *See* Banswasi Seva Ashram

Association of Power Producers, 153

Bahuguna, V. K., 61–62

Bahujan Samaj Party (BSP), viii, 20, 91, 95–96, 110, 148

Baiga. *See* British East India Company

Bakhtin, Mikhail, 12. *See also* chronotopes

Banswasi Seva Ashram, 38–39, 50–55, 86–90, 104–7, 122–23; and Bhoodan politics, 100–103

bauxite. *See* coal mining

Below Poverty Level (BPL) card, 104, 116. *See also* poverty

Bhai, Prem, 38, 49, 51–52, 101–2

Bharatiya Janata Party (BJP), 68–69, 158–59

Bharatiya Kisan Union (BKU), 115

Bhave, Vinoba, 38, 102

Bhoodan. *See* forest dwellers; Sarvodaya movement

Bhuiyas, 90, 92, 123. *See also* Scheduled Tribes

Bihar, 27, 32, 34, 41, 52, 69, 86, 90, 102

Bombay Natural History Society, 142–44

BRICs (Brazil, Russia, India, and China), 146

British East India Company, 30–32, 163n2

bureaucratic indifference, 156

Campaign for Survival and Dignity (CSD), 59, 63–85, 94, 119, 129–31, 144

capital accumulation: conservationist rationale for, 65; by dispossession, 27, 64, 94, 141–42, 146, 150; dynamics of, 24, 156; enclosure and, 145–49; and popular struggle, 149–52; regimes of, 6. *See also* India's forests: capital accumulation of; property

casteism. *See* jativadi

cement manufacturing, vii, 6, 50, 88, 103, 125. *See also* coal mining; UP Cement Corporation

censorship. *See* State of Emergency: censorship during

Chamar (caste), 90, 92, 123, 132. *See also* Dalit; Ramnagar

Chandrapur Super Thermal Power Station, 48, 54

Chidambaram, Finance Minister, 154

China, 145–46. *See also* BRICs

chronotopes, 12–13. *See also* word traps: as chronotopes

citizenship, 4, 7, 157–59, 165

clearances, 48, 152–55. *See also* property

coal mining, vii, 3, 6, 28, 33, 36–37, 46, 48, 50, 54, 152–56, 164n6. *See also* Sonbhadra

collective action: Campaign for Survival and Dignity and, 84–85; as coalition building, 54, 87, 100, 132; co-optation of, 117, 156; defined, 15; dual operability of, 18, 23, 29, 161; infrastructure of, 54, 56, 159; law as product of, xi, 7–10, 13–18, 27, 87, 97 141, 159–60; political authority of, 4, 22, 24, 58, 134, 155; of state actors, 135–38; tentative achievements of, 16. *See also* lawmaking: and collective action; methodology: and theories of collective action

Common Minimum Programme, 71

Communist Party of India CPI(M), 44–45, 53, 69, 77, 88, 95, 101, 115, 130, 148; student vs. trade union wing, 26

Communist Party of India Marxist-Leninist CPI(ML), 27, 91

Confederation of Indian Industry, 153

www.ingramcontent.com/pod-product-compliance
Lightning Source LLC
Chambersburg PA
CBHW032350280326
41935CB00008B/523